AN INTRODUCTION
TO EFFICIENCY AND
PRODUCTIVITY ANALYSIS

AN INTRODUCTION TO EFFICIENCY AND PRODUCTIVITY ANALYSIS

by

Tim Coelli
D. S. Prasada Rao
George E. Battese

Kluwer Academic Publishers
Boston/Dordrecht/London

Distributors for North America:
Kluwer Academic Publishers
101 Philip Drive
Assinippi Park
Norwell, Massachusetts 02061 USA

Distributors for all other countries:
Kluwer Academic Publishers Group
Distribution Centre
Post Office Box 322
3300 AH Dordrecht, THE NETHERLANDS

Library of Congress Cataloging-in-Publication Data

A C.I.P. Catalogue record for this book is available from the Library of Congress.

Printed on acid-free paper.

Printed in the United States of America

To
Michelle, Visala and Marilyn

TABLE OF CONTENTS

FIGURES

TABLES

PREFACE

This book is designed to be a "first port of call" for people wishing to study efficiency and productivity analysis. The book provides an accessible introduction to the four principal methods involved, namely, least-squares econometric production models, index numbers, data envelopment analysis (DEA) and stochastic frontiers. For each method, we provide a detailed introduction to the basic method, give a simple numerical example to illustrate the concepts and then discuss some of the more important extensions to the basic methods and indicate some references for further reading. We also describe a number of detailed empirical applications using real data to illustrate these methods.

The book may be used as a textbook or as a reference text. As a textbook it could be used in an advanced-undergraduate or graduate-level course. Two early chapters are devoted to a review of production economics. These chapters could be skimmed quickly in a course for graduate economics majors, but they should prove very useful to undergraduate students and those doing a major in another field, such as business management, health studies, etc.

There have been several excellent books written on performance measurement in recent years, such as Färe, Grosskopf and Lovell (1985, 1994), Fried, Lovell and Schmidt (1993), Charnes et al (1995) and Färe, Grosskopf and Russell (1997). The present book is not designed to compete with these books, but to provide a lower-level bridge to the material contained within them, and many other books and journal articles written on this topic.

We believe this book contains three features unique to books in this field.

1. It is an introductory text.

2. It contains detailed discussion and comparison of all of the four principal methods.

3. It provides detailed advice on computer programs which can be used to calculate the various measures. This involves a number of presentations of computer instructions and output listings for the SHAZAM, TFPIP, DEAP and FRONTIER computer programs.

The book has evolved from a set of notes for short courses which were given by the authors to a number of Government agencies in Australia during 1995 and 1996. Particular mention should be made of the NSW Treasury where the first of these short courses was presented.   We thank John Pierce from NSW Treasury for proposing the idea for a short course on this topic and for the encouragement he has given staff of the Centre for Efficiency and Productivity Analysis (CEPA).   We are grateful to the many people from: NSW Treasury, Bureau of Industry Economics, Industry Commission, Victorian Treasury, Queensland Treasury, the Australian Bureau of Statistics and a number of other staff from NSW Government agencies who attended these courses and provided valuable feedback and suggestions.   We are also particularly indebted to Bert Balk, Rolf Färe, Knox Lovell and Chris O'Donnell for making valuable comments on various drafts of this manuscript.

Tim Coelli
D.S. Prasada Rao
George E. Battese

Centre for Efficiency and
Productivity Analysis,
University of New England,
Armidale, N.S.W., Australia.

1. INTRODUCTION

1.1 Introduction

This book is concerned with measuring the performance of firms, which convert inputs into outputs. An example of a firm is a shirt factory which uses materials, labour and capital (inputs) to produce shirts (output). The performance of this factory can be defined in many ways. A natural measure of performance is a productivity ratio: the ratio of outputs to inputs, where larger values of this ratio are associated with better performance. Performance is a relative concept. For example, the performance of the factory in 1996 could be measured relative to its 1995 performance or it could be measured relative to the performance of another factory in 1996, etc.

The methods of performance measurement that are discussed in this book can be applied to a variety of "firms".[1] They can be applied to private sector firms producing goods, such as the factory discussed above, or to service industries, such as travel agencies or restaurants. The methods may also be used by a particular firm to analyse the relative performance of units within the firm (e.g., bank branches or chains of fast food outlets or retail stores). Performance measurement can also be applied to non-profit organisations, such as schools or hospitals.

---

[1] In some of the literature on productivity and efficiency analysis the rather ungainly term "decision making unit" (DMU) is used to describe a productive entity in instances when the term "firm" may not be entirely appropriate. For example, when comparing the performance of power plants in a multi-plant utility, or when comparing bank branches in a large banking organisation, the units under consideration are really *parts* of a firm rather than firms themselves. In this book we have decided to use the term "firm" to describe any type of decision making unit, and ask that readers keep this more general definition in mind as they read the remainder of this book.

All of the above examples involve micro-level data. The methods we consider can also be used for making performance comparisons at higher levels of aggregation. For example, one may wish to compare the performance of an industry over time or across geographical regions (e.g., shires, counties, cities, states, countries, etc.).

We discuss the use and the relative merits of a number of different performance measurement methods in this book. These methods differ according to the type of measures they produce; the data they require; and the assumptions they make regarding the structure of the production technology and the economic behaviour of decision makers. Some methods only require data on quantities of inputs and outputs while other methods also require price data and various behavioural assumptions, such as cost minimisation, profit maximisation, etc.

But before we discuss these methods any further, it is necessary for us to provide some informal definitions of a few terms. These definitions are not very precise, but they are sufficient to provide readers, new to this field, some insight into the sea of jargon in which we swim. Following this we provide an outline of the contents of the book and a brief summary of the principal performance measurement methods that we consider.

1.2 Some Informal Definitions

In this section we provide a few informal definitions of some of the terms which are frequently used in this book. More precise definitions will be provided later in the book. The terms are:

- productivity;
- technical efficiency;
- allocative efficiency;
- technical change;
- scale economies;
- total factor productivity (TFP);
- production frontier; and
- feasible production set.

We begin by defining the **productivity** of a firm as the ratio of the output(s) that it produces to the input(s) that it uses.

$$\text{productivity} = \text{outputs/inputs} \qquad (1.1)$$

When the production process involves a single input and a single output, this calculation is a trivial matter. However, when there is more than one input (which is often the case) then a method for aggregating these inputs into a single index of inputs must be used to obtain a ratio measure of productivity.[2] In this book, we discuss some of the methods that are used to aggregate inputs (and/or outputs) for the construction of productivity measures.

When we refer to productivity, we are referring to **total factor productivity**, which is a productivity measure involving all factors of production.[3] Other traditional measures of productivity, such as labour productivity in a factory, fuel productivity in power stations, and land productivity (yield) in farming, are what is known as *partial* measures of productivity. These partial productivity measures can provide a misleading indication of overall productivity when considered in isolation.

The terms, **productivity** and **efficiency,** have been used frequently in the media over the last ten years by a variety of commentators. They are often used interchangeably, but this is unfortunate because they are not precisely the same things. To illustrate the distinction between the terms, it is useful to consider a simple production process in which a single input (x) is used to produce a single output (y). The line OF′ in Figure 1.1 represents a **production frontier** which may be used to define the relationship between the input and the output. The production frontier represents the maximum output attainable from each input level. Hence it reflects the current state of technology in the industry. More is stated about its properties in later sections. Firms in that industry operate either on that frontier, if they are **technically efficient**, or beneath the frontier if they are not technically efficient. Point A represents an inefficient point whereas points B and C represent efficient points. A firm operating at point A is inefficient because technically it could increase output to the level associated with the point B without requiring more input.[4]

We also use Figure 1.1 to illustrate the concept of a **feasible production set** which is the set of all input-output combinations that are feasible. This set consists of all points between the production frontier, OF′, and the x-axis (inclusive of these bounds).[5] The points along the production frontier define the efficient subset of this feasible production set. The primary advantage of the *set representation* of a production technology is made clear when we discuss multi-input/multi-output production and the use of distance functions in later chapters.

---

[2] The same problem occurs with multiple outputs.

[3] It also includes all outputs in a multiple-output setting.

[4] Or alternatively, it could produce the same level of output using less input (i.e., produce at point C on the frontier).

[5] Note that this definition of the production set assumes free disposability of inputs and outputs. These issues will be discussed further in subsequent chapters.

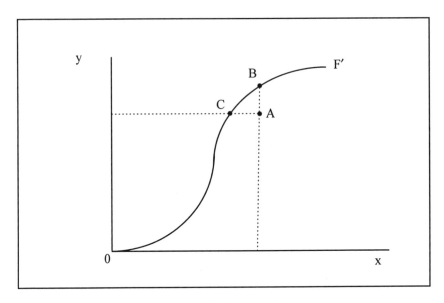

Figure 1.1 Production Frontiers and Technical Efficiency

To illustrate the distinction between technical efficiency and productivity we utilise Figure 1.2. In this figure, we use a ray through the origin to measure productivity at a particular data point. The slope of this ray is y/x and hence provides a measure of productivity. If the firm operating at point A were to move to the technically efficient point B, the slope of the ray would be greater, implying higher productivity at point B. However, by moving to the point C, the ray from the origin is at a tangent to the production frontier and hence defines the point of maximum possible productivity. This latter movement is an example of exploiting **scale economies**. The point C is the point of (technically) optimal scale. Operation at any other point on the production frontier results in lower productivity.

From this discussion, we conclude that a firm may be technically efficient but may still be able to improve its productivity by exploiting scale economies. Given that changing the scale of operations of a firm can often be difficult to achieve quickly, technical efficiency and productivity can be given short-run and long-run interpretations.

The discussion above does not include a time component. When one considers productivity comparisons through time, an additional source of productivity change, called **technical change,** is possible. This involves advances in technology which may be represented by an upward shift in the production frontier. This is depicted in Figure 1.3 by the movement of the production frontier from $0F_0'$ in period 0 to $0F_1'$ in period 1. In period 1, all firms can technically produce more output for each level of input, relative to what was possible in period 0. An example of technical change is the installation of a new boiler for a coal-fired power plant which extends the plant productivity potential beyond previous limits. [6]

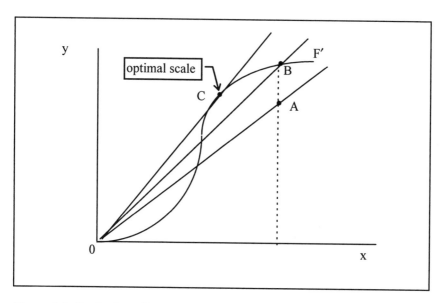

Figure 1.2 Productivity, Technical Efficiency and Scale Economies

When we observe that a firm has increased its productivity from one year to the next, the improvement need not have been from efficiency improvements alone, but may have been due to technical change or the exploitation of scale economies or from some combination of these three factors.

Up to this point, all discussion has involved physical quantities and technical relationships. We have not discussed issues such as costs or profits. If information on prices is available, and a behavioural assumption, such as cost minimisation or profit maximisation, is appropriate, then performance measures can be devised which incorporate this information. In such cases it is possible to consider **allocative efficiency,** in addition to technical efficiency. Allocative efficiency in input selection involves selecting that mix of inputs (e.g., labour and capital) which produce a given quantity of output at minimum cost (given the input prices which prevail). Allocative and technical efficiency combine to provide an overall economic efficiency measure.[7]

---

[6] This is an example of embodied technical change, where the technical change is embodied in the capital input. Disembodied technical change is also possible. One such example, is that of the introduction of legume/wheat crop rotations in agriculture in recent decades.

[7] In the case of a multiple-output industry, allocative efficiency in output mix may also be considered.

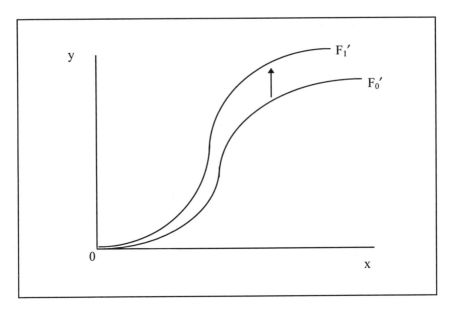

Figure 1.3 Technical Change Between Two Periods

Now that we are armed with this handful of informal definitions we briefly describe the layout of the book and the principal methods which we consider in subsequent chapters.

1.3 Overview of Methods

There are essentially four major methods discussed in this book:

1. least-squares econometric production models;

2. total factor productivity (TFP) indices;

3. data envelopment analysis (DEA); and

4. stochastic frontiers.

The first two methods are most often applied to aggregate time-series data and provide measures of technical change and/or TFP. Both of these methods assume all firms are technically efficient. Methods 3 and 4, on the other hand, are most often applied to data on a sample of firms (at one point in time) and provide measures of relative efficiency among those firms. Hence these latter two methods do not assume that all firms are technically efficient. However, multilateral TFP indices can also be used to compare the relative productivity of a group of firms at one point in time. Also DEA and stochastic frontiers can be used to measure both technical change and efficiency change, if panel data are available.

Thus we see that the above four methods can be grouped according to whether they recognise inefficiency or not. An alternative way of grouping the methods is to note that methods 1 and 4 involve the econometric estimation of parametric functions, while methods 2 and 3 do not. These two groups may therefore be termed "parametric" and "non-parametric" methods, respectively. These methods may also be distinguished in several other ways, such as by their data requirements, their behavioural assumptions and by whether or not they recognise random errors in the data (noise). These differences are discussed in later chapters.

1.4 Outline of Chapters

In this section we provide an outline of the contents of the subsequent ten chapters in this book. As noted above, we consider four different methodologies, least-squares econometric production models, index numbers, DEA and stochastic frontiers. Each of these methods have two chapters devoted to it. For each method we first describe the basic methodology and provide a simple numerical illustration. We then describe extensions to the basic method and provide a detailed description of an empirical application. In addition to these eight chapters, there is a chapter which describes the application of efficiency measurement methods to TFP measurement (Chapter 10) and a conclusions chapter (Chapter 11).

It should also be noted that the material on least-squares econometric production models is primarily included to provide a balanced view of productivity measurement methods. This material is discussed in many other texts and hence is not discussed in great detail. In fact, Chapters 2 and 3 are more concerned with a review of production economics than with the least-squares methods themselves.

The outline of the contents of the subsequent chapters is as follows.

Chapter 2. Production Economics: This is a review of production economics at the level of an undergraduate microeconomics course. It includes a discussion of production, cost and profit functions, and reviews a variety of concepts, such as technical change, returns to scale and optimisation rules. The chapter concludes with a discussion of econometric estimation of production functions and technical change measurement.

Chapter 3. Additional Topics in Production Economics: Here we provide an introduction to the dual relationship between production functions and cost, profit and distance functions. We illustrate how the analysis of these alternative functions permit information on the structure of the production technology to be extracted. We extend our single-output discussion in Chapter 2 to the multi-output case. A discussion of econometric estimation and technical change measurement concludes the chapter.

Chapter 4. Index Numbers and Productivity Measurement: This chapter introduces index number methods. We describe the familiar Laspeyres and Paasche index numbers which are often used for price index calculations (such as a consumer price index). We also describe Tornqvist and Fisher indices and discuss why they may be preferred when calculating indices of input and output quantities and TFP. We also cover the issue of transitivity in spatial comparisons and discuss how one may transform a non-transitive index into a transitive (multilateral) index. The various index number methods are illustrated using a simple numerical example. The chapter concludes with a detailed empirical example.

Chapter 5. Economic Theory and Index Numbers: In this chapter we discuss the economic theory which underlies the various index number methods. We look at the economic theory associated with input price indices, output price indices, input quantity indices, output quantity indices, and finally TFP indices.

Chapter 6. Efficiency Measurement using DEA: In this chapter we provide an introduction to DEA, the mathematical programming approach to the estimation of frontier functions and the calculation of efficiency measures. We discuss the basic DEA models (input- and output- orientated models under the assumptions of constant returns to scale and variable returns to scale) and illustrate these methods using simple numerical examples.

Chapter 7. Additional Topics on DEA: Here we extend our discussion of DEA models to include the issues of environmental variables, allocative efficiency and the treatment of slacks. The chapter concludes with a detailed empirical application.

Chapter 8. Efficiency Measurement using Stochastic Frontiers: This is an alternative approach to the estimation of frontier functions using econometric techniques. It has advantages over DEA when data noise is a problem. The basic stochastic frontier model is introduced and illustrated using a simple example.

Chapter 9. Additional Topics on Stochastic Frontiers: In this chapter we extend the discussion of stochastic frontiers to cover allocative efficiency, panel data models, the inclusion of environmental and management variables, and other issues. The chapter concludes with a detailed empirical example.

Chapter 10. Productivity Measurement using Efficiency Measurement Methods: In this chapter we discuss how one may use efficiency measurement methods (such as DEA and stochastic frontiers) in the analysis of panel data for the purpose of measuring TFP growth. We discuss how the TFP measures may be decomposed into technical efficiency change and technical change. The chapter concludes with a detailed empirical application.

Chapter 11. Concluding Comments.

1.5 What is Your Economics Background?

When writing this book we had two groups of readers in mind. The first group contains postgraduate economics majors who have recently completed a graduate course on microeconomics, while the second group contains people with less knowledge of microeconomics. This second group might include undergraduate students, MBA students and researchers in industry and government who do not have a strong economics background (or who did their economics training a number of years ago). The first group may quickly review Chapters 2 and 3. They should take note of the notation that is used and also read the sections on econometric estimation of production models. The second group of readers should read Chapters 2 and 3 carefully. Depending on your background, you may also need to supplement your reading with some of the reference texts that are suggested in these chapters.

2. REVIEW OF PRODUCTION ECONOMICS

2.1 Introduction

The primary purpose of this chapter is to provide a review of some key production economics results at the level one would expect an undergraduate economics student to achieve. This chapter draws heavily upon a number of economics textbooks, which are referenced throughout the chapter, especially Call and Holahan (1983) and Beattie and Taylor (1985).

When writing this chapter we had to make an early decision regarding the approach we would take. In particular we had to decide if we would continue to follow the traditional approach to teaching production economics which uses functions to describe the production technology (this approach is used in many past and present economics texts) or should we choose the alternative approach which uses sets to describe the production technology (e.g., see Varian, 1992; and Färe and Primont, 1995). After some thought we decided to focus on the function approach to seek conformity with what we expect most readers to be familiar with, and also because it facilitates graphical representation (but restricts us to single output technologies). However, set concepts are also introduced in Chapter 3 when we discuss multi-output technologies and distance functions.

This chapter begins with a discussion of production functions and related concepts. We then introduce price information and discuss optimal decisions associated with cost-minimising and profit-maximising behaviour. The chapter concludes with a discussion of econometric estimation of production functions.

2.2 Production Functions

We begin our discussion with the definition of a production function. The production function describes the technical relationship between the inputs and outputs of a production process. A production function defines the maximum output(s) attainable from a given vector of inputs.[1] Much of the discussion in this chapter considers a production process which involves the production of a single output from two inputs, where one input is variable in the short run (which we call labour) and one is fixed in the short run but variable in the long run (which we call capital). This simple production process is assumed so that we can introduce a variety of production concepts without requiring excessive mathematical rigour.

This two-input and single-output production process is obviously a significant simplification of many, if not all, production processes. For example, consider the railways. We could specify the output as being number of passengers (tickets sold) and the inputs as labour and capital (rolling stock, lines and stations), but there are many problems with this description of the production process. For example, we do not account for other important inputs such as fuel, electricity and other consumables; we ignore the freight side of output; and also ignore the heterogeneity of rail tickets, in that some could be for inter-city trips while others may only be for a simple commuter trip from one suburb to the next. Furthermore, once we divide the inputs into fixed and variable groups, the specification of labour as a variable input may not be appropriate in an industry in which labour unions have traditionally been quite strong.

This example is introduced to make it clear that we believe the single-output, two-input model is rarely applicable in reality. However, it is assumed in much of this chapter because it allows us to simplify the discussion of many production economics concepts. Furthermore, all of these concepts can subsequently be shown (in some cases, with a large quantity of algebra required) to be applicable to more general production processes. Discussion of cases involving more than two inputs and more than one output is presented in Chapter 3.

Following Beattie and Taylor (1985, p5), the following assumptions are made in this chapter:

- The production process is monoperiodic;
- All inputs and outputs are homogenous;
- The production function is twice continuously differentiable;

---

[1] The majority of economics textbooks refer to the technical relationship between inputs and output as a *production function* rather than as a *production frontier*. The two terms refer to identical things. The efficiency measurement literature tends to use the term *frontier* to stress the maximal property of the function.

- The production function and output and input prices are known with certainty;

- There is no budget constraint; and

- The goal of the firm is to maximise profit (or minimise cost for a specified output level).

These are obviously quite strong assumptions. We discuss some of the implications of violation of these assumptions later.

Production functions are usually represented by a mathematical function or by a graph. We could specify a two-input, single output production function as:

$$y = f(x_1, x_2) \qquad (2.1)$$

where y is output; x_1 is a variable input (which we call *labour*); x_2 is a fixed input (which we call *capital*); and f(.) is a suitable function, such as those discussed later in this chapter. If we assume that x_2 is fixed in the short run[2] (such that $x_2 = x_{20}$), then the short run production function can be represented by

$$y = f(x_1 | x_2 = x_{20}) \qquad (2.2)$$

or by a 2-dimensional graph, such as the line marked TP_1 in Figure 2.1.[3] That is, the line TP_1 represents the maximum quantity of output that can be produced using different quantities of labour, with capital fixed at x_{20}. If one wished to represent the *long-run production function,* where capital is also variable, using a graph, one could either draw a number of different short-run curves for differing levels of x_2 (see Figure 2.2), or one could plot the entire production surface in three dimensions (for example, refer to the 3D plots on pages 18 and 20 of Beattie and Taylor 1985).

2.2.1 Product Curves

The graph of a (short-run) production function, depicted in the uppermost graph in Figure 2.1, is also referred to as the *total product* (TP) curve. To help discuss some of the properties of a production function we view aspects of this production technology through *average product* (AP) and *marginal product* (MP) concepts. The average product of labour is simply the quantity of output produced divided by the quantity of labour used:

$$AP_1 = y/x_1 = f(x_1 | x_2 = x_{20})/x_1. \qquad (2.3)$$

---

[2] The concepts of *short run* and *long run* in production economics are quite fluid concepts. Essentially the short run is a length of time during which quantities of variable inputs can be varied but quantities of fixed inputs cannot. The long run is the length of time in which quantities of all inputs may be varied.

[3] Throughout this chapter we assume that inputs and outputs are infinitely divisible, and hence continuous (smooth) functions exist. In reality inputs and/or outputs can sometimes be quite "lumpy". For example, it would be very difficult to add some fraction of a bus to a transport fleet!

This is depicted in Figure 2.1, where we note that the AP is equivalent to the slope of the ray from a point on the TP curve to the origin. The marginal product (MP) of labour can be approximately interpreted as the quantity of extra output produced by each extra unit of labour (with capital held constant). This is equal to the slope of the TP curve, which is equivalent to the derivative of the TP curve with respect to labour:

$$MP_1 = \frac{\partial y}{\partial x_1} = \frac{\partial}{\partial x_1} f(x_1 | x_2 = x_{20}) \qquad (2.4)$$

The MP curve is also depicted in Figure 2.1. Note that MP increases as labour increases until the inflection point on the TP curve is reached. Following this, the MP decreases until it becomes zero (at the quantity of labour at which the TP curve is at its maximum). The decline in the MP curve in Figure 2.1 is a graphical representation of the *law of diminishing marginal returns*. This law states that when one factor is held fixed (e.g., capital) and another factor (e.g., labour) is increased, the MP of each additional unit of the variable factor must eventually decline, due to congestion in the use of the fixed factor.

2.2.2 The Three Stages of Production

We can divide the above graphs into three distinct "stages" of production. These stages are:

    I. increasing AP;

    II. decreasing AP while MP is positive; and

    III. negative MP.

These three stages are identified in Figure 2.1. The profit-maximising firm operates in Stage II, because Stages I and III can be shown to be inefficient. Stage III is obviously inefficient because the addition of an extra unit of x_1 results in a decline in output. Stage I is inefficient because the addition of an extra unit of labour results in an increase in the average product of all labour units employed. A firm should never produce where AP_1 is rising since this implies that the firm could increase average labour productivity by employing more labour. Thus the firm should produce somewhere in Stage II.

The selection of the optimal (profit maximising) point within Stage II not only requires knowledge of the production technology but also requires knowledge of the output and input prices. The selection of the optimal levels of inputs (and output) is discussed further in Section 2.3.

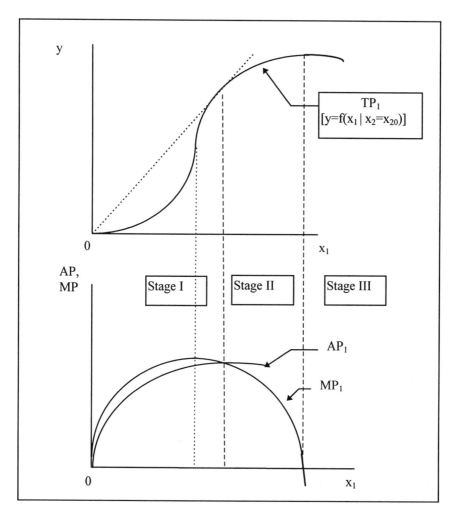

Figure 2.1 TP, AP and MP Curves and Three Stages of Production

2.2.3 Long-Run Production Functions and Isoquants

In the long run, the quantities of all inputs are variable. Thus the long-run production function is represented by equation 2.1, rather than equation 2.2 (where capital, x_2, is set at a fixed level). Although a full graphical representation of a long-run production function requires a three-dimensional graph, it can still be represented in two dimensions in one of two ways: by a family of short run production functions, where each corresponds to a different level of capital (refer to Figure 2.2); or by a family of isoquants in input/input space, where each isoquant corresponds to a different level of output.

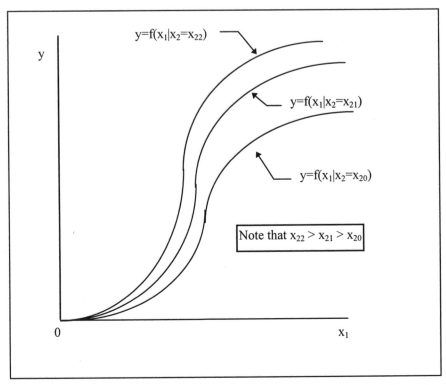

Figure 2.2 A Long-Run Production Function Represented by a Family of Short-Run Production Functions

An isoquant depicts all combinations of labour and capital (x_1 and x_2) that could be used to produce a particular quantity of output (say $y=y_0$).[4] Each level of output has an associated isoquant. An isoquant is algebraically derived from equation 2.1 by making x_2 the subject of the equation and setting y to a fixed value, such as y_0. An isoquant curve is depicted in Figure 2.3. Isoquants have the following properties:

- they are negatively sloped in the efficient stage of production (Stage II);

- they are non-intersecting; and

- they are convex to the origin.

---

[4] This definition of an isoquant is similar to that found in most introductory economics texts. It assumes that all firms are technically efficient and hence that they must operate on the isoquant. This assumption is relaxed in later chapters when we allow for inefficiency and the isoquant becomes the boundary of the input set.

The isoquants must be negatively sloped in Stage II of production, as depicted in Figure 2.3, because otherwise the firm could reduce the quantities of both inputs and still produce the same quantity of output. This is depicted in Figure 2.4 where the ranges, AA′ and BB′, correspond to Stage III production, for x_2 and x_1, respectively. These ranges indicate that there is congestion in the use of one of the inputs to the extent that its MP is negative.

The slope of the isoquant is known as the *marginal rate of technical substitution (MRTS)*. It reflects the rate at which labour can be substituted for capital, while holding output constant. It can be shown to be equal to the negative of the ratio of the marginal product of labour (MP_1) to the marginal product of capital (MP_2):

$$\text{MRTS} = \frac{dx_2}{dx_1} = -\frac{MP_1}{MP_2} \tag{2.5}$$

The remaining two properties of isoquants, listed above, are essentially common sense. The "non-intersecting" property of isoquants follows immediately from the definition of an isoquant. The intersection of two isoquants contradicts the definition because it implies that a particular combination of inputs can (efficiently) produce two levels of output. Lastly, the convexity of an isoquant is a consequence of the diminishing marginal product property of stage II of production. For example, as more labour is substituted for capital (a movement down the isoquant in Figure 2.4) the increased use of limited capital results in a decline in the MP of labour and hence a decline in the MRTS.

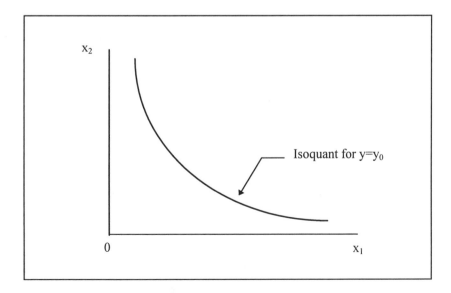

Figure 2.3 An Isoquant

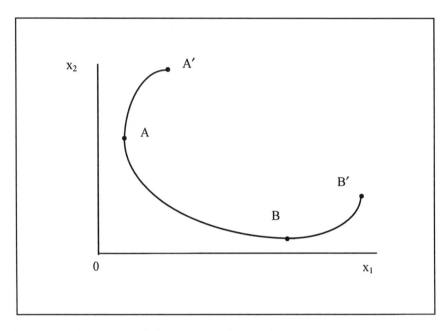

Figure 2.4 An Isoquant Reflecting Input Congestion

2.2.4 Returns to Scale and Other Measures

Returns to scale (RTS) is a long-run concept which reflects the degree to which a proportional increase in all inputs increases output. *Constant RTS* occurs when a proportional increase in all inputs results in the same proportional increase in output. For example, if doubling labour and capital results in a doubling of output, then this is evidence of constant RTS. *Increasing RTS* occurs when a proportional increase in all inputs results in a <u>more than</u> proportional increase in output, while *decreasing RTS* exists when a proportional increase in all inputs results in a <u>less than</u> proportional increase in output.

In algebraic terms, these are expressed by:

Returns to Scale	Definition ($\alpha > 1$)
Constant	$f(\alpha x_1, \alpha x_2) = \alpha f(x_1, x_2)$
Increasing	$f(\alpha x_1, \alpha x_2) > \alpha f(x_1, x_2)$
Decreasing	$f(\alpha x_1, \alpha x_2) < \alpha f(x_1, x_2)$

There are many reasons why a particular firm may possess certain RTS properties. The most commonly used example relates to a small firm exhibiting increasing RTS because it can gain by having additional staff specialise in particular tasks. One possible reason for decreasing returns to scale is the case where a firm has become so large that the management is not able to exercise close control over all aspects of the production process (as may be possible in a smaller firm).

Empirical analyses of production routinely investigate RTS by estimating the *total elasticity of production* (ε). They also often present estimates of the *partial production elasticities* (E$_i$) of each input and the *elasticity of substitution* (σ) between the two inputs. The partial production elasticities measure the proportional change in output resulting from a proportional increase in the i-th input, with all other input levels held constant. The production elasticity of the i-th input is defined as

$$E_i = \frac{\partial y}{\partial x_i} \frac{x_i}{y}. \tag{2.6}$$

One would normally expect to find that E$_i$ > 0. A negative production elasticity would be against expectations since it would imply that an increase in the i-th input (with other inputs held fixed) results in a <u>decrease</u> in output. This is the Stage III production region discussed earlier.

The total elasticity of production (sometimes referred to as the *elasticity of scale*) measures the proportional change in output resulting from a unit proportional increase in all inputs. The total elasticity of production can be shown to be equal to the sum of all the partial production elasticities. In the case of two inputs this is equal to

$$\varepsilon = E_1 + E_2. \tag{2.7}$$

The value of ε is related to RTS in the following manner:

Returns to Scale	Total Elasticity of Production (ε)
Constant	= 1
Increasing	> 1
Decreasing	< 1

In econometric analyses, the value of ε can vary for different input values if the production function is *non-homogenous* (e.g. the translog functional form) or will be fixed for all input values if the functional form is *homogenous* (e.g. the Cobb-

Douglas functional form).[5] The properties of a number of popular functional forms are discussed later in this chapter.

The elasticity of substitution (σ) is closely related to the MRTS. The MRTS measures the <u>slope</u> of the isoquant while σ measures the <u>curvature</u> of the isoquant. The elasticity of substitution is defined as the proportionate rate of change in the input ratio (x_2/x_1) divided by the proportionate rate of change in MRTS. That is,

$$\sigma = \frac{d(x_2 / x_1)}{(x_2 / x_1)} \bigg/ \frac{d(MP_1 / MP_2)}{(MP_1 / MP_2)} . \tag{2.8}$$

The elasticity of substitution is a unit-less measure of the substitution behaviour between the inputs. In Stage II of production (i.e. convex isoquants) σ lies between 0 and ∞, with a larger value of σ implying greater substitutability between the inputs. A value of $\sigma=\infty$ occurs when the inputs are perfect substitutes while $\sigma=0$ occurs when the inputs must be used in fixed proportions. Examples of isoquants which have $\sigma = 0$, 1, and ∞ are presented below in Figure 2.5. Note that when $\sigma = 0$ the isoquant has a right-angle shape and no substitution is possible. The inputs are used in the fixed proportions defined by the corner of the isoquant because operation at any other point on the isoquant results in the use of more of one input with no reduction in the other input and no gain in output. Also note that when $\sigma = \infty$ the isoquant is a straight line and the two inputs are hence infinitely substitutable.

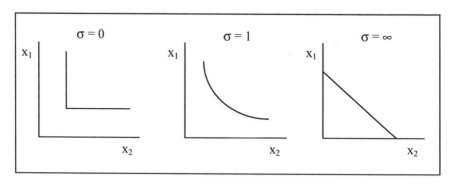

Figure 2.5 Elasticities of Substitution and Isoquant Shapes

---

[5] A function is said to be *homogenous of degree* λ if increasing all RHS variables by a factor $\alpha>0$ results in an increase in the LHS variable by a factor of α^{λ}.

2.2.5 A Simple Numerical Example

To illustrate some of these concepts we introduce a simple numerical example. Assume that the production function has the mathematical form:

$$y = 2x_1^{0.5}x_2^{0.4} \qquad (2.9)$$

This is an example of a Cobb-Douglas production function. This is quite a simple functional form which has a number of restrictive properties which are discussed later in this chapter. The partial production elasticities for this function are:

$$E_1 = \frac{\partial y}{\partial x_1}\frac{x_1}{y} = 0.5 \times 2x_1^{0.5-1}x_2^{0.4} \times \frac{x_1}{y} = 0.5 \times 2x_1^{0.5}x_2^{0.4}y^{-1} = 0.5 \qquad (2.10)$$

and

$$E_2 = \frac{\partial y}{\partial x_2}\frac{x_2}{y} = 0.4 \times 2x_1^{0.5}x_2^{0.4-1} \times \frac{x_2}{y} = 0.4 \times 2x_1^{0.5}x_2^{0.4}y^{-1} = 0.4 \qquad (2.11)$$

for labour and capital, respectively. Note that in the case of the Cobb-Douglas, the partial production elasticities are equal to the powers of the inputs in the production function.

The returns to scale is equal to the sum of these partial elasticities:

$$\varepsilon = E_1 + E_2 = 0.5 + 0.4 = 0.9. \qquad (2.12)$$

This value is less than 1 indicating decreasing returns to scale. We check this observation by doubling all inputs and seeing what happens to output. We obtain:

$$y = 2(2x_1)^{0.5}(2x_2)^{0.4} = 2^{0.5+0.4} \times 2x_1^{0.5}x_2^{0.4} = 2^{0.9}y \qquad (2.13)$$

which is a less than proportional increase in output.

Using some further calculus, it can be shown that the elasticity of substitution, σ, for this (or any Cobb-Douglas) production function is equal to 1, irrespective of the values of the parameters (i.e., if we change the numbers: 2, 0.5 and 0.4 in equation 2.9 to alternative numbers we will still obtain $\sigma=1$). This is one of the restrictive properties of the Cobb-Douglas functional form.

2.3 Price Information and Cost Minimisation and Profit Maximisation

Up until this point in the chapter we have only discussed the production function and physical aspects of production. We now introduce information on the prices of inputs and outputs and also make assumptions regarding the economic behaviour of the firm. We assume that the firm faces perfectly competitive input and output markets. That is, the firm faces particular prices and the behaviour of one firm cannot influence the price of any good (i.e., the size of the firm is very small relative to the size of the market).

We consider optimal input and output decisions under four different sets of behavioural assumptions:

    1.   short-run (SR) cost minimisation;

    2.   long-run (LR) cost minimisation;

    3.   SR profit maximisation; and

    4.   LR profit maximisation.

The first three of these options are special cases of the fourth. Under LR profit maximisation labour, capital and output are all variable and hence their values may be chosen by the firm so as to maximise profit. In the first three cases, at least one of these variables is assumed fixed. The assumptions are summarised below for the simple one-output, two-input example, which we consider in this chapter.

case	description	variable quantities	fixed quantities
1	SR cost minimisation	labour	capital, output
2	LR cost minimisation	labour, capital	output
3	SR profit maximisation	labour, output	capital
4	LR profit maximisation	labour, capital, output	none

Before we go on to discuss how to select optimal input and output levels in these four cases, we first note that in some instances it may be very difficult to assume one of these behavioural objectives and/or it may be very difficult to obtain information on prices. A publicly-funded university is an example of a productive unit where the above behavioural objectives are unlikely to apply (output maximisation given a fixed budget is perhaps closer to reality) and output prices (of university degrees and research papers) are very difficult to specify. In such instances, it may be wisest to ignore any (imperfect) price information and to focus on the technical efficiency side of things.[6]

Putting the above non-profit case aside, we now discuss how to select optimal input and/or output quantities, given one of the above behavioural assumptions, along with given price levels and knowledge of the production function. We firstly use graphical methods to solve the optimisation problem, and then demonstrate a solution using calculus.

2.3.1 Cost Minimisation

To begin, we specify the notation that is used to represent prices. We use p, w_1 and w_2 to represent the prices of output, labour and capital, respectively.

Before discussing optimal input and/or output choices further it is useful to first define a few cost curves. Cost curves traditionally have cost on the vertical axis and output on the horizontal axis. Many of our short-run cost curves can be derived by inverting a product curve from Section 2.2 and multiplying it by the price of labour.[7] For example, we can derive the *total variable cost (TVC)* curve by making labour (x_1) the subject of equation 2.2

$$x_1 = f^{-1}(y|x_2=x_{20}) \tag{2.14}$$

and then multiplying this by the wage rate (w_1) to provide

$$TVC = w_1x_1 = w_1f^{-1}(y|x_2=x_{20}). \tag{2.15}$$

In graphical terms, we take the TP curve from Figure 2.1, swap the output and labour axes around and then multiply the inverted curve by the wage rate to provide the TVC curve in Figure 2.5. This curve represents the total variable cost (in this case the labour cost) associated with each level of output.

The (short run) *total fixed cost (TFC)* curve is easy to derive. It is simply the quantity of capital used (x_{20}) multiplied by the price (or implicit rental rate) of capital (w_2). That is,

$$TFC = w_2x_{20} \tag{2.16}$$

which can be represented by a horizontal line as depicted in Figure 2.5.

---

[6] See Pestieau and Tulkens (1993) for further discussion of performance measurement in non-profit organisations.

[7] This can be done because we have only one variable input, and we assume perfect competition, and hence that the firm is a price taker in input markets.

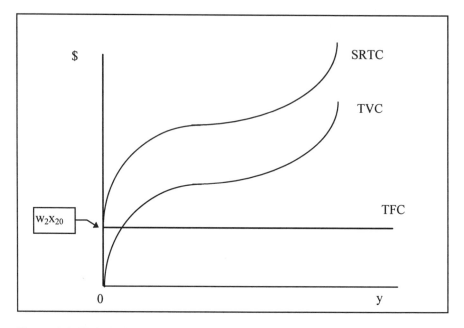

Figure 2.6 TVC, TFC and SRTC Curves

The *short run total cost (SRTC)* curve is simply the sum of TVC and TFC. That is,

$$\begin{aligned} \text{SRTC} &= \text{TVC} + \text{TFC} = w_1x_1 + w_2x_{20} \\ &= w_1f^1(y, x_2=x_{20}) + w_2x_{20} \\ &= c(y), \end{aligned} \tag{2.17}$$

where $c(y)$ represents the functional relationship between SRTC and output (y). In Figure 2.6 we show that the SRTC curve is simply the TVC curve shifted up by the amount w_2x_{20}.

Long-Run Cost Curves

As was the case with product curves, there are two ways in which we can extend our short run analysis of costs to the long run (when all input quantities are variable). We can plot a family of SRTC curves (each corresponding to different levels of capital), or we could use isoquant and isocost curves.

We begin by considering the first of these two options. Figure 2.7 shows the SRTC curves corresponding to three different levels of capital. The segments of these curves which form the lower boundary of the three curves (i.e., the lines which join the points A, B, C and D) trace out the *long-run total cost (LRTC)* curve. If we were to plot an infinite number of SRTC curves (each corresponding to a different level of the fixed input), the resulting LRTC curve would be a smooth curve, as depicted in Figure 2.8. Note that the smooth LRTC curve passes through the origin, because this corresponds to the point where no capital and labour are used.

The *long-run average cost (LRAC)* curve can be derived from the LRTC curve as

$$\text{LRAC} = \text{LRTC}/y. \tag{2.18}$$

The LRAC curve is depicted in Figure 2.8. Note that the height of this curve for any value of y is equal to the slope of a ray from the origin to the LRTC curve corresponding to y. The optimal (minimum cost) scale of plant is indicated by the minimum of the LRAC curve.

The *long-run marginal cost (LRMC)* curve can be derived from the LRTC curve using differentiation

$$\text{LRMC} = \frac{\partial}{\partial y} \text{LRTC} . \tag{2.19}$$

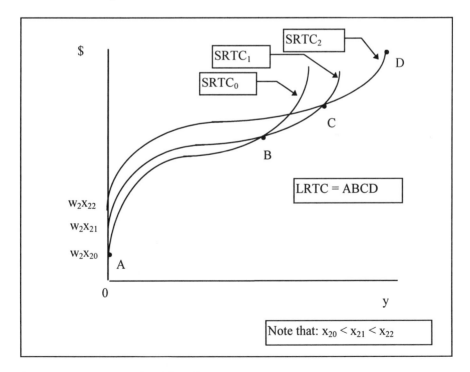

Figure 2.7 Long Run Total Cost Curve

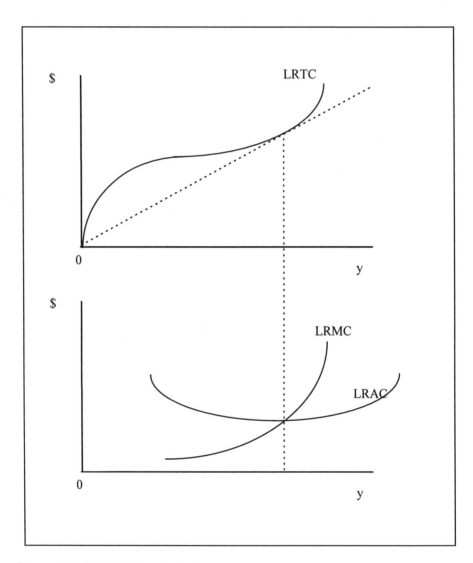

Figure 2.8 LRAC, LRTC and LRMC Curves

The LRMC curve intersects the LRAC curve at the minimum of the LRAC curve, as depicted in Figure 2.8.[8]

Isoquants and Cost Minimisation

Another method of illustrating long-run cost information on a diagram is to add information on factor prices (in the form of isocost lines) to the isoquants presented in Section 2.2. An isoquant and an isocost line are plotted in Figure 2.8. The isocost line in Figure 2.9 is drawn for a total cost level of $C=C_0$. It is a straight line with slope equal to $-(w_2/w_1)$, the negative of the ratio of the input prices, and vertical and horizontal intercepts of C_0/w_2 and C_0/w_1, respectively. These intercepts correspond to the quantities of these inputs that could be purchased if all of C_0 was spent on that input. One could obviously specify a large number of isocost curves, each corresponding to a different level of total costs, with each line having the same slope. We have chosen to draw that isocost line which happens to be at a tangent to the selected isoquant so that we can use this diagram to also discuss producer optimisation.

Consider the case where a firm wishes to produce the output level $y=y_0$. The least-cost method of producing this level of output is defined by the point of tangency between the isoquant and an isocost line. In Figure 2.9 this is defined by the point A. This implies that the firm should use x_1* of labour and x_2* of capital to produce the desired output. The combination of inputs in any other proportions would result in production at some point on the isoquant other than point A. This "other" point must, by definition, intersect an isocost line which lies to the right of the isocost line, depicted in Figure 2.9, and hence involve a larger cost than C_0. Thus the point A defines the least-cost method of producing output y_0.

By observing that the slope of the isocost line is $-(w_2/w_1)$ and the slope of the isoquant is equal to $-(MP_1/MP_2)$, we see that the optimisation rule is expressed as:

$$-\frac{MP_1}{MP_2} = -\frac{w_1}{w_2}$$

or as

$$\frac{MP_1}{w_1} = \frac{MP_2}{w_2}.$$ (2.20)

That is, the marginal products per dollar spent on all inputs must be equal.

---

[8] Average and marginal cost curves can also be defined for the short-run case. See Call and Holahan (1983) or any undergraduate microeconomics text for examples.

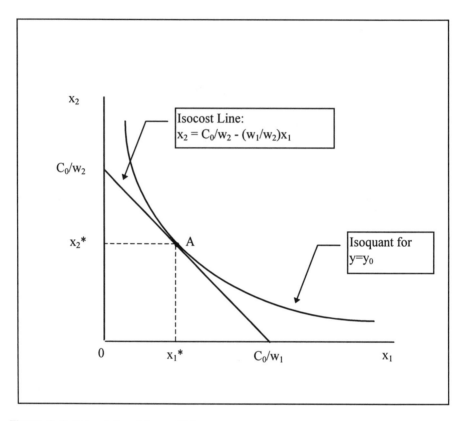

Figure 2. 9 Isoquant and Isocost Line

This same rule can also be derived using calculus. The values of x_1 and x_2 that provide minimum total cost, for a given output level, can be obtained by finding the first partial derivatives of a Lagrangean function (involving the cost function and the production function constraint), setting these equal to zero and solving for x_1 and x_2.[9] This is illustrated using a simple example later in this chapter.

Note that the above discussion involves LR cost minimisation (where all inputs are variable and output is fixed). SR cost minimisation is not illustrated here because it is a trivial exercise when there is only one variable input. The labour level that is required can be obtained directly from the production function (i.e., without needing price information). One simply reads the quantity of labour corresponding to the given output level, y_0, from the TP curve (such as that in Figure 2.1) which is drawn for the given capital level, x_{20}. If we had two variable inputs (say labour and materials) then the selection of optimal quantities of labour and materials depend

---

[9] If the Lagrangian function has more than one stationary point then the second partial derivatives can be used to identify the minimum point(s).

upon their relative prices and the method involved is similar to that described above for LR cost minimisation.

We have seen how the LRTC curve can be derived by plotting a large number of SRTC curves. An alternative way of deriving the LRTC curve is to repeat the above cost minimisation approach for a number of different output levels and then plot the resulting cost and output combinations on a graph (as in Figure 2.8). The two methods obtain the same LRTC.

2.3.2 Profit Maximisation

The profit of the firm is defined as total revenue (TR) minus total costs. In the case of perfect competition, the TR curve is simply a straight line with slope equal to the output price, p, which passes through the origin. The LR profit curve is equal to the TR curve minus the LRTC curve. These three curves are depicted in Figure 2.10. Note that the largest gap between the TR and LRTC curves corresponds to the highest point on the LR profit curve. Thus we can use this profit curve to identify the LR profit-maximising level of output.

The graphical solution of the SR profit maximisation case is identical to the LR case depicted above except we replace the LRTC curve with the SRTC curve from Figure 2.5. This provides graphs very similar to those depicted in Figure 2.10 except that the SR profit curve intersects the vertical axis at a distance of w_2x_{20} below the origin (instead of passing through the origin as the LR profit curve does). The SR profit curve is not illustrated so as to conserve space.

The selection of an optimal level of output to produce can also be determined using the marginal curves. The profit-maximising rule is to equate the long run marginal curves. That is,

$$MR = LRMC \tag{2.21}$$

In the case of perfect competition, MR is equal to the price of output (p). Figure 2.11 illustrates the profit-maximising rule using the marginal curves. It is evident from Figure 2.11, that production at any point other than y* would result in a lowering of profits. This is obvious for larger outputs, because marginal cost will exceed marginal revenue when output exceeds y*. Profit will also fall if output is reduced below y* because at any point below y* the producer could still increase profits by producing an extra unit of output because the marginal revenue (the price) obtained for that extra unit would be greater than the marginal cost of producing that extra unit.

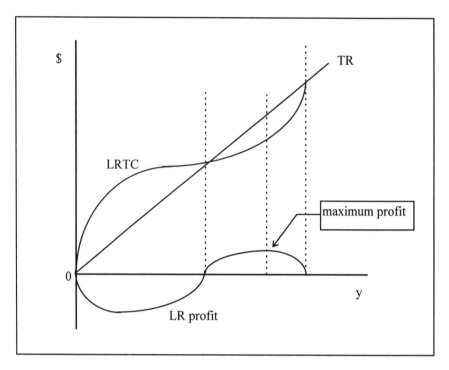

Figure 2.10 LR profit curve

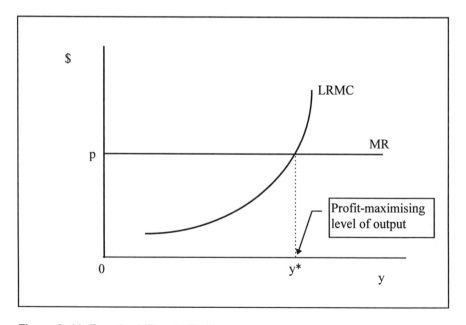

Figure 2. 11 Equating MR and LRMC

2.3.3 A Simple Numerical Example

In this section we use the simple Cobb-Douglas production function example introduced earlier to illustrate how one can use calculus (instead of graphs) to select optimal input and/or output quantities. Recall that our example production function from equation 2.9 is:

$$y = 2x_1^{0.5}x_2^{0.4} \tag{2.22}$$

We assume that the price levels are 4, 4 and 2 for p, w_1 and w_2, respectively.

LR Cost Minimisation

In this case output is fixed and the two inputs are variable. Assuming that an output quantity of y = 10 is required, we can set up a Lagrangean function to minimise the cost

$$C = w_1x_1 + w_2x_2 \tag{2.23}$$

of producing this output level, subject to the production function constraint. The Lagrangean function is:

$$L = w_1x_1 + w_2x_2 + \lambda(y - 2x_1^{0.5}x_2^{0.4}). \tag{2.24}$$

To minimise this function we find the first partial derivatives with respect to the input quantities and with respect to the Lagrangean multiplier, λ, and set them all to zero.

$$\frac{\partial L}{\partial x_1} = w_1 - \lambda x_1^{-0.5}x_2^{0.4} = 0 \tag{2.25}$$

$$\frac{\partial L}{\partial x_2} = w_2 - \lambda 0.8x_1^{0.5}x_2^{-0.6} = 0 \tag{2.26}$$

$$\frac{\partial L}{\partial \lambda} = y - 2x_1^{0.5}x_2^{0.4} = 0 \tag{2.27}$$

We can simplify these expressions by inserting the information we know on input prices and output quantities. This provides us with:

$$4 - \lambda x_1^{-0.5}x_2^{0.4} = 0 \tag{2.28}$$

$$2 - \lambda 0.8x_1^{0.5}x_2^{-0.6} = 0 \tag{2.29}$$

$$10 - 2x_1^{0.5}x_2^{0.4} = 0 \tag{2.30}$$

Now from equation 2.28 we obtain

$$\lambda = 4(x_1^{-0.5}x_2^{0.4})^{-1}. \tag{2.31}$$

Substituting this into the 2nd equation, we obtain

$$2 - 4(x_1^{-0.5}x_2^{0.4})^{-1}0.8x_1^{0.5}x_2^{-0.6} = 0$$

which after re-arrangement becomes

$$2 - 3.2x_1x_2^{-1} = 0$$

or

$$x_2 = 1.6x_1. \tag{2.32}$$

Now substituting this into the production function (equation 2.30) we obtain

$$10 - 2x_1^{0.5}(1.6x_1)^{0.4} = 0$$

or

$$x_1 = (5/(1.6)^{0.4})^{1/0.9} = 4.85 \tag{2.33}$$

and then using this in equation 2.32 we obtain

$$x_2 = 1.6 \times 4.85 = 7.76. \tag{2.34}$$

Hence the cost-minimising quantities of labour and capital are 4.85 and 7.76, respectively (when $y=10$, $w_1=4$ and $w_2=2$).

LR Profit Maximisation

In this case both the output and the two inputs are variable. Profit is defined as:

$$\pi = TR - TC = py - (w_1x_1 + w_2x_2). \tag{2.35}$$

We begin by substituting in the production constraint ($y = 2x_1^{0.5}x_2^{0.4}$), providing:

$$\pi = p(2x_1^{0.5}x_2^{0.4}) - (w_1x_1 + w_2x_2). \tag{2.36}$$

To maximise this function we find the first partial derivatives with respect to the input quantities and set them both equal to zero.

$$\frac{\partial \pi}{\partial x_1} = px_1^{-0.5}x_2^{0.4} - w_1 = 0 \tag{2.37}$$

$$\frac{\partial \pi}{\partial x_2} = 0.8px_1^{0.5}x_2^{-0.6} - w_2 = 0 \tag{2.38}$$

We can simplify these expressions by inserting the information we know on input and output prices. This provides us with:

$$4x_1^{-0.5}x_2^{0.4} - 4 = 0 \tag{2.39}$$

$$3.2x_1^{0.5}x_2^{-0.6} - 2 = 0 \tag{2.40}$$

Now from equation 2.39 we obtain

$$x_2 = (x_1^{0.5})^{2.5} = x_1^{1.25} \tag{2.41}$$

and substituting this into equation 2.40 we obtain:

$$3.2x_1^{0.5}(x_1^{1.25})^{-0.6} - 2 = 0$$

which after re-arrangement becomes

$$3.2x_1^{-0.25} - 2 = 0$$

or

$$x_1 = (1.6)^4 = 6.55 \tag{2.42}$$

and then using this in equation 2.41 we obtain

$$x_2 = 6.55^{1.25} = 10.49. \tag{2.43}$$

Now substituting these two values into the production function we obtain

$$y = 2 \times 6.55^{0.5} \times 10.49^{0.4} = 13.11. \tag{2.44}$$

Thus the profit-maximising levels of labour, capital and output are 6.55, 10.49 and 13.11, respectively (when $p=4$, $w_1=4$ and $w_2=2$).

One important point to note regarding this simple example is that the empirical production function we have chosen (equation 2.9) is concave. This guarantees that the derived profit and cost curves have a maximum point and a minimum point, respectively. If we had chosen an empirical production function which was convex.

For example, a Cobb-Douglas exhibiting increasing returns to scale, then both of these curves would be unbounded.

In fact, in the above simple numerical example we have not been very rigorous. We have only discussed the first-order optimising conditions. We have not mentioned the second-order optimising conditions that involve the use of the second-order partial derivatives to check if the stationary point obtained is a maximum or a minimum. We also did not mention that if profit is everywhere negative, then the firm will chose to produce nothing at all. For a more complete discussion of these issues refer to Beattie and Taylor (1985).

2.4 Econometric Estimation of Production Functions

Production functions can be estimated from sample data. This data may involve observations on a number of firms in a particular time period (cross-sectional data); aggregate industry-level data observed over a number of time periods (time-series data); or observations on a number of firms in a number of time periods (panel data). To estimate a production function, information on output and input quantities is required.

One may either estimate a *parametric* function using econometric (statistical) methods, or a *non-parametric* function using mathematical programming. The parametric approach has been, by far, most frequently used in applied economic analysis to date. However, the non-parametric approach has been equally, if not more, popular in analyses of efficiency.

2.4.1 Functional Form

The first step in any parametric empirical application is to select an appropriate functional form for the production function. A variety of functional forms have been used in applied production analyses. These range from simple forms, such as the Cobb-Douglas:

$$y = Ax_1^{b_1} x_2^{b_2},$$ (2.45)

or equivalently as

$$\ln y = \ln A + b_1 \ln x_1 + b_2 \ln x_2,$$ (2.46)

to more complex forms, such as the translog:[10]

---

[10] See Jorgenson, Christensen and Lau (1973).

$$\ln y = b_0 + b_1 \ln x_1 + b_2 \ln x_2 + (1/2)[b_{11}(\ln x_1)^2 + b_{22}(\ln x_2)^2] + b_{12}\ln x_1 \ln x_2$$
$$(2.47)$$

The Cobb-Douglas is easy to estimate and mathematically manipulate but is restrictive in the properties it imposes upon the production structure (such as a fixed RTS value and an elasticity of substitution equal to unity). The translog does not impose these restrictions upon the production structure,[11] but this comes at the cost of a having a form which is more difficult to mathematically manipulate and which can suffer from degrees of freedom and multicollinearity problems. There are a number of functional forms which lie between these two extremes. These include the constant elasticity of substitution (CES) function:

$$y = A[bx_1^{-g} + (1-b)x_2^{-g}]^{-v/g}$$
$$(2.48)$$

which relaxes the assumption of unitary elasticity of substitution, and the Zellner-Revankar[12] form:

$$ye^{\theta y} = Ax_1^{b_1}x_2^{b_2}$$
$$(2.49)$$

which allows RTS to vary across output levels.

For further information on the properties of various functional forms, see Section 2.5 in Beattie and Taylor (1985), especially Table 2.1, which lists a number of the properties of some commonly used production functions.

2.4.2 Technical Change Measurement

If time-series data (or cross-section/time-series data) are available, then the rate of technological change in an industry may be estimated by including a time-trend variable in an econometric production function. For example, the Cobb-Douglas production function in equation 2.46 would become

$$\ln y = b_0 + b_1 \ln x_1 + b_2 \ln x_2 + b_t t,$$
$$(2.50)$$

where t is a time trend (t=1,2,...,T). The estimate of the coefficient, b_t, provides an estimate of the annual percentage change in output resulting from technological change.

The translog production function in equation 2.47 can be adjusted in a similar manner to account for technological change. However, since the translog is a

---

[11] The translog functional form is one of a class of functional forms known as *flexible* functional forms. These provide a second-order local approximation to any functional form. Another example of a flexible form is the quadratic.

[12] See Zellner and Revankar (1969).

second-order approximation, we usually introduce both t and t^2 into the equation to obtain

$$\ln y = b_0 + b_1\ln x_1 + b_2\ln x_2 + b_{12}\ln x_1\ln x_2 + (1/2)[b_{11}(\ln x_1)^2 + b_{22}(\ln x_2)^2]$$
$$+ b_t t + b_{tt}t^2. \tag{2.51}$$

An estimate of the annual percentage change in output resulting from technological change is provided by the first partial derivative of equation 2.51 with respect to t: $b_t + 2tb_{tt}$. This value will vary for different values of t. It will decrease over the sample period if b_{tt} is negative and increase if it is positive.

These production functions can be easily estimated using any number of computer packages. We utilise the SHAZAM econometrics package (White, 1993) to illustrate a few things in this book. SHAZAM code is listed in Table 2.1. In this example it is assumed that time-series data are available on one output and two inputs for a particular industry. The data are assumed to be stored in columns in a text file, named *eg.dta*. In this SHAZAM code, we read in the data, generate columns containing the logs of the data, generate a time trend variable, and then estimate a Cobb-Douglas production function using ordinary least squares (OLS) regression. Following this we generate the squares and cross-products of relevant variables and then estimate the translog function using OLS.

Table 2.1 SHAZAM Instructions for Production Function Estimation

	SHAZAM Code	**Description**
1	read(eg.dta) y x1 x2	read in data on output and 2 inputs from the data file
2	genr ly=log(y)	obtain logarithm of y
3	genr lx1=log(x1)	obtain logarithm of x1
4	genr lx2=log(x2)	obtain logarithm of x2
5	genr t=time(0)	construct a time trend, t=1,2,...,T.
6	* Cobb-Douglas:	comment line
7	ols ly lx1 lx2 t	obtain OLS estimates of the coefficients of the Cobb-Douglas production function
8	genr lx12=lx1*lx2	obtain cross-product
9	genr lx11=0.5*lx1**2	obtain 0.5 times the square of log(x1)
10	genr lx22=0.5*lx2**2	obtain 0.5 times the square of log(x2)
11	genr t2=t**2	obtain square of time trend
12	* translog:	comment line
13	ols ly lx1 lx2 lx12 lx11 lx22 t t2	obtain OLS estimates of the coefficients of the translog production function

Note that *Hicks-neutral technological change* is assumed in equations 2.50 and 2.51. This essentially implies that the isoquants are shifting each year without any change in the shape of the isoquants. That is, the marginal products remain the same. Non-neutral technological change can be considered by also including the cross-products of t and the logged inputs into equation 2.51. Non-neutral technological change is discussed in the following chapter.

2.5 Conclusions

This chapter gives a summary of some results in production economics. If you feel your knowledge of production economics is a bit rusty, then you are strongly advised to consult a microeconomics textbook and read the relevant chapters on production economics. Any text which is presently in use in a university should suffice. The texts that we have primarily relied upon are:

- Call and Holahan (1983) - Chapters 5 and 6;

- Beattie and Taylor (1985) - Chapters 2, 3 and 4;

- Varian (1992) - Chapters 1-5; and

- Henderson and Quandt (1980) - Chapters 4 and 5.

Call and Holahan (1983) primarily uses graphs to illustrate the concepts and hence may be a good point to start if you do not have strong mathematics skills. However, if you have reasonable mathematics skills then you may find the other texts more appealing.

In the next chapter we extend this introductory discussion of production economics to include the duality between a production function and a (minimum) cost function or (maximum) profit function representation of a technology. We also extend our discussion of single-output technologies to accommodate multiple-output technologies and distance function representations of these technologies.

3. ADDITIONAL TOPICS IN PRODUCTION ECONOMICS

3.1 Introduction

The production economics concepts discussed in Chapter 2 should provide sufficient background for many of the basic efficiency and productivity measurement methods discussed in this book. Much of the Chapter 2 material is similar to what one would be likely to encounter in an undergraduate microeconomics course. The present chapter reviews some additional, more advanced, production economics material. Our primary focus in this chapter is on duality and multiple-input, multiple-output distance functions. An appreciation of the material in this chapter will ensure a deeper understanding of the basic productivity and efficiency measurement methods, and will also assist with the interpretation of more advanced methods, such as the measurement of allocative efficiency using stochastic frontier cost functions, which is discussed in Chapter 9.

This chapter is organised as follows. In Section 3.1 we discuss the duality between the production function and cost and profit functions and their properties. Following this we discuss econometric estimation of cost and profit functions in Section 3.2 and then introduce multi-output technologies and distance functions in Section 3.3. The chapter ends with some concluding remarks in Section 3.4.

3.2 Duality in Production

In this section we discuss the dual relationship between the production function representation of a production technology and the minimum cost or maximum profit function representations of a production technology.[1] It should be noted that the term *duality* is not used solely in production economics. It is also used in many other areas of study to describe two methods of approaching the same question. For example, it is used in consumer theory to describe the relationship between utility functions and expenditure functions.[2] It is also used in linear programming to describe how any maximisation (minimisation) problem can be expressed as an equivalent minimisation (maximisation) problem.

The discussion of duality in production economics (hereafter termed simply "duality") in this chapter is based primarily upon Chapter 6 in Beattie and Taylor (1985) and to a lesser extent upon Chambers (1988). Further relevant readings are listed in the final section of this chapter.

3.2.1   A Digression on Input Demand and Output Supply Functions

Two concepts that should be defined prior to our discussion of duality are those of input demand equations and output supply equations. We did not consider these concepts in Chapter 2 but came very close to doing so. We assumed that prices (both for inputs and output) were fixed at certain values.[3] Hence, when we used both graphs and calculus to obtain the quantities of inputs and output that maximise profits, we had, in fact, obtained the quantities corresponding to one point on each of:

- the output supply curve;

- the labour input demand curve; and

- the capital input demand curve.[4]

That is, we had identified those points corresponding to the price levels we had assumed.

We now describe how these profit-maximising output supply and input demand functions can be derived using either graphs or calculus. Following this we will also describe how conditional input demand curves can also be derived when cost minimisation is assumed.

---

[1] One may also represent a production technology in other ways, such as by a revenue function or by a cost indirect revenue function or a revenue indirect cost function, however, the cost and profit approaches have been the ones most often considered. For a comprehensive discussion of various dual production representations and their inter-relationships see Fare and Primont (1995).

[2] Cornes (1992) provides an excellent discussion of the many uses of duality in economics.

[3] Recall our example involved two inputs (labour=x_1, capital=x_2) and one output (y), with prices w_1, w_2 and p, respectively. In this Chapter we will assume we are dealing with the long run and hence that all inputs are variable. Results involving one or more fixed factors can also be derived, but these would be more messy than the case where all inputs are variable. All assumptions made in Chapter 2 are also made in this chapter, unless otherwise stated.

[4] Note that these curves represent the quantities supplied and demanded by a single firm not those of the entire industry.

Profit Maximisation

Recall that the profit-maximising level of output was obtained by equating MR and LRMC, as depicted in Figure 2.11. To derive the entire output supply curve (not just a single point) we could hold input prices (w_1 and w_2) fixed at some level and vary the output price (p), repeatedly solving the profit-maximisation problem, obtaining an output quantity (y) for each output price level (p), and hence tracing out the output supply curve of this profit-maximising firm. It is fairly obvious that this supply curve will be equivalent to the LRMC curve in Figure 2.11. However, keep in mind that this supply curve assumes the input prices have been fixed at particular levels. If we had considered different input prices, this would result in a different cost curve and hence a different supply function. Thus we should note that the supply curve does not only depend upon the output price, but also upon the two input prices. We could represent this supply function by:

$$y^* = y^*(p, w_1, w_2) \tag{3.1}$$

where y^* represents the profit maximising quantity of y and $y^*(.)$ represents the functional relationship between y^* and the prices.

We could also derive the input demand curves for labour (x_1) and capital (x_2) in a similar manner. For an illustration of this refer to Chapter 11 in Call and Holahan (1983). Essentially we find that the input demand equations of the profit-maximising firm are also a function of all three prices. Thus we could write them as:

$$x_1^* = x_1^*(p, w_1, w_2) \tag{3.2}$$

and

$$x_2^* = x_2^*(p, w_1, w_2) \tag{3.3}$$

where x_i^* represents the profit maximising level of the i-th input and $x_i^*(.)$ represents the functional relationship between x_i^* and the prices.

The above three functions can also be derived by using calculus to determine the levels of x_1, x_2 and y which maximise profit (given particular prices). The profit maximising firm is attempting to maximise profit, given the production technology and prices. Profit is defined as

$$\pi = TR - TC = py - (w_1 x_1 + w_2 x_2). \tag{3.4}$$

Now to find those values of x_1 and x_2 (and subsequently y) which maximise profit [given the production technology $y = f(x_1, x_2)$] we substitute the production function into equation 3.4 to obtain

$$\pi = p.f(x_1,x_2) - (w_1x_1 + w_2x_2). \tag{3.5}$$

We then find the first partial derivatives of this with respect to each of the input quantities, set these equal to zero and solve simultaneously for x_1 and x_2 to obtain equations 3.2 and 3.3, the input demand equations. Lastly, to obtain the output supply equation, we substitute these two input demand equations into the production function

$$y = f(x_1,x_2) = f(x_1^*(p,w_1,w_2),x_2^*(p,w_1,w_2)) \tag{3.6}$$

to obtain the output supply function (equation 3.1).

We can therefore use equations 3.1 to 3.3, the input demand and output supply equations, to read off the quantities of inputs and output that would maximise profit, for a given set of prices.[5]

Cost Minimisation

In some instances cost minimisation, given an output level, can be a more appropriate behavioural assumption than profit maximisation.   For example, consider the case of a power plant that is contracted to produce a certain amount of power.   In such cases the output supply function is not an issue (since output is exogenously fixed).[6]   The input demand functions can be derived by specifying the (total) cost function

$$c = w_1x_1 + w_2x_2 \tag{3.7}$$

and deriving the input levels which would minimise cost subject to the production function constraint.[7]   This restricted minimisation problem may be solved by forming a Lagrangean function

$$L = w_1x_1 + w_2x_2 + \lambda(y-f(x_1,x_2)), \tag{3.8}$$

finding the first partial derivatives of this with respect to x_1, x_2 and λ, setting these equal to zero, and solving simultaneously for x_1 and x_2 to derive the conditional input demand functions:

$$x_1^c = x_1^c(y,w_1,w_2) \tag{3.9}$$

---

[5]There are many other possible uses of these output supply and input demand equations. For example, they are often used to derive industry level supply and demand equations to assess the likely impact of various policies, such as taxes and subsidies, upon production decisions.

[6] An *exogenous* variable is one whose value is assumed fixed. That is, determined by factors outside the system.

[7]This was illustrated graphically in Figure 2.9 where the optimal input combinations were obtained from the point of tangency between the isoquant and the isocost line.

and

$$x_2^c = x_2^c(y, w_1, w_2),$$ (3.10)

where x_i^c denotes the cost-minimising level of the i-th input and $x_i^c(.)$ represents the functional relationship between x_i^c and the input prices and output. The main difference to note between these conditional input demand functions and the demand functions obtained under profit maximisation (see equations 3.2 and 3.3) is that the output quantity (y) appears as an argument instead of output price (p).

3.2.2 How is Duality Useful?

The above section describes how, with knowledge of the production function, output supply and input demand equations, which are consistent with a firm's optimisation objective, may be derived. The above approach is called the *primal approach*. It requires one to obtain an estimate of the production function (perhaps using econometric methods). There is an alternative approach which is known as the *dual approach*. It involves deriving output supply and input demand equations directly from an estimated profit or cost function. These derivations are much simpler than is the case with the primal approach. There is no need for construction of Lagrangean functions or the solution of sets of simultaneous equations, as is required in the primal approach. One simply specifies an objective function (such as a maximum profit function or a minimum cost function) and the input demand and output supply equations are obtained using partial differentiation, with no other algebraic manipulations required.

This is one example of how duality theory can be of assistance. Before we discuss duality further, it would be beneficial to list some of its many applications in the analysis of production, productivity and efficiency, so that we can see the potential benefit of this section. Some of the ways in which we can use duality are:

- Duality can provide an easier method of obtaining output supply and input demand equations (as discussed above).

- Duality theory is used to help identify the economic properties of popular TFP index number methods, such as the Tornqvist index (see Chapter 5).

- Duality theory can be used to decompose the cost inefficiency estimates obtained from a frontier cost function into its technical and allocative components (see Chapter 9).

- In some instances, when one wishes to measure the characteristics of a production technology using econometric methods, one may find that it may be more convenient or more appropriate to estimate a cost or profit function instead of the production function. Possible reasons include:

- ◆ It may be easier to obtain information on costs and prices than to obtain information on input quantities.

- ◆ Some authors argue that direct econometric estimation of a production function may suffer from simultaneous equations bias if the input quantities are not exogenous to the optimisation decision. Hence the estimation of a profit or cost function, which has the (arguably) *exogenous* prices on the right hand side (RHS) of the estimating equation, may be more appropriate from a statistical perspective.[8]

- ◆ In recent years, some researchers have begun estimating multiple output production technologies using distance functions. Prior to this development, researchers faced with multiple output production would usually either: (i) aggregate the outputs into a single output measure and estimate a production function, or (ii) they would turn to dual methods where cost and profit functions can accommodate multiple outputs with ease.

More will be said on many of these issues later in this chapter and in other chapters. We shall now discuss the dual methods in more detail, beginning with the profit maximisation case.

3.2.3 Profit Functions and Hotelling's Lemma

A profit function is defined as the <u>maximum</u> profit associated with particular input and output prices. It may be obtained by substituting the profit-maximising input demand and output supply equations derived in the primal approach (i.e., equations 3.1 to 3.3) into the definition of profit (equation 3.4) to obtain:

$$\pi^* = p[y(p,w_1,w_2)] - \{w_1[x_1(p,w_1,w_2)] + w_2[x_2(p,w_1,w_2)]\}$$

$$= \pi^*(p,w_1,w_2) \qquad\qquad\qquad (3.11)$$

where the notation π^* is used to indicate <u>maximum</u> profit while $\pi^*(.)$ represents the relationship between π^* and prices.

This derivation of a profit function is used to illustrate the concept of the profit function. You would be unlikely to actually derive a profit function in this way in practice, because a principal advantage of the dual approach is the avoidance of the necessity to use the primal approach. In practice, one would normally specify a profit function (which has appropriate properties that will be defined shortly), estimate the function using sample data (say using econometrics), and then use *Hotelling's Lemma* to derive the output supply and input demand equations.

---

[8]In the cost minimisation case the (fixed) output will also appear on the RHS.

Hotelling's Lemma

Hotelling's Lemma, which is derived from the *envelope theorem*,[9] states that the first partial derivatives of the profit function with respect to each of the input prices define the negative of the input demand functions. That is,

$$\frac{\partial \pi^*}{\partial w_1} = -x_1^*(p,w_1,w_2) \tag{3.12}$$

and

$$\frac{\partial \pi^*}{\partial w_2} = -x_2^*(p,w_1,w_2). \tag{3.13}$$

Hotelling's Lemma also states that the first partial derivative of the indirect profit function with respect to output price provides the output supply equation:

$$\frac{\partial \pi^*}{\partial p} = y^*(p,w_1,w_2) \tag{3.14}$$

This result also generalises to the case of K inputs and M outputs.

Symmetry

The symmetry between the cross partial derivatives of these input demand and output supply functions follows as direct result of *Young's Theorem*, which states that a second partial derivative should be invariant to the order of differentiation. That is, for any twice differential function, $g(z_1, z_2)$

$$\frac{\partial^2 g(z_1,z_2)}{\partial z_1 \partial z_2} = \frac{\partial^2 g(z_1,z_2)}{\partial z_2 \partial z_1}. \tag{3.15}$$

Using this we can show that

$$-\frac{\partial x_1^*(p,w_1,w_2)}{\partial w_2} = \frac{\partial^2 \pi^*(p,w_1,w_2)}{\partial w_1 \partial w_2} = \frac{\partial^2 \pi^*(p,w_1,w_2)}{\partial w_2 \partial w_1} = -\frac{\partial x_2^*(p,w_1,w_2)}{\partial w_1} \tag{3.16}$$

and also that

---

[9] See Beattie and Taylor (1985, pp.227) for the definition and a proof of the envelope theorem.

$$-\frac{\partial x_i{}^*(p, w_1, w_2)}{\partial p} = \frac{\partial^2 \pi^*(p, w_1, w_2)}{\partial w_i \partial p} = \frac{\partial^2 \pi^*(p, w_1, w_2)}{\partial p \partial w_i} = \frac{\partial y^*(p, w_1, w_2)}{\partial w_i}.$$

$$(3.17)$$

When a production technology is estimated by estimating a system of output supply and input demand functions using econometric methods (e.g., Coelli 1996), the analyst should ensure that these symmetry restrictions are imposed, or alternatively a hypothesis test could be conducted to determine if symmetry holds for that particular data set. If symmetry is found to be violated this may be a consequence of data quality or perhaps a result of one or more of the assumptions underlying the approach being incorrect (e.g. competitive markets).[10]

3.2.4   Cost Functions and Shephard's Lemma

A cost function is defined in a similar manner to the profit function. A cost function is defined as the <u>minimum</u> cost of producing a particular output with given input prices.   It may be obtained by substituting the cost-minimising input demand equations derived in the primal approach (i.e. equations 3.9 and 3.10) into the cost definition (equation 3.7) to obtain:

$$c^* = w_1[x_1{}^c(y,w_1,w_2)] + w_2[x_2{}^c(y,w_1,w_2)]$$

$$= c^*(y,w_1,w_2) \qquad\qquad (3.18)$$

where the notation c^* is used to indicate <u>minimum</u> cost while $c^*(.)$ represents the relationship between c^* and the exogenous variables (input prices and output).

Again it should be stressed, as we did above for the profit function, that this derivation of a cost function is used to illustrate the concept of the cost function. You would be unlikely to actually derive a cost function in this way in practice, because a principle advantage of the approach is the avoidance of having to use the primal approach. In practice, one would normally specify a cost function (which has appropriate properties that will be defined shortly), estimate the function using sample data (say using econometrics), and then use *Shephard's Lemma* to derive the input demand equations.

Shephard's Lemma

Shephard's Lemma, which is also derived from the *envelope theorem*, states that the first partial derivative of the cost function with respect to each of the input prices

---

[10] One should also ensure that the estimated output supply and input demand functions are homogenous of degree zero in prices and that the properties of monotonicity and convexity are satisfied. For more on these properties see section 3.5.1.

defines the conditional input demand functions (i.e. conditional upon the output level, y). That is,

$$\frac{\partial c*}{\partial w_1} = x_1^c(y, w_1, w_2) \tag{3.19}$$

and

$$\frac{\partial c*}{\partial w_2} = x_2^c(y, w_1, w_2). \tag{3.20}$$

This result also generalises to the case of K inputs and M outputs.

Symmetry

The symmetry between the cross partial derivatives of the conditional input demand functions follows as direct result of *Young's Theorem*. It can be shown that

$$\frac{\partial x_1^c(y, w_1, w_2)}{\partial w_2} = \frac{\partial^2 c*(y, w_1, w_2)}{\partial w_1 \partial w_2} = \frac{\partial^2 c*(y, w_1, w_2)}{\partial w_2 \partial w_1} = \frac{\partial x_2^c(y, w_1, w_2)}{\partial w_1}. \tag{3.21}$$

3.2.5 Properties of Cost and Profit Functions

As mentioned in the previous section, a profit or cost function must satisfy a number of properties to ensure that it is consistent with the assumed optimising behaviour. They should be twice continuously differentiable and should also be symmetric (as defined earlier). Some other properties which they should possess are discussed below.

Properties of Profit Functions

In the following statement of properties we will use the notation x and w to represent a vector of input quantities and prices, respectively. Thus in the case of two inputs we would have $x=(x_1, x_2)'$ and $w=(w_1, w_2)'$. If the underlying production technology satisfies a number of fairly weak properties [see Chambers (1988) for details] then the profit function possesses the following properties.

1. $\pi*(p, w) \geq 0$, for $p, w \geq 0$.

2. $\pi*(p^a, w) \geq \pi*(p^b, w)$, for $p^a \geq p^b$.

3. $\pi*(p, w^a) \leq \pi*(p, w^b)$, for $w^a \geq w^b$.

4. $\pi*(p, w)$ is homogenous of degree one in all prices.

5. $\dfrac{\partial \pi^*(p, w)}{\partial p}$ and $\dfrac{\partial \pi^*(p, w)}{\partial w_i}$ are homogenous of degree zero in all prices.

6. $\pi^*(p, w)$ is convex in all prices if the production function, $y = f(x)$, is strictly concave.[11,12]

The first three properties are straightforward. The first property makes sense when one recalls that all input quantities are assumed variable, hence one should never achieve a negative profit when one could produce nothing and achieve a zero profit. Properties 2 and 3 state that when output price increases profit cannot fall and that when an input price increases profit cannot rise. These properties are often referred to as the *monotonicity* property.

Property 4 states that the profit function should be homogenous of degree one. This implies that if we double all prices we will exactly double profit. This follows directly from the definition of profit (see equation 3.4).

Property 5 follows directly from property 4, because the first derivative of a function that is homogenous of degree λ, will provide a function that is homogenous of degree λ-1. Property 5 can also be viewed from the point that the producer will not be fooled by inflation. That is, a proportional increase in all prices will not cause the producer to alter the input mix nor will it encourage him/her to produce more output. The producer will only respond to real price changes.

A rough explanation of Property 6 is that it is necessary for the profit function to have a maximum (refer to the discussion following equation 3.5). If the production function does not eventually exhibit decreasing returns to scale, the producer would be able to indefinitely increase the scale of operations and hence to have no limit to profit.

More detailed discussions and proofs of these properties may be found in Beattie and Taylor (1985, pp.245).

Properties of Cost Functions

If the underlying production technology satisfies a number of fairly weak properties (see Chambers 1988 for details) then the cost function possesses the following properties.

---

[11] For example, a homogenous production function with decreasing returns to scale is strictly concave. See Beattie and Taylor (1985, pp.59) for definitions of various forms of concavity and convexity.

[12] In an empirical analysis, this concavity need only be in the neighbourhood of the sample data. Thus one could have an S-shaped production function which has both concave and convex regions, as long as the sample data is confined to the concave regions (i.e., not in Stage I).

1. $c^*(y,w) \geq 0$, for $w \geq 0$ and $y > 0$.

2. $c^*(y,w^a) \geq c^*(y,w^b)$, for $w^a \geq w^b$.

3. $c^*(y,w)$ is homogenous of degree one in all prices.

4. $\dfrac{\partial c^*(y,w)}{\partial w_i}$ is homogenous of degree zero in all prices.

5. $c^*(y,w)$ is weakly concave in input prices if the production function, $y=f(x)$, is strictly quasi-concave.[13]

Discussion of the relevance of these properties would follow similar lines to the discussion of the profit case above. The interested reader is again referred to Beattie and Taylor (1985, pp.242) for more on these properties.

3.2.6 A Simple Numerical Illustration

The best way to obtain a concrete feel for duality is get one's hands dirty with an example. In this example we begin by specifying a simple production function (a Cobb-Douglas example) and use the primal approach to derive input demand and output supply equations. We then insert these back into the profit definition to obtain a profit function, and then finally derive the input demand and output supply equations from it using Hotelling's Lemma, hopefully illustrating that the resulting output supply and input demand functions are identical to those obtained using the primal approach.[14]

The idea for this example is borrowed from Beattie and Taylor (1985, p.237). However, in our example we use a different production function and supply a number of extra lines of derivation. We begin by recalling our production function example from equation 2.9

$$y = 2x_1^{0.5}x_2^{0.4}. \tag{3.22}$$

This is a one-output, two-input example. We firstly illustrate how the input demand and output supply equations consistent with the profit maximising objective can be derived using the *primal* approach.

The definition of profit is

$$\pi = TR - TC = py - (w_1x_1 + w_2x_2). \tag{3.23}$$

Substituting the production function into this we obtain

---

[13] For example, the traditional 3-stage S-shaped production function is strictly quasi-concave.

[14] Again, it should be stressed that this is not a typical example of how duality would be used in practice. One would normally begin a dual analysis by specifying an indirect profit or cost function and estimating it.

$$\pi = p[2x_1^{0.5}x_2^{0.4}]- (w_1x_1 + w_2x_2). \tag{3.24}$$

The values of x_1 and x_2 for which π is maximised may be obtained by finding the first partial derivatives of equation 3.24 with respect to each of the x_i and setting these to zero:

$$\frac{\partial \pi}{\partial x_1} = px_1^{-0.5}x_2^{0.4} - w_1 = 0 \tag{3.25}$$

$$\frac{\partial \pi}{\partial x_2} = 0.8px_1^{0.5}x_2^{-0.6} - w_2 = 0. \tag{3.26}$$

These are then solved simultaneously to obtain the input demand functions.[15] For example, one could make x_2 the subject of equation 3.26 to obtain:

$$x_2 = [w_2/(0.8px_1^{0.5})]^{-5/3} \tag{3.27}$$

and then substitute this into equation 3.25 to obtain:

$$px_1^{-0.5}\{[w_2/(0.8px_1^{0.5})]^{-5/3}\}^{0.4} - w_1 = 0.$$

By making x_1 the subject of this equation (which involves a few lines of algebra) we obtain the labour input demand equation:

$$x_1^* = 0.41p^{10}w_1^{-6}w_2^{-4}. \tag{3.28}$$

Substitution of this into equation 3.27 provides the capital input demand equation:

$$x_2^* = [w_2/(0.8p\{0.41p^{10}w_1^{-6}w_2^{-4}\}^{0.5})]^{-5/3}$$

which after rearrangement (involving a few more lines of algebra) becomes:

$$x_2^* = 0.33p^{10}w_1^{-5}w_2^{-5}. \tag{3.29}$$

The output supply equation can be obtained by substituting these two demand equations (3.28 and 3.29) into the production function (equation 3.22) to obtain:

$$y^* = 2(0.41p^{10}w_1^{-6}w_2^{-4})^{0.5}(0.33p^{10}w_1^{-5}w_2^{-5})^{0.4}$$

which after rearrangement becomes:

---

[15]Note that the above partial derivatives were also obtained in Chapter 2. However, in Chapter 2 we then went on to solve these equations to obtain the profit maximising quantities corresponding to particular price levels. In this chapter we will solve these equations to derive input demand and output supply functions so we are then able to specify what the profit maximising quantities will be for any arbitrary set of prices.

$$y^* = 0.82p^9w_1^{-5}w_2^{-4}.$$ (3.30)

Thus we have derived the input demand and output supply equations for the profit-maximising firm using the *primal* approach outlined in Section 3.1.1. We now substitute these three equations (3.28 to 3.30) into the profit definition (equation 3.23) to obtain the profit function implied by this example:

$$\pi^* = py^* - [w_1x_1^* + w_2x_2^*]$$

$$= p(0.82p^9w_1^{-5}w_2^{-4})-[w_1(0.41p^{10}w_1^{-6}w_2^{-4}) + w_2(0.33p^{10}w_1^{-5}w_2^{-5})]$$

which after rearrangement becomes:

$$\pi^* = 0.082p^{10}w_1^{-5}w_2^{-4}.$$ (3.31)

Again we stress that this is not something that is normally done in practice. One would usually not know the input demand and output supply equations. One would normally specify a profit function (which possesses appropriate properties) and estimate it so as to be able to extract the input demand and output supply equations, along with other information.

We now use the dual approach to derive the output supply and input demand equations from the profit function defined in equation 3.31. According to Hotelling's Lemma, the output supply equation may be obtained by setting the first partial derivative of the profit function with respect to output price equal to output quantity. That is,

$$\frac{\partial \pi^*}{\partial p} = 0.82p^9w_1^{-5}w_2^{-4} = y^*.$$ (3.32)

Furthermore, Hotelling's Lemma states that the input demand equations are be obtained by setting the first partial derivatives of the profit function with respect to input prices equal to the negatives of the respective input quantities. That is,

$$\frac{\partial \pi^*}{\partial w_1} = -0.41p^{10}w_1^{-6}w_2^{-4} = -x_1^*$$ (3.33)

and

$$\frac{\partial \pi^*}{\partial w_2} = -0.33p^{10}w_1^{-5}w_2^{-5} = -x_2^*.$$ (3.34)

A quick comparison of these three equations (3.32 to 3.34) with the output supply and input demand equations obtained using the primal approach (equations 3.28 to 3.30) confirms that the two approaches have come up with identical equations. This is an illustration of Hotelling's Lemma.

In the above derivations we have shown the derivation of a profit function from a production function. We could complete the circle by showing how the production function could be derived from the profit function. That is, let us say the profit function in equation 3.31 was obtained using econometric estimation, and that we now wish to obtain the underlying production function. We can do this by first deriving the input demand and output supply equations from the profit function using Hotelling's Lemma (which we have already done - see equations 3.32 to 3.34). We then simultaneously solve these three equations to eliminate the three prices. This process will leave us with the production function defined in equation 3.22.

This example could also be repeated for the cost-minimisation case. The interested reader is advised to consult Beattie and Taylor (1985, p.239) to see a similar process repeated for cost minimisation.

The above discussion of duality suggests that in order to estimate a production technology all we need to do is specify some sort of profit or cost function, estimate it in some way (say using econometric methods) and then we will be able to recover all relevant information about the underlying production technology. Although this is generally the case, we must make a few qualifications:

- Not all functional forms used in econometric analyses of profit and cost allow one to derive an explicit expression for the underlying production function. This does not mean the production function does not exist - only that the mathematical derivation of its form is intractable. An example of such a functional form is the translog. The Cobb-Douglas functional form, however, is an example of a functional form for which the underlying production function can be derived. The point should also be made that not being able to obtain an explicit expression for the underlying production function does not prevent a researcher from being able to derive estimates of key measures, such as technological change, elasticities of substitution and the total elasticity of production.[16]

- The form of the profit or cost function must satisfy a number of properties to ensure that it is consistent with the assumed optimising behaviour. These properties were listed in the previous section.

---

[16] Note that some texts refer to the total elasticity of production as the scale elasticity or as the function coefficient.

3.3 Econometric Estimation of Cost and Profit Functions

3.3.1 Functional Forms

Econometric estimation of a profit or cost function requires the selection of an appropriate functional form. This functional form would hopefully be:

1. sufficiently flexible so that it can accommodate various production structures; and

2. satisfy the properties discussed in the previous section (or permit the imposition of these properties through the application of appropriate constraints).

These two objectives are often in conflict. The imposition of constraints upon a flexible functional form to achieve appropriate theoretical properties can subsequently reduce the flexibility of many popular flexible functional forms (see Diewert and Wales, 1987).

Many of the functional forms discussed in Chapter 2 in reference to production functions have been used to specify cost and profit functions in empirical analyses. An example of a Cobb-Douglas profit function was used in the illustration in the previous section. In general form, this profit function could be expressed as:

$$\pi^* = A w_1^{\beta_1} w_2^{\beta_2} p^{\beta_3} \tag{3.35}$$

which may also be expressed in log form as:

$$\ln\pi^* = \ln A + \beta_1 \ln w_1 + \beta_2 \ln w_2 + \beta_3 \ln p. \tag{3.36}$$

A translog profit function could be expressed as:

$$\ln\pi^* = \beta_0 + \beta_1 \ln w_1 + \beta_2 \ln w_2 + \beta_3 \ln p + \beta_{12} \ln w_1 \ln w_2 + \beta_{13} \ln w_1 \ln p +$$

$$\beta_{23} \ln w_2 \ln p + (1/2)[\beta_{11}(\ln w_1)^2 + \beta_{22}(\ln w_2)^2 + \beta_{33}(\ln p)^2]. \tag{3.37}$$

The translog is but one example of a flexible functional form that has become popular in dual analyses of production. Others include the normalised quadratic, the generalised Leontief, and the generalised McFadden. The last of these has recently become popular because it permits the imposition of curvature properties (i.e., concavity/convexity) without loss of second order flexibility. Refer to Fuss and McFadden (1978) and Diewert and Wales (1987) for more on the properties of various flexible functional forms.

It should be noted that many of the popular flexible functional forms are such that one cannot derive the production function implied by the cost or profit functions.

As noted earlier, this is not a problem because all of the key measures, such as technical change, substitution elasticities and the total elasticity of production, can still be derived.

3.3.2 Some Estimation Issues

This section could be very long, but we will limit ourselves to a few points. The first point relates to exogeneity of regressors and simultaneous equation bias.

Regressor Exogeneity

Consider the least squares (LS) regression equation:

$$z = g(r, \beta) + v, \tag{3.38}$$

where the dependent variable (z) is assumed to be *endogenous* (i.e., determined within the system), the RHS variables (denoted by the vector, r) are assumed to be *exogenous* variables (i.e., their values are determined outside the system), $g(.)$ represents the functional form, β is a vector of parameters to be estimated, and v is an appended error term, which is usually assumed to be independently and identically distributed with mean 0 and variance σ^2. Given these assumptions, the LS estimates of β will be unbiased. However, if one or more of the RHS variables are not exogenous, then the resulting LS estimates of β will be biased.[17]

If we consider a production function:

$$y = f(x) + v \tag{3.39}$$

and assume that the firm is attempting to select the input and output quantities that will maximise profits, given prices, then both x and y are endogenous. Hence LS estimates of this equation may suffer from simultaneous equations bias.[18]

One way of addressing this issue is to estimate a cost or profit function instead. The cost function has output quantity and input prices on the RHS, which are both assumed exogenous; and the profit function has only (exogenous) prices on the RHS. The exogeneity of these prices hinges, of course, on the assumption of competition (or price regulation). One of the earliest empirical studies to estimate a dual cost function was the study by Nerlove (1963) which estimated a Cobb-Douglas cost function to investigate scale economies in US electric power generation.

---

[17] For more on this see Griffiths, Hill and Judge (1993, ch 18).

[18] Zellner, Kmenta and Dreze (1966) show that direct estimation of a production function will not suffer from simultaneous equations bias if it is appropriate to assume that the producer is attempting to maximise *expected* rather than *actual* profit. Their arguments are often used to justify the direct econometric estimation of production functions.

Systems Estimation

When estimating a flexible dual function, for example a translog cost function, the cost equation can become quite complex. For example, consider the translog cost function:

$$\ln c^* = \beta_0 + \beta_1 \ln w_1 + \beta_2 \ln w_2 + \beta_3 \ln y + \beta_{12} \ln w_1 \ln w_2 + \beta_{13} \ln w_1 \ln y +$$

$$\beta_{23} \ln w_2 \ln y + (1/2)[\beta_{11}(\ln w_1)^2 + \beta_{22}(\ln w_2)^2 + \beta_{33}(\ln y)^2] + v. \qquad (3.40)$$

where we have only one output and two inputs, yet there are 10 unknown parameters to estimate. LS estimation of similar functions involving more inputs and/or outputs is likely to suffer from degrees of freedom and multicollinearity problems resulting in inefficient estimates. More efficient estimates can be obtained by simultaneously estimating the cost function with the input demand equations (derived using Shephard's Lemma). This is usually done using iterated Zellner SUR estimation.[19] As noted in Christensen and Greene (1976), the input demand equations derived from a translog cost function have the cost shares as the dependent variables. The input demand equations (or share equations) derived from equation 3.40 can be shown to be

$$(w_1 x_1 / c) = \beta_1 + \beta_{11} \ln w_1 + \beta_{12} \ln w_2 + \beta_{13} \ln y + v_1 \qquad (3.40a)$$

$$(w_2 x_2 / c) = \beta_2 + \beta_{12} \ln w_1 + \beta_{22} \ln w_2 + \beta_{23} \ln y + v_2 \qquad (3.40b)$$

where $(w_i x_i / c)$ is the cost share of the i-th input.

The parameters in equations 3.40, 3.40a and 3.40b can be estimated by iterated Zellner SUR using any number of econometric packages. Example SHAZAM code is listed in Table 3.1. The equations are estimated using SHAZAM's SYSTEM command with cross-equation restrictions imposed using the RESTRICT option. Note that we have only imposed restrictions such as $\beta_1 = \beta_1$, etc. Theoretical restrictions such as homogeneity could be imposed in a similar manner (and also tested using the TEST command if required). For details of the parametric forms of these restrictions see Christensen and Greene (1976, p.660). Note also that we have dropped one of the share equations from the estimated system in Table 3.1. This is done because the covariance matrix will be singular if all share equations are included. Also note that the iterated Zellner SUR results are not affected by which share equation is dropped.

---

[19] For more on this estimation method see Griffiths, Hill and Judge (1993, ch 17).

Data Issues

One important point to make is that one cannot estimate a regression equation unless the RHS variables (the regressors) vary between observations. Thus if we have data on a number of firms for a particular year where they all face the same input and output prices we cannot estimate cost and profit functions of the form discussed above. The price data must vary for some reason (e.g., geography or over time).

Table 3.1 SHAZAM Instructions for SUR Estimation of a Translog Cost Function

	SHAZAM Code	**Description**
1	read(eg2.dta) y x1 x2 c w1 w2	read in data on output, 2 inputs, cost and input prices from a data file
2	genr lc=log(c)	obtain logarithm of c
3	genr lw1=log(w1)	obtain logarithm of w1
4	genr lw2=log(w2)	obtain logarithm of w2
5	genr ly=log(y)	obtain logarithm of y
6	genr lw12=lw1*lw2	obtain cross-product
7	genr lw1y=lw1*ly	obtain cross-product
8	genr lw2y=lw2*ly	obtain cross-product
9	genr lw11=0.5*lw1**2	obtain 0.5 times the square of log(w1)
10	genr lw22=0.5*lw2**2	obtain 0.5 times the square of log(w2)
11	genr lyy=0.5*ly**2	obtain 0.5 times the square of log(y)
12	genr s1=w1*x1/c	obtain cost share for input 1
13	genr s2=w2*x2/c	obtain cost share for input 2
14	genr one=1	generate a column of 1's (so that cross-equation restrictions can later be imposed which involve the intercept term)
15	system 2 / restrict nocons	estimate a system of 2 equations with restrictions and with no intercept terms.
16	ols lc one lw1 lw2 ly lw12 lw1y lw2y lw11 lw22 lyy	translog cost function
17	ols s1 one lw1 lw2 ly	share equation for input 1
18	restrict one:2-lw1:1=0	ensure beta1=beta1
19	restrict lw1:2-lw11:1=0	ensure beta11=beta11
20	restrict lw2:2-lw12:1=0	ensure beta12=beta12
21	restrict ly:2-lw1y:1=0	ensure beat13=beta13
22	end	end of system command

Many empirical studies have used aggregate (i.e., industry level) time series data to estimate cost and profit functions. Price variation will occur in this data. However, time series data introduces many other problems, such as questions regarding aggregation effects, price expectations, multi-period (dynamic) optimisation and technological change, to name a few.

Multi-Output Production

Up until now we have dealt entirely with the single output production process. One of the primary advantages of the dual approach is in it's ability to deal with multi-output technologies. Hotelling's Lemma and Shephard's Lemma both apply to the multi-output, multi-input case. These Lemmas are formally stated for this general case in Beattie and Taylor (1985, ch6).

Multi-output functional forms for indirect cost and profit functions are simple extensions of the single product cases. For example, a two-input, two-output translog profit function is expressed as:

$$\ln\pi^* = \beta_0 + \beta_1 \ln w_1 + \beta_2 \ln w_2 + \beta_3 \ln p_1 + \beta_4 \ln p_2 + \beta_{12} \ln w_1 \ln w_2 + \beta_{13} \ln w_1 \ln p_1 +$$

$$\beta_{14} \ln w_1 \ln p_2 + \beta_{23} \ln w_2 \ln p_1 + \beta_{24} \ln w_2 \ln p_2 + \beta_{34} \ln p_1 \ln p_2 +$$

$$(1/2)[\beta_{11}(\ln w_1)^2 + \beta_{22}(\ln w_2)^2 + \beta_{33}(\ln p_1)^2 + \beta_{44}(\ln p_2)^2] + v. \quad (3.41)$$

Multi-output production is discussed further in Section 3.3.

3.3.3 Technical Change Measurement

Econometric analyses of production (be they primal or dual) which involve time series data (or panel data) can be used to obtain parametric measures of the rate of technical change. This is normally achieved by including a time trend in the estimating equation(s). For example, consider the translog cost function in equation 3.40. It is common to include a time trend (t) and its square (t^2) to account for the possibility of techical change:[20]

$$\ln c^* = \beta_0 + \beta_1 \ln w_1 + \beta_2 \ln w_2 + \beta_3 \ln y + \beta_{12} \ln w_1 \ln w_2 + \beta_{13} \ln w_1 \ln y + \beta_{23} \ln w_2 \ln y$$

$$+ (1/2)[\beta_{11}(\ln w_1)^2 + \beta_{22}(\ln w_2)^2 + \beta_{33}(\ln y)^2] + \beta_t t + \beta_{tt} t^2 + v. \quad (3.42)$$

The partial derivative of cost with respect to time (t) will then provide an indication of the rate of movement in the cost function over time. For technical progress to occur, the sign of this value should be negative, indicating the cost function is shifting down over time (and hence the production function is rising over time, as depicted in Figure 1.3).

The inclusion of time in the manner depicted in equation 3.42 accounts for what is known as *Hicks-neutral technical change*. That is, the functions shift up and

---

[20] The t^2 term is included to provide consistency with the second order approximation notion of the translog form.

down but their slopes (e.g. the MRTS) do not alter. *Non-neutral techical change* can be accounted for by also including terms involving the interactions of the other regressors and time:

$$\ln c^* = \beta_0 + \beta_1 \ln w_1 + \beta_2 \ln w_2 + \beta_3 \ln y + \beta_{12} \ln w_1 \ln w_2 + \beta_{13} \ln w_1 \ln y +$$

$$\beta_{23} \ln w_2 \ln y + (1/2)[\beta_{11}(\ln w_1)^2 + \beta_{22}(\ln w_2)^2 + \beta_{33}(\ln y)^2]$$

$$+ \beta_{1t} \ln w_1 t + \beta_{2t} \ln w_2 t + \beta_{3t} \ln y t + \beta_t t + \beta_{tt} t^2 + v. \qquad (3.43)$$

Non-neutral technical change is also often termed *biased technical change*, in that the movement in the functions will be biased in favour of certain input(s) and/or output(s) and against others. This can be visualised using the isoquants depicted in Figure 3.1.

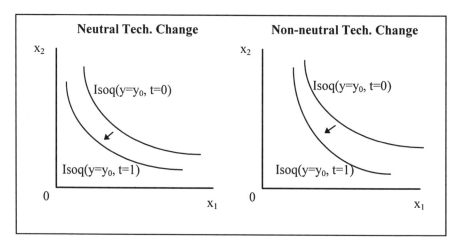

Figure 3.1 Technical Change and the Isoquant

It is stated above that one can estimate a cost or profit function and then use this estimated function to measure the technical characteristics of the underlying technology. We have illustrated how one can obtain measures of neutral technical change. If one assumes non-neutral technical change then one can also obtain measures of the biases in technical change. For an illustration of this see Weaver (1983), Antle (1984) and Coelli (1996). One can also measure scale economies, elasticities of substitution and other properties. The interested reader is advised to consult Christensen and Greene (1976), Fuss and McFadden (1978) and Blackorby and Russell (1989) for discussions of these methods.

3.4 Multi-output Production and Distance Functions

In the previous section we made some reference to the fact that one could easily generalise the single output cost and profit functions to accommodate multiple output situations. Of course we cannot establish a dual relationship between a single-output production function and a multiple-output indirect cost or profit function: we must specify a multi-output production function. Now to avoid potential confusion we will reserve the term *production function* for the case of a single output technology. Hence, when we refer to a multiple output production process we will refer to the multiple output production *technology* (not to a production function).

Now a convenient way to describe a multi-input, multi-output production technology is using the technology set, S. Following Färe and Primont (1995), we use the notation x and y to denote a non-negative K×1 input vector and a non-negative M×1 output vector, respectively. The technology set is then defined as:

$$S = \{(x,y) : x \text{ can produce } y\}. \tag{3.44}$$

That is, the set of all input-output vectors (x,y), such that x can produce y.

Now before we use this notion of a technology set to define multi-input, multi-output distance functions we will first ensure that we are comfortable with the notion of a production possibility curve which we now discuss in a brief digression.

3.4.1 A Digression on Production Possibility Curves and Revenue Maximisation

A multi-output production technology can be very difficult to conceptualise or to visualise. We can attempt to provide some understanding by using a simple 1-input, 2-output example. In this instance we can specify a input requirement function where we express the single input as a function of the two outputs:

$$x_1 = g(y_1, y_2). \tag{3.45}$$

This one-input, two-output case can be used to illustrate the idea of a *production possibility curve* (PPC), which is the output counterpart of the isoquant. The isoquant represents the various combinations of inputs that could be used to produce a given output level. The production possibility curve, on the other hand, depicts the various output combinations that could be produced using a given input level. An example of a production possibility curve is provided in Figure 3.2.

A discussion of the properties of this curve would follow similar lines to our discussion of the isoquant, so we shall omit much of it. Obviously a production possibility curve could be drawn for each input level. Furthermore, we shall observe that the combination of outputs which maximise profit, given an input level, will be equivalent to that which maximises revenue.[21] The revenue equivalent to the isocost line is the *isorevenue line,* which has slope equal to the negative ratio of the output prices ($-p_1/p_2$). The optimal (revenue maximising) point will be determined by the point of tangency between this line and the production possibility curve, as depicted in Figure 3.3.

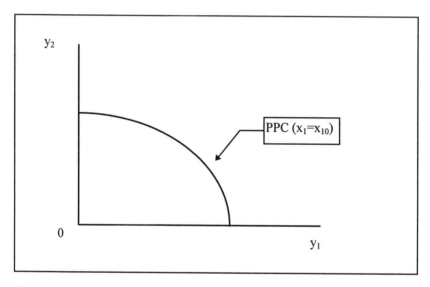

Figure 3.2 Production Possibility Curve

Production at any point on the production possibility curve other than point A in Figure 3.3 will coincide with an isorevenue curve which is closer to the origin and hence imply lower total revenue (and thus lower profit).

Before we return to our discussion of production sets and distance functions we will quickly make note of the fact that our discussion of biased technical change in the previous section can be extended to include multiple output situations. Technical change can favour the production of one commodity over another. This concept is illustrated in Figure 3.4 which is the output counterpart to Figure 3.1.

---

[21] This is similar to the notion that selecting input levels so as to minimise the cost of producing a given output level, is equivalent to maximising profit (given the output constraint).

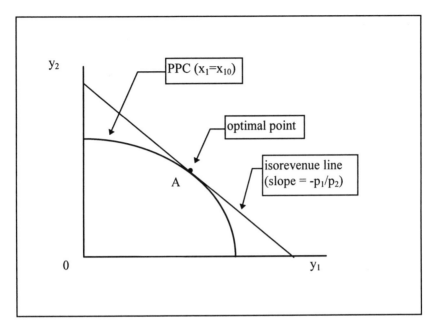

Figure 3.3 The Production Possibility Curve and Revenue Maximisation

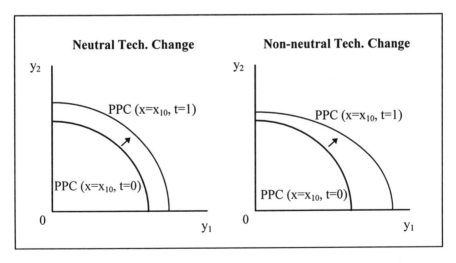

Figure 3.4 Technical Change and the Production Possibility Curve

3.4.2 Output Distance Functions

Distance functions allow one to describe a multi-input, multi-output production technology without the need to specify a behavioural objective (such as cost-minimisation or profit-maximisation).   One may specify both input distance functions and output distance functions. An input distance function characterises the production technology by looking at a minimal proportional contraction of the input vector, given an output vector. An output distance function considers a maximal proportional expansion of the output vector, given an input vector. We consider an output distance function first.

We begin by noting that the production technology defined by the set, S, may be equivalently defined using output sets, $P(x)$, which represents the set of all output vectors, y, which can be produced using the input vector, x. That is,

$$P(x) = \{y : x \text{ can produce } y\}. \tag{3.46}$$

The properties of this set are summarised as follows. For each x, the output set $P(x)$ is assumed to satisfy:

(i) $0 \in P(x)$: nothing can be produced out of a given set of inputs (i.e., inaction is possible);

(ii) non-zero output levels cannot be produced from zero level of inputs;

(iii) $P(x)$ satisfies strong disposability of outputs: if $y \in P(x)$ and $y^* \leq y$ then $y^* \in P(x)$;[22]

(iv) $P(x)$ satisfies strong disposability of inputs: if y can be produced from x, then y can be produced from any $x^* \geq x$;[23]

(v) $P(x)$ is closed;

(vi) $P(x)$ is bounded; and

(vii) $P(x)$ is convex.

Similar assumptions, with the exception of "boundedness", are made regarding the input sets defined for the inputs sets, $L(y)$.

---

[22] An alternative assumption to strong disposability is "weak disposability", which states that if a vector of outputs, y, can be produced from a given input vector, x, then any contraction of y, λy, with $0<\lambda<1$, can also be produced with x. It is easy to see that strong disposability implies weak disposability, but not vice versa.

[23] Since x^* and x are vectors, $x^* \geq x$ holds when all elements of x^* are greater than or equal to the corresponding elements in x, but strictly greater for at least one element.

The assumption of closedness is essentially a mathematical requirement, but bounded nature of P(x) implies that we cannot produce unlimited levels of outputs with a given set of inputs. Convexity implies that if two combinations of output levels can be produced with a given input vector x, then any average of these output vectors can also be produced. This assumption implicitly requires the commodities to be continuously divisible.

The output distance function is defined on the output set, P(x), as:[24]

$$d_o(x,y) = \min\{\delta : (y/\delta) \in P(x)\}. \tag{3.47}$$

A few simple properties of $d_o(x,y)$ can be stated. These properties follow directly from the axioms on the technology set. The properties are:

(i) $d_o(x,y)$ is non-decreasing in y and increasing in x;

(ii) $d_o(x,y)$ is linearly homogeneous in y;

(iii) if y belongs to the production possibility set of x (i.e., $y \in P(x)$), then $d_o(x,y) \leq 1$; and

(iv) distance is equal to unity (i.e., $d_o(x,y) = 1$) if y belongs to the "frontier" of the production possibility set (the PPC curve of x).[25]

It is useful to illustrate the concept of an output distance function using an example where two outputs, y_1 and y_2, are produced using the input vector, x. Now for a given input vector we can represent the production technology on the two dimensional diagram in Figure 3.5. Here the production possibility set, P(x), is the area bounded by the production possibility frontier, PPC-P(x), and the y_1 and y_2 axes. The value of the distance function for the firm using input level x to produce the outputs defined by the point A is equal to the ratio $\delta = 0A/0B$.

This distance measure is the inverse of the factor by which the production of all output quantities could be increased while still remaining within the feasible production possibility set for the given input level.[26] We also observe that the points B and C are on the production possibility surface, denoted by PPC-P(x), and hence would have distance function values equal to 1.

---

[24] Note that the definition of the output distance function in equation (3.47) could be made more rigorous by replacing "min" (which stands for "minimum") with "inf" (which stands for "infimum"). This allows for the possibility that the minimum does not exist (i.e., that $\delta = +\infty$ is possible). We shall, however, continue to use the less precise term "min" in this book in the interests of ease of reading.

[25] These properties play a major role in the ensuing chapters which focus on efficiency measurement.

[26] Note that this distance measure is the inverse of the Farrell-type output-orientated measure of technical efficiency which is defined in Chapter 6.

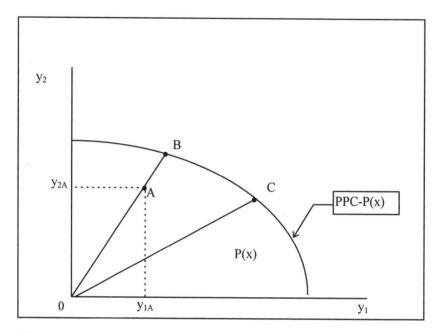

Figure 3.5 Output Distance Function and Production Possibility Set

3.4.3 Input Distance Functions

The input distance function, which involves the scaling of the input vector, is defined in a similar manner. It can be defined on the input set, $L(y)$, as:[27]

$$d_i(x,y) = \max\{\rho : (x/\rho) \in L(y)\}, \tag{3.48}$$

where the input set $L(y)$ represents the set of all input vectors, x, which can produce the output vector, y. That is,

$$L(y) = \{x : x \text{ can produce } y\}. \tag{3.49}$$

The properties of the input distance function can be easily derived using the assumptions made with respect to the production technology. Given the general axioms listed in the previous section, it is easy to show that:

---

[27] Note that the definition of the input distance function in equation (3.48) could be made more rigorous by replacing "max" (which stands for "maximum") with "sup" (which stands for "supremum"). This allows for the possibility that the maximum does not exist (i.e., that $\rho = +\infty$ is possible). We shall, however, continue to use the less precise term "max" in this book in the interests of ease of reading.

(i)   the input distance function is non-decreasing in x and increasing in y;

(ii)   it is linearly homogeneous in x;

(iii) if x belongs to the input set of y (i.e., $x \in L(y)$) then $d_i(x,y) \geq 1$; and

(iv)   distance is equal to unity (i.e., $d_i(x,y) = 1$) if x belongs to the "frontier" of the input set (the isoquant of y).

We can illustrate the input distance function using an example where two inputs, x_1 and x_2, are used in producing output vector, y. Now for a given output vector we can represent the production technology on the two dimensional diagram in Figure 3.6. Here the input set, L(y), is the area bounded from below by the isoquant, Isoq-L(y). The value of the distance function for the point, A, which defines the production point where firm A uses x_{1A} of input 1 and x_{2A} of input 2, to produce the output vector y, is equal to the ratio $\rho = 0A/0B$.

Having defined output distance functions in the previous section, it is useful to state a couple of results which connect the input and output distance functions. The first point we can make is that if $y \in P(x)$, that is, if y belongs to the production possibility set associated with input vector x, then x belongs to the feasible input set associated with output vector y, that is $x \in L(y)$. Using this we can state that

$$d_i(x,y) \geq 1 \text{ if and only if } d_o(x,y) \leq 1.$$

Further, if the technology exhibits global returns to scale then we can state that, for all x and y,

$$d_i(x,y) = 1/d_o(x,y).$$

This means that, under constant returns to scale, the input distance function is the reciprocal of the output distance function, for any (x, y).

3.4.4   Uses of Distance Functions

Output and input distance functions have a number of uses. They can be used to define a variety of index numbers, as discussed in some of the following chapters. They can also be directly estimated by either econometric or mathematical programming methods. Coelli and Perelman (1996a,b) provide a discussion of these estimation methods and illustrate their use in an analysis of technical efficiency in European railways. Estimated distance function have also been used in some recent analyses seeking measures of shadow prices (Färe et al 1989, 1993).

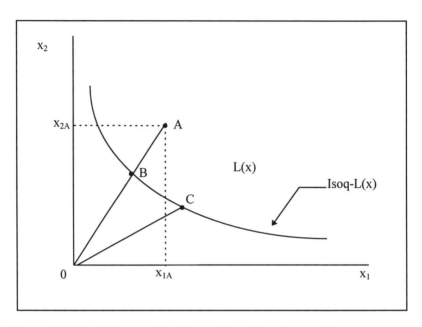

Figure 3.6 Input Distance Function and Input Requirement Set

3.5 Conclusions

The discussion of production economics in this chapter is selective and far from rigorous. Our intention was to provide the reader with some basic knowledge of profit, cost and distance functions to assist with the comprehension of some of the efficiency and productivity measures discussed in later chapters. The intention was not to write a three volume set on production economics. Hence there have been a number of omissions. Some topics which we have not discussed in any detail include: additional functional forms, such as the generalised Leontief, normalised quadratic, and others; producer behaviour under imperfect competition; and short-run dual models, where some inputs may be assumed quasi-fixed. For discussion of these and a variety of other extensions see Fuss and McFadden (1978), Chambers (1988) and Beattie and Taylor (1985).

Furthermore, this chapter has also only dealt with a subset of the ten dual functions which Färe and Primont (1995) list in their "duality diamond". Additional functions discussed in that book include the revenue function, revenue indirect cost function, cost indirect revenue function, indirect input distance function and indirect output distance function. The interested reader is encouraged to refer to Färe and Primont (1995) for a more comprehensive treatment of the material introduced in this chapter.

However, having just described what issues have not been covered in Chapters 2 and 3, we conclude this chapter with the observation that the production economics results reviewed in these two chapters should provide the reader with sufficient background to aid the comprehension of the various efficiency and productivity measurement methods discussed in the coming chapters.

4. INDEX NUMBERS AND PRODUCTIVITY MEASUREMENT

4.1 Introduction

Index numbers are the most commonly used instruments to measure changes in levels of various economic variables. Index numbers relating to various economic phenomena are regularly compiled and published. The consumer price index (CPI), which measures the changes in prices of a range of consumer goods and services, is the most widely used economic indicator. Other important index numbers include the price deflators for national income aggregates; financial indices such as the All Ordinaries Index (Australia) and the Dow Jones Index (U.S.A.); and indices of import and export prices.

The principal aim of this chapter is to provide a simple exposition to various index numbers that are relevant in the context of measuring productivity changes over time and space. Based on the discussion in the preceding chapters, it is evident that measuring productivity changes necessarily involves measuring changes in the levels of output and the associated changes in the input usage. Such changes are easy to measure in the case of a single input and a single output, but are more difficult when multi-output and multi-input cases are considered.

We see three principal areas in productivity measurement where index numbers play a major role. The first and foremost is the use of index numbers in the measurement of changes in total factor productivity (TFP) leading to the popular TFP index numbers. TFP index numbers in turn require separate output and input quantity index numbers.

The second use of index numbers in productivity measurement is an indirect role. It concerns the use of index numbers in generating required data which can be used in the application of Data Envelopment Analysis (DEA) or in the estimation of the Stochastic Frontiers. These two techniques are discussed in Chapters 6 to 9. Application of these techniques using very detailed data on inputs and outputs becomes impossible due to lack of degrees of freedom. In most practical applications of these techniques, it becomes necessary to "aggregate" data into a smaller set of input and output variables. For example, different types of labour inputs are usually aggregated into one single labour input. Outputs of commodities that belong to a particular group are usually aggregated into a single output aggregate for the group. For example, in agriculture, items such as wheat, rice etc. are grouped to form the output of "cereals". This type of aggregation, which is essentially an intermediate step in the process of assessing efficiency and productivity change, requires the use of index numbers. Usually such aggregates take the form of "value aggregates at constant prices" or just "constant price series".

The third issue concerns the type of index numbers that are required in handling panel data sets, with price and quantity data over time and space. Comparison of spatial observations usually requires some basic consistency requirements such as "transitivity" and "base invariance". These requirements in turn stipulate that formulae used for purpose of generating index numbers, of the type discussed in the preceding two paragraphs, need to satisfy some additional requirements.

The principal aim of this chapter is to familiarise the reader with various formulae in the index number literature, such as the Laspeyres, Paasche, Fisher and Tornqvist index numbers, and then to focus on the construction of price and quantity index numbers. Quantity index number formulae are applied to input and output data leading to quantity index numbers which are in turn used in defining the TFP index.

Chapter 5 deals with the micro-economic theoretic foundations to the measurement of input and output index numbers and examines the relationship between the TFP index numbers and measures of efficiency and technical change. Malmquist index numbers based on distance measures are introduced in Chapter 5 with a view to connecting the index number measures to those resulting from DEA and other techniques.

4.2 Conceptual Framework and Notation

An index number is defined as a real number that measures changes in a set of related variables. Conceptually, index numbers may be used for comparisons over time or space or both. Index numbers are used to measure price and quantity changes over time, as well as to measure differences in the levels across firms, industries, regions or countries. Price index numbers may refer to consumer prices, input and output prices, export and import prices, etc., whereas quantity index numbers may be measuring changes in quantities of outputs produced or inputs used by a firm or industry over time or across firms.

Index numbers have a long and distinguished history in economics, with some of the most important contributions due to Laspeyres and Paasche dating back to the late nineteenth century. The Laspeyres and Paasche formulae are still commonly used by national statistical offices around the world. But it is the work of Irving Fisher and his book, *The Making of Index Numbers* published in 1922, that recognised the possibility of using many statistical formulae to derive appropriate index numbers. The Tornqvist (1936) index is a formula that plays a major role in productivity measurement. Chapter 2 of Diewert and Nakamura (1993) provides an excellent exposition of the historical background to index number construction.

Notation

We use the following notation throughout this chapter. Let p_{ij} and q_{ij} represent, respectively, the price and quantity of the i-th commodity (i = 1,2,...,N) in the j-th period (j = s,t). Without loss of generality, s and t may refer to two firms instead of time periods, and quantities may refer to either inputs or outputs.

Conceptually, all index numbers measure changes in the levels of a set of variables from a reference period. The reference period is denoted at the "base period". The period for which the index is calculated is referred to as the "current period". Let I_{st} represent a general index number for current period, t, with s as the base period. Similarly, let V_{st}, P_{st} and Q_{st} represent value, price and quantity index numbers, respectively.

The General Index Number Problem

The value change from period s to t is the ratio of the value of commodities in periods s and t, valued at respective prices. Thus

$$V_{st} = \frac{\sum_{i=1}^{N} p_{it}q_{it}}{\sum_{i=1}^{N} p_{is}q_{is}}. \tag{4.1}$$

The index, V_{st}, measures the change in the value of the basket of quantities of N commodities from period s to t. Obviously V_{st} is the result of changes in the two components, prices and quantities. While V_{st} is easy to measure, it is more difficult to disentangle the effects of price and quantity changes. We may want to disentangle these effects so that, for example, the quantity component can be used in measuring the quantity change.

If we are operating in a single commodity world, then such a decomposition is very simple to achieve. We have

$$V_{st} = \frac{p_t q_t}{p_s q_s} = \frac{p_t}{p_s} \times \frac{q_t}{q_s} \; .$$

Here the ratios p_t/p_s and q_t/q_s measure the relative price and quantity changes and there is no index number problem.

In general, when we have $N \geq 2$, commodities we have a problem of aggregation. For each commodity, i (i = 1,2,...,N), the price relative, p_{it}/p_{is}, measures the change in the price level of the i-th commodity and the quantity relative, q_{it}/q_{is}, measures the change in the quantity level of the i-th commodity.

Now the problem is one of combining the N different measures of price (quantity) changes, into a single real number, called a *price (quantity) index*. This problem is somewhat similar to the problem of selecting a suitable measure of central tendency. In the next two sections we briefly examine some of the more commonly used formulae for measuring price and quantity index changes.

4.3 Formulae for Price Index Numbers

We first focus on the price index number construction and then illustrate how these formulae can also be used in the construction of quantity index numbers.

Laspeyres and Paasche Formulae

These formulae represent the most widely used formulae in practice. The Laspeyres price index uses the base period quantities as weights, whereas, the Paasche index uses the current period weights to define the index.

$$\text{Laspeyres index} = P_{st}^L = \frac{\sum\limits_{i=1}^{N} p_{it} q_{is}}{\sum\limits_{i=1}^{N} p_{is} q_{is}} = \sum_{i=1}^{N} \frac{p_{it}}{p_{is}} \times \omega_{is}, \tag{4.2}$$

where $\omega_{is} = p_{is} q_{is} \Big/ \sum\limits_{i=1}^{N} p_{is} q_{is}$ is the value share of i-th commodity in the base period.

Equation 4.2 suggests two alternative interpretations. First, the Laspeyres index is the ratio of two value aggregates resulting from the valuation of the base-period quantities at current and base-period prices. The second interpretation is that the index is a value-share weighted average of the N-price relatives. The value shares reflect the relative importance of each commodity in the basket. The value shares used here refer to the base period.

A natural alternative to the use of base-period quantities in the definition of the Laspeyres index is an index number formula that uses current-period quantities. The Paasche formula, which makes use of the current-period quantities, is given by

$$\text{Paasche index} = P_{st}^P = \frac{\sum\limits_{i=1}^{N} p_{it} q_{it}}{\sum\limits_{i=1}^{N} p_{is} q_{it}} = \frac{1}{\sum\limits_{i} \frac{p_{is}}{p_{it}} \times \omega_{it}} .$$ (4.3)

The first part of equation 4.3 shows that the Paasche index is the ratio of the two value aggregates resulting from the valuation of period-t quantities at the prices prevailing in periods t and s. Alternatively, the last part of the equation suggests that the Paasche index is a weighted harmonic mean of price relatives, with current period value shares as weights.

From equations 4.2 and 4.3 it can be seen that the Laspeyres and Paasche formulae, in a sense, represent two extremes, one formula placing emphasis on base period quantities and the other on current period quantities. These two indices coincide if the price relatives do not exhibit any variation, that is, if $p_{it}/p_{is} = c$, then the Laspeyres and Paasche indices coincide, equal to the constant c. These indices tend to diverge when price relatives exhibit a large variation. The extent of divergence also depends on quantity relatives and the statistical correlation between price and quantity relatives. Bortkiewicz (1924) provides a decomposition of the Laspeyres-Paasche gap.

The Laspeyres and Paasche indices are quite popular since they are easy to compute and they provide "bounds" for the *true index* which is defined using economic theory (see Chapter 5). Most national statistical agencies use these formulae or some minor variations of these indices in computing various indices, such as the CPI. In particular, use of the Laspeyres index is more prevalent. A point to note here is that if published price indices are being used for purposes of deflating a given value series, then the resulting deflated series will exhibit definite characteristics depending on which formula is used in constructing the price index numbers. This issue is further elaborated in Section 4.4, where indirect measurement of quantity changes are discussed.

The Fisher Index

The gap between the Laspeyres and Paasche indices led Fisher (1922) to define a geometric mean of the two indices as a possible index number formula:

$$\text{Fisher index} = P_{st}^F = \sqrt{P_{st}^L \times P_{st}^P} .$$ (4.4)

Though the Fisher index is an artificial construct, which is between the two extremes, it possesses a number of desirable statistical and economic theoretic properties. Diewert (1992) demonstrates the versatility of the Fisher index. In view of the many favourable properties it has, the Fisher index is also known as the *Fisher ideal index.*

The Tornqvist Index

The Tornqvist index has been used in many total factor productivity studies that have been conducted in the last decade. In this section we define the Tornqvist price index, while in the next section we define the Tornqvist quantity index. The Tornqvist price index is a weighted geometric average of the price relatives, with weights given by the simple average of the value shares in periods s and t,

$$
P_{st}^T = \prod_{i=1}^N \left[\frac{p_{it}}{p_{is}} \right]^{\frac{\omega_{is}+\omega_{it}}{2}} .
\tag{4.5}
$$

The Tornqvist index is usually presented and applied in its log-change form

$$
\ln P_{st}^T = \sum_{i=1}^N \left(\frac{\omega_{is} + \omega_{it}}{2} \right) \left[\ln p_{it} - \ln p_{is} \right].
\tag{4.6}
$$

The log-change form offers a convenient computational form. In log-change form, the Tornqvist index is a weighted average of logarithmic price changes. Furthermore, the log-change in the price of the i-th commodity

$$
\ln p_{it} - \ln p_{is} = \ln \frac{p_{it}}{p_{is}} \cong \left(\frac{p_{it}}{p_{is}} - 1 \right),
$$

represents the percentage change (inflation rate) in the price of the i-th commodity. Hence the Tornqvist price index, in its log-change form, provides an indication of the overall growth rate in prices.

There are many more formulae in the index number literature, we restrict our attention to these four formulae as they represent the most commonly used formulae. We return to discuss some of the properties of these index numbers in Section 4.5, after a brief description of quantity index numbers.

4.4 Quantity Index Numbers

Two approaches can be used in measuring quantity changes. The first approach is a direct approach, where we derive a formula that measures overall quantity change from individual commodity specific quantity changes, measured by q_{it}/q_{is}. The Laspeyres, Paasche, Fisher and Tornqvist indices can be applied directly to quantity relatives. The second approach is an indirect approach, which uses the basic idea that price and quantity changes are two components that make up the value change over the periods s and t. So if price changes are measured directly using the formulae in the previous section, then quantity changes can be indirectly obtained after discounting the value change for the price change. This approach is discussed below in Section 4.4.2.

4.4.1 The Direct Approach

Various quantity index formulae may be defined using price index numbers, by simply interchanging prices and quantities. The formulae described above yield

$$Q_{st}^{L} = \frac{\sum_{i=1}^{N} p_{is} q_{it}}{\sum_{i=1}^{N} p_{is} q_{is}}, \qquad Q_{st}^{P} = \frac{\sum_{i=1}^{N} p_{it} q_{it}}{\sum_{i=1}^{N} p_{it} q_{is}}, \quad \text{and} \quad Q_{st}^{F} = \sqrt{Q_{st}^{L} \times Q_{st}^{P}}. \tag{4.7}$$

The Tornqvist quantity index, in its multiplicative and additive (log-change) forms, is given below:

$$Q_{st}^{T} = \prod_{i=1}^{N} \left[\frac{q_{it}}{q_{is}} \right]^{\frac{\omega_{is} + \omega_{it}}{2}}, \tag{4.8}$$

$$\ln Q_{st}^{T} = \sum_{i=1}^{N} \left(\frac{\omega_{is} + \omega_{it}}{2} \right) (\ln q_{it} - \ln q_{is}). \tag{4.9}$$

The Tornqvist index in equation 4.8 is the most popular index number used in measuring changes in output quantities produced and input quantities used in production over two time periods s and t. The log-change form of the Tornqvist index in equation 4.9 is the formula generally used for computational purposes. Preference for the use of the Tornqvist index formula is due to the many important economic-theoretic properties attributed to the index by Diewert (1976, 1981) and Caves, Christensen and Diewert (1982b). Economic theory issues are discussed further in the following chapter.

4.4.2 The Indirect Approach

The indirect approach is commonly used for purposes of quantity comparisons over time. This approach uses the basic premise that the price and quantity changes measured must account for value changes.

Value change = Price change × Quantity change

$$V_{st} = P_{st} \times Q_{st.} \tag{4.10}$$

Since V_{st} is defined from data directly as the ratio of values in periods t and s, Q_{st} can be obtained as a function of P_{st}, as shown below in equation 4.11:

$$Q_{st} = \frac{V_{st}}{P_{st}} = \frac{\sum_{i=1}^{N} p_{it} q_{it}}{\sum_{i=1}^{N} p_{is} q_{is}} \Bigg/ P_{st} \qquad (4.11)$$

$$= \frac{\sum_{i=1}^{N} p_{it} q_{it} \Big/ P_{st}}{\sum_{i=1}^{N} p_{is} q_{is}} = \frac{\text{value in period t, adjusted for price change}}{\text{value in period s}}$$

$$\therefore Q_{st} = \frac{\text{value in period t (at constant period s prices)}}{\text{value in period s (at period s prices)}}.$$

The numerator in this expression corresponds to the constant price series commonly used in many statistical publications. Basically, this approach states that quantity indices can be obtained from ratios of values, aggregated after removing the effect of price movements over the period under consideration.

A few important features and applications of indirect quantity comparisons are discussed below.

Constant Price Aggregates and Quantity Comparison

A direct implication of equation 4.11 and the indirect approach is that value aggregates, adjusted for price changes over time, can be considered as aggregate quantities or quantities of a composite commodity. Such price deflated series are abundant in the publications of statistical agencies. Examples of such aggregates are: gross domestic product (GDP); output of sectors, such as agriculture and manufacturing; investment series; and exports and imports of good and services.

Time series and cross section data on such aggregates are often used as data series for use in the estimation of least squares econometric production models, stochastic frontiers, and also in DEA calculations, where it is necessary to reduce the dimensions of the output and input vectors. This means that, even if index number methodology is not used in measuring productivity changes directly, it is regularly used in creating intermediate data series.

"Self-Duality" of Formulae for Direct and Indirect Quantity Comparisons

Let us examine the implications of the choice of formula for price comparisons on indirect quantity comparisons. Suppose we construct our price index numbers using a Laspeyres formula. Then the indirect quantity index, defined in equation 4.11, can be algebraically shown to be the Paasche Quantity index, defined in equation 4.7. This means that Laspeyres-price and Paasche-quantity indices form a pair that will together exactly decompose the value change. In that sense, the Paasche-quantity index can be considered as the dual of the Laspeyres-price index.

It is also easy to show that the Paasche-price index and Laspeyres-quantity index together decompose the value index, and therefore are dual to each other. An important question that arises is: "Are there self-dual index number formulae such that the same formula for price and quantity index numbers decompose the value index exactly?" The answer to this is in the affirmative. The Fisher index for prices and Fisher index for quantities together form a dual pair. This implies that the direct quantity index obtained using the Fisher formula is identical to the indirect quantity index derived by deflating the value change by the Fisher price index. This property is sometimes referred to as the *factor reversal test*. We consider this property in the next section.

The Tornqvist index, due to the geometric nature of its formula, does not have the property of self-duality. This means that if we use the Tornqvist price index, then the indirect quantity index derived would be different from the quantity index derived using the Tornqvist index in equation 4.8 directly.

If the direct and indirect approaches lead to different answers, or different numerical measures of quantity changes, a problem of choice often arises as to which approach should be used in a given practical application. This problem is discussed below.

Direct versus Indirect Quantity Comparisons

Some of the analytical issues involved in a choice between direct and indirect quantity comparisons are discussed in Allen and Diewert (1981). From a practical point of view, such a choice depends on the type of data available, the variability in the price and quantity relatives, as well as the theoretical framework used in the quantity comparisons.

From a practical point of view, a researcher will rarely have the luxury of choosing between direct and indirect comparisons. If the problem involves the use of aggregative data, then quantity data are usually only available in the form of constant price series. In such cases data unavailability solves the problem.

The second point concerns the reliability of the underlying index. Since an index number is a scalar value representation of changes observed for different commodities, the reliability of such a representation depends upon the variability observed in price and quantity changes for the different commodities. If price changes tend to be uniform over different commodities, then the price index provides a reliable measure of the price change. A similar conclusion can be drawn for the quantity index numbers. The relative variability in the price and quantity ratios, p_{it}/p_{is} and q_{it}/q_{is} ($i = 1,2,...,N$) provides a useful clue as to which index is more reliable. If the price ratios exhibit less variability (relative to the quantity ratios), then an indirect quantity index can be advocated, and if quantity relatives show less variability, then a direct quantity index should be preferred. Variability in these ratios can be measured using standard variance measures.

Following on from this important consideration, it is worth noting that over time price changes tend to be more uniform across commodities, than commodity changes. Price changes for different commodities are usually deviations from an underlying rate of overall price change. In contrast, quantity ratios tend to exhibit considerable variation across different commodities, even in the case of changes over time.

Another point of significance is that if price (quantity) ratios exhibit little variability then most index number formulae lead to very similar measures of price (quantity) change. There is more concurrence of results arising out of different formulae, and therefore the choice of a formula has less impact on the measure of price (quantity) change derived.

Finally, in the context of output and productivity comparisons, direct quantity comparisons may offer theoretically more meaningful indices as they utilise the constraints underlying the production technologies. Work by Diewert (1976, 1983) and Caves, Christensen and Diewert (1982a) suggests that direct input and output quantity indices, based on the Tornqvist index formula, are theoretically superior under certain conditions. Diewert (1992) shows that the Fisher index performs very well with both theoretical and test properties. An additional point in favour of the Fisher index is that it is self-dual, in that it satisfies the factor-reversal test. In addition, the Fisher index is defined using the Laspeyres and Paasche indexes. Therefore, the index is easier to understand and it is also capable of handling zero quantities in the data set.

Some recent work by Balk (1997) suggests that under the assumption of behaviour under revenue constraints, productivity indexes are best computed using indirect quantity measures. Given these results, from a theoretical point of view, the choice between direct and indirect quantity (input or output) should be based on the assumptions on the behaviour of the firm or decision making unit.

All the evidence and discussion on this issue of choice between direct and indirect quantity comparisons suggests that a decision needs to be made on pragmatic considerations as well as on pure analytical grounds.

4.5 Properties of Index Numbers: The Test Approach

In view of the existence of numerous index number formulae, Fisher (1922) proposed a number of intuitively meaningful criteria, called tests, to be satisfied by the formulae. These tests are used in the process of choosing a formula for purposes of constructing price and quantity index numbers. An alternative (yet closely related) framework is to state a number of properties, in the form of axioms, and then to find an index number that satisfies a given set of axioms. This approach is known as the *axiomatic approach* to index number construction. Eichorn and Voeller (1976) provides a summary of the axiomatic approach. Balk (1995) provides a recent summary of some of the axiomatic price index number theory. Diewert (1992) provides a range of axioms for consideration in productivity measurement and recommends the use of the Fisher index. It is not within the scope of this intermediate text to provide details of the axiomatic approach nor to delve deeply into various tests originally proposed by Fisher. The main purpose of this brief section is to provide the reader with an intuitive and non-rigorous treatment of some of the tests and state two results of some importance to productivity measurement.

Let P_{st} and Q_{st} represent price and quantity index numbers which are both real-valued functions of the prices and quantities (N commodities) observed in periods s and t, denoted by N-dimensional column vectors, p_s, p_t, q_s, q_t. Some of the basic and commonly used axioms are listed below.

Positivity: The index (price or quantity) should be everywhere positive.

Continuity: The index is a continuous function of the prices and quantities.

Proportionality: If all prices (quantities) increase by the same proportion then P_{st} (Q_{st}) should increase by that proportion.

Commensurability or Dimensional invariance: The price (quantity) index must be independent of the units of measurement of quantities (prices).

Time-reversal test: For two periods s and t: $\qquad P_{st} = \dfrac{1}{P_{ts}}$.

Mean-value test: The price (or quantity) index must lie between the respective minimum and maximum changes at the commodity level.

Factor-reversal test: A formula is said to satisfy this test if the *same* formula is used for direct price and quantity indices and the product of the resulting indices is equal to the value ratio.

Circularity test (transitivity): For any three periods, s, t and r, this test requires that: $P_{st} = P_{sr} \times P_{rt}$. That is, a direct comparison between s and t yields the same index as an indirect comparison through r.

The following two results describe the properties of Fisher and Tornqvist indices, and thus offer justification for the common use of these indices in the context of productivity measurement.

Result 4.1:   The Fisher index satisfies all the properties listed above, with the exception of the circularity test (transitivity).

In fact Diewert (1992) shows that the Fisher index satisfies many more properties.   The Fisher index satisfies the factor-reversal test which guarantees a proper decomposition of value change into price and quantity changes.   This justifies the label of "ideal index" attached to the Fisher formula.   The factor-reversal property shows that the direct Fisher quantity index is the same as the indirect quantity index derived by deflating the value index by the Fisher price index.   The Fisher index exhibits the "self-dual" property.   Diewert (1976, 1981) show that the Fisher index is *exact* and *superlative.*[1]

Result 4.2:   The Tornqvist index satisfies all the tests listed above with the exception of the factor-reversal and circularity tests.

This result and other results are proved in Eichorn and Voeller (1983).   Proofs of these statements are highly mathematical but the final results are quite useful.   Theil (1973, 1974) shows that the Tornqvist index fails the factor-reversal test by only a small order of approximation.   Failure to satisfy the factor-reversal test is not considered to be very serious as there is no necessity for the price and quantity index numbers to be *self-dual*, and no real analytical justification for the use of the same type of formula for price as well as quantity comparisons.

Fixed Base versus Chain Base Comparisons

We now briefly touch upon the issue of comparing prices, quantities and productivity over time.   In the case of temporal comparisons, in particular within the context of productivity measurement, we are usually interested in comparing each year with the previous year, and then combining annual changes in productivity to measure changes over a given period.   The index constructed using this procedure is known as a *chain index*.   To facilitate a formal definition, let I(t,t+1) define an index of interest for period t+1 with t as the base period.   The index can be applied to a time series with t = 0, 1, 2, . . , T.   Then a comparison between period t and a fixed base period, 0, can be made using the following chained index of comparisons for consecutive periods.

$$I(0, t) = I(0, 1) I(1, 2) \ldots I(t-1, t)$$

---

[1] These terms are explained in the next chapter which deals with the theoretical foundations of some of the index numbers. At this time we note that these terms, *exact* and *superlative*, refer to properties related to the economic theory underlying price and quantity index number measurement.

As an alternative to the chain-base index, it is possible to compare period 0 with period t using any one of the formulae described earlier. The resulting index is known as the *fixed-base index*.

Most national statistical offices make use of a fixed-base Laspeyres index mainly because the weights will remain the same for all the fixed-base index computations. Usually the base periods are shifted on a regular basis.

There is a considerable index number literature focusing on the relative merits of fixed- and chain-base indices. A good survey of the various issues can be found in Forsyth (1978), Forsyth and Fowler (1981) and Szulc (1983). From a practical angle, especially with respect to productivity measurement, a chain index is more suitable than a fixed-base index. Since the chain index involves only comparisons with consecutive periods, the index is measuring smaller changes. Therefore, some of the approximations involved in the derivation of theoretically meaningful indices are more likely to hold. Another advantage is that comparisons over consecutive periods would mean that the Laspeyres-Paasche spread is likely to be small indicating that most index number formulae result in indexes which are very similar in magnitude. The only drawback associated with the chain index is that the weights used in the indexes need to be revised every year.

The use of a chained index does not result in transitive index numbers. Even though transitivity is not considered essential for temporal comparisons, it is necessary in the context of multilateral comparisons. The question of transitivity in multilateral comparisons is considered in some detail in Section 4.7, as multilateral TFP studies are now quite common.

Which formula to choose?

The foregoing discussion indicates that the choice of formula is essentially between the Fisher and Tornqvist indices. Both of these formulae possess important properties and satisfy a number of axioms. If published aggregated data are used then it is necessary to check what formula was used in creating the series. It is very likely that Laspeyres or Paasche indices are used in such data series. If the indices are being computed for periods which are not far apart then differences in the numerical values of Fisher and Tornqvist indices are likely to be quite minimal. Further, both of these indices also have important theoretical properties. While in practice the Tornqvist index seems to be preferred, use of the Fisher index may be recommended due to its additional self-dual property and its ability to accommodate zeros in the data.

4.6 A Simple Numerical Example

At this point we introduce a simple example which is used throughout the remainder of this chapter. Table 4.1 contains five years of price and quantity data from a hypothetical firm called Billy's Bus Company.[2] This company uses three inputs: labour, capital and "other", to produce two outputs: metropolitan passenger kilometres and long distance passenger kilometres.[3]

The calculations in this example are conducted using the SHAZAM econometrics package (White, 1993), which has an INDEX command that calculates the Laspeyres, Paasche, Fisher and Tornqvist indices automatically. Note, however, that any standard spreadsheet program, such as EXCEL or LOTUS, or any statistical package, such as MINITAB or SAS, are also adequate for computational purposes.

Table 4.1: Data for Billy's Bus Company

	INPUTS					
	quantity			price		
year	labour	capital	other	labour	capital	other
1990	145	67	39	39	100	100
1991	166	75	39	41	110	97
1992	162	78	43	42	114	103
1993	178	89	42	46	121	119
1994	177	93	51	46	142	122
	OUTPUTS					
	quantity		price			
year	metropolitan	long distance	metropolitan	long distance		
1990	471	293	27	18		
1991	472	290	28	17		
1992	477	278	34	17		
1993	533	277	32	20		
1994	567	289	34	23		

We illustrate the calculation of price and quantity indices by calculating the relevant output price and output quantity indices for this firm. The SHAZAM instructions are presented in Table 4.2a. The commands are quite simple. To calculate a price index, the INDEX command requires that the price and quantity data columns are listed together in pairs (ie., price1, quantity1, price2, quantity 2, etc.)

---

[2] It should be noted that this example was inspired by the excellent Choochoo Railway example presented in Industry Commission (1992).
[3] Note that in most real applications we would have most probably begun with data on the values (i.e., expenditures or receipts) for all five variables, quantities for the two outputs and for the labour input, and price deflators (most likely obtained from a statistical agency) for the capital and "other" inputs. We would have then derived implicit quantities for the capital and "other" inputs and implicit prices for the two outputs and labour input.

The SHAZAM output listing is presented in Table 4.2b. It is important to note that SHAZAM uses the term "Divisia" to describe the Tornqvist index.[4] This term is used because the Tornqvist index is a discrete approximation to the Divisia index. The output of the INDEX command lists the four price indices first, followed by four indirect quantity indices. Note that the price indices all have the value 1 in the first year (1990). This is the base year which is used by the INDEX command unless another base year is specified (for more on this see the SHAZAM User's Manual, White 1993).

Table 4.2a SHAZAM Instructions for Output Price and Quantity Indices

	Shazam Command	**Description**
1.	sample 1 5	indicates that there are 5 observations
2	read yr y1 y2 p1 p2	read data on Year (Yr), 2 outputs quantities and prices
3 4 5 6 7	1990 471 293 27 18 1991 472 290 28 17 1992 477 278 34 17 1993 533 277 32 20 1994 567 289 34 23	data set - note that data can be read from a file instead of listing in the program.
8	** output price indices	comment line
9	index p1 y1 p2 y2	calculates chained price index numbers using different formulae
10	** output quantity indices	comment line
11	index y1 p1 y2 p2	calculates chained quantity index numbers using different formulae

The SHAZAM INDEX command can also be used to calculate direct quantity indices by simply changing the order that prices and quantities are listed on the command line. This is illustrated by the second INDEX command listed in Tables 4.2a and 4.2b. Be sure to note that SHAZAM incorrectly labels the quantity index as a price index and vice versa, in this instance.

---

[4] Note that the SHAZAM INDEX command automatically produces a chained Divisia (Tornqvist) index. For all other formulae, we need to give the CHAIN option to created chained indices. Unless otherwise specified, indices for Laspeyres, Paasche and Fisher are calculated using the first period as the base period.

Table 4.2b SHAZAM Output for Output Price and Quantity Indices

---

```
|_sample 1 5
|_read yr y1 y2 p1 p2
    5 VARIABLES AND                5 OBSERVATIONS STARTING AT OBS        1

|_** output price indices
|_index p1 y1 p2 y2

REQUIRED MEMORY IS PAR=     1 CURRENT PAR=   500
BASE PERIOD IS OBSERVATION       1
                      PRICE INDEX                           QUANTITY
DIVISIA PAASCHE  LASPEYRES  FISHER    DIVISIA       PAASCHE     LASPEYRES
FISHER
1    1.000    1.000    1.000    1.000    0.1799E+05  0.1799E+05    0.1799E+05
0.1799E+05
2    1.010    1.010    1.010    1.010    0.1797E+05  0.1796E+05    0.1797E+05
0.1797E+05
3    1.169    1.171    1.167    1.169    0.1792E+05  0.1788E+05    0.1795E+05
0.1792E+05
4    1.159    1.166    1.163    1.165    0.1949E+05  0.1938E+05    0.1942E+05
0.1940E+05
5    1.256    1.264    1.265    1.264    0.2064E+05  0.2051E+05    0.2050E+05
0.2051E+05
|_** output quantity indices
|_index y1 p1 y2 p2

REQUIRED MEMORY IS PAR=     1 CURRENT PAR=   500
BASE PERIOD IS OBSERVATION       1
                      PRICE INDEX                           QUANTITY
      DIVISIA PAASCHE LASPEYRES FISHER   DIVISIA       PAASCHE   LASPEYRES
FISHER
   1    1.000    1.000    1.000    1.000    0.1799E+05  0.1799E+05    0.1799E+05
0.1799E+05
   2    0.999    0.999    0.998    0.999    0.1817E+05  0.1817E+05    0.1817E+05
0.1817E+05
   3    0.996    0.998    0.994    0.996    0.2103E+05  0.2099E+05    0.2107E+05
0.2103E+05
   4    1.083    1.079    1.077    1.078    0.2086E+05  0.2093E+05    0.2098E+05
0.2096E+05
   5    1.147    1.139    1.140    1.140    0.2261E+05  0.2275E+05    0.2274E+05
0.2275E+05
```

4.7 Transitivity in Multilateral Comparisons

In this section we consider the problem of deriving price and quantity index numbers over space at a given point of time. This problem arises when we are interested in output, input and productivity level comparisons across a number of countries, regions, firms, plants, etc. In such cases, we are typically interested in all pairs of comparisons, ie., comparisons across all pairs of firms. Suppose we derive an index, I_{st}, for a pair of firms (s,t), using a formula of our choice. We consider all pairs (s,t) with s,t = 1,2,...,M. Then we have a matrix of comparisons between all pairs of firms,

$$\begin{bmatrix} I_{11} & I_{12} & \cdots & I_{1M} \\ I_{21} & I_{22} & \cdots & I_{2M} \\ \vdots & & & \\ I_{M1} & I_{M2} & \cdots & I_{MM} \end{bmatrix}. \qquad (4.12)$$

This matrix represents all multilateral comparisons involving M firms and ideally we would like these comparisons to be internally consistent, ie., to satisfy the property of transitivity.

Internal consistency requires that a direct comparison between any two firms s and t, should be the same as a possible indirect comparison between s and t through a third firm r. Thus we require, for any r, s and t,

$$I_{st} = I_{sr} \times I_{rt} . \qquad (4.13)$$

For example, if a matrix of index numbers shows that firm s produces 10% more than firm r and firm r produces 20% more than firm t, then we should always find that firm s produces 32% ($1.1 \times 1.2 = 1.32$) more than firm t.

Unfortunately, none of the index number formulae, including Fisher and Tornqvist, satisfy the transitivity property, given in equation 4.13. Remember, however, that these two indices do satisfy the time-reversal test: $I_{st} = 1/I_{ts}$.

The problem then is: how do we obtain consistent multilateral comparisons between firms? A simple solution is to generate transitive indices from a set of non-transitive multilateral comparisons using a technique due to Elteto-Koves (1964) and Szulc (1964). This method is known as the EKS method.[5] Caves, Christensen and Diewert (1982a) uses the EKS method to derive multilateral Tornqvist indices that are transitive.

We illustrate the conversion of non-transitive indices into transitive indices as follows. Suppose we start with Tornqvist indices, I_{st}^{T}, for all pairs s,t. Then for all firms s and t, we use the EKS method to convert the Tornqvist indices into multilateral Caves, Christensen and Diewert (CCD) indices by calculating:

$$I_{st}^{CCD} = \prod_{r=1}^{M} \left[I_{sr}^{T} \times I_{rt}^{T} \right]^{\frac{1}{M}} \qquad (4.14)$$

---

[5] This method was suggested in the context of deriving transitive index numbers for comparisons of prices across countries. This procedure is currently one of the methods used by the OECD for generating internationally comparable statistics on gross domestic product and its components. We do not consider the EKS method in detail. For details see Rao and Banerjee (1984). Only an application of this method in the context of productivity comparisons due to Caves, Christensen and Diewert (1982a) is considered here.

These indices satisfy the following properties:

(i) I_{st}^{CCD}, for s,t = 1,2,...,M, are transitive.

(ii) The new indices, I_{st}^{CCD}, deviate the least from the original Tornqvist indices in a least-squares sense.

(iii) If we focus on quantity indices based on the Tornqvist formula then the CCD index in log-change form can be shown to be equal to

$$\ln Q_{st}^{CCD} = \frac{1}{M} \sum_{r=1}^{M} \left[\ln Q_{sr}^{T} + \ln Q_{rt}^{T} \right]$$

$$= \frac{1}{2} \sum_{i=1}^{N} (\omega_{it} + \overline{\omega}_{i})(\ln q_{it} - \overline{\ln q_{i}}) - \frac{1}{2} \sum_{i=1}^{N} (\omega_{is} + \overline{\omega}_{i})(\ln q_{is} - \overline{\ln q_{i}}),$$

(4.15)

where $\overline{\omega}_{i} = \frac{1}{M} \sum_{j=1}^{M} \omega_{ij}$ and $\overline{\ln q_{i}} = \frac{1}{M} \sum_{j=1}^{M} \ln q_{ij}$.

The formula in equation 4.15 is the form proposed in Caves, Christensen and Diewert (1982a) and this is the form used in most empirical analyses of total factor productivity measurement conducted during the past decade.

(iv) The formula in equation 4.15 has an intuitive interpretation. A comparison between two firms is obtained by first comparing each firm with the average firm and then comparing the differences in firm levels relative to the average firm.

Although the question of transitivity is quite important, the rationale behind the CCD multilateral index is rarely spelt out. In this section we attempt to examine the main logic behind the CCD index. From this viewpoint, although equation 4.15 is the most popular form for a multilateral Tornqvist index, it is desirable to use the form in equation 4.14 as the root of the multilateral index.

Equation 4.14 provides an approach which can be applied to binary indices without detailed price and quantity data. To elaborate, suppose we have a matrix of binary Fisher or Tornqvist price and quantity indices. Then how do we generate transitive indices? The formula in equation 4.15 is not very useful in such cases because it requires all the basic price and quantity data. Even if basic data are not available, it is feasible to apply equation 4.14 and derive multilateral comparisons that are transitive.

It is not obvious from equation 4.14 how this procedure can be applied if the preferred index formula is different from the Tornqvist index. Suppose we are working with Fisher index numbers for output index numbers between firms. Let Q_{st}^{F} represent the Fisher index for firm t with firm s as base. Obviously Q_{st}^{F} for s, t = 1,2,...,M do not satisfy transitivity. The EKS procedure in equation 4.14 can be applied to yield consistent indices as:

$$Q_{st}^{F-EKS} = \prod_{r=1}^{M} \left[Q_{sr}^{F} \times Q_{rt}^{F} \right]^{\frac{1}{M}}.$$

The resulting quantity index numbers, Q_{st}^{F-EKS}, satisfy the transitivity property.

It is important to bear in mind that the condition of transitivity is an operational constraint preserving internal consistency. The imposition of the transitivity condition implies that a quantity (or price) comparison between two firms, s and t, will be influenced by price and quantity data for not just the two firms s and t but all the other firms in the analysis. Hence, the addition of an extra firm to the sample will necessitate the recalculation of *all* indices.

4.8 TFP Measurement Using Index Numbers

The main focus of this chapter, thus far, has been on the mechanics of constructing price and quantity index numbers. In terms of measuring productivity changes, index numbers are used in measuring changes in the levels of output produced and levels of inputs used in the production process over two time periods or across two firms. This can be achieved by using a suitable formula to compute input and output quantity index numbers.

A total factor productivity (TFP) index measures change in total output relative to the change in the usage of all inputs. A TFP index is preferred over partial productivity measures, such as output per unit of labour, since partial measures can provide a misleading picture of performance.

The main purpose of this section is to briefly describe the computational methods used in deriving an index of TFP, either over time or across firms or enterprises. A TFP index may be applied to binary comparisons, where we wish to compare two time periods or two cross-sectional units, or it may be applied to a multilateral situation where the TFP index is computed for several cross-sectional units.

4.8.1 Binary Comparisons

Consider the TFP index for two time periods or enterprises, s and t. We define the TFP index as,[6]

$$\ln \text{TFP}_{st} = \ln \frac{\text{Output Index}_{st}}{\text{Input Index}_{st}}, \tag{4.27}$$

---

[6] This definition is similar to the Hicks-Moorsteen productivity index defined in Chapter 5.

where the output and input indices are computed using any of the formulae discussed in Sections 4.3 and 4.4.

For the purposes of this section, we let ys and xs represent output and input quantities, and ωs and υs represent value shares for outputs and inputs, respectively. Subscripts, s and t, stand for firms or time periods, and i is used to denote the i-th output commodity and j to denote the j-th input commodity.

In most empirical applications, where TFP indices are calculated, the Tornqvist index formula is used for purposes of output and input index calculations. Then the Tornqvist TFP index[7] is defined, in its logarithmic form as

$$\ln \text{TFP}_{st} = \ln \frac{\text{Output Index}_{st}}{\text{Input Index}_{st}} = \ln \text{Output Index}_{st} - \ln \text{Input Index}_{st}$$

$$= \frac{1}{2} \sum_{i=1}^{N} (\omega_{is} + \omega_{it})(\ln y_{it} - \ln y_{is}) - \frac{1}{2} \sum_{j=1}^{K} (\upsilon_{js} + \upsilon_{jt})(\ln x_{jt} - \ln x_{js}),$$

$$(4.28)$$

where the first part of the right-hand side of equation 4.28 is the logarithmic form of the Tornqvist index applied to output data, and the second part is the input index, calculated using input quantities and the corresponding cost shares.

Equation 4.28 suggests that it is possible to replace the Tornqvist index by any other suitable formula. Diewert (1992) suggests the use of the Fisher index which has many desirable properties. In many respects, the Fisher index is more intuitive than the Tornqvist index and, more importantly, it decomposes the value index exactly into price and quantity components. The fact that it is in an additive format also makes the Fisher index more easily understood. In this case, the TFP index is given by

$$\text{TFP}_{st} = \frac{\text{Output Index}_{st} \ (\text{Fisher})}{\text{Input Index}_{st} \ (\text{Fisher})}.$$

Since the Fisher and Tornqvist indices both provide reasonable approximations to the "true"[8] output and input quantity index numbers, in most practical applications involving time series data, both formulae yield very similar numerical values for the TFP index (Diewert 1992).

---

[7] It appears that in many cases, the Tornqvist TFP index is considered to be essentially the same as the TFP index. But we here make a distinction between these two. Equation 4.27 defines a general TFP index and equation 4.28 is a particular case where indices are derived using the Tornqvist index formula.
[8] The concept of "true" quantity and price index numbers is introduced in the next chapter.

4.8.2 A Simple Numerical Example

Continuing on with our Bus Company example, we can easily obtain a Tornqvist TFP index by finding the ratio of the output quantity and input quantity indices. These calculations could be performed using SHAZAM, as we did before, or one could use spreadsheet software, such as EXCEL or LOTUS. However, we use TFPIP Version 1.0, which is a computer program recently developed for the purpose of computing index numbers for input and output quantities, as well as the resulting TFP index numbers. The TFPIP program produces index numbers calculated using either the Fisher or the Tornqvist formulae.[9] The program produces chained index numbers for comparisons over time. An option to produce transitive multilateral comparisons is also available in TFPIP V 1.0. The TFPIP program is discussed in the Appendix.

We now turn our attention the data on Billy's Bus Company. To calculate the TFP index and the underlying input and output quantity index numbers, we need to prepare a data file and an instruction file. Note that all files used by TFPIP are text files. The data file for this example is given in Table 4.3a below. The data file consists of five annual observations, each row representing a year's observation. The first two columns represent quantities of the two outputs in the example, the next three columns show the input quantities. Price data are in the last five columns, again the first two columns representing the two output commodities and the last three columns containing the prices of the input commodities.

Table 4.3a Listing of Data file, EX1.DTA

471	293	145	67	39	27	18	39	100	100
472	290	166	75	39	28	17	41	110	97
477	278	162	78	43	34	17	42	114	103
533	277	178	89	42	32	20	46	121	119
567	289	177	93	51	34	23	46	142	122

The instruction file is listed in Table 4.3b below. Comments provided on each line explain the meaning of each instruction. The first two lines identify the location of the data and output files. The last two rows allow us to pick the formula we wish to use and the type of comparisons we wish to make.

---

[9] It is anticipated that future versions of this program will have the capability of producing index numbers derived using different formulae.

Table 4.3b Listing of Instruction File, EX1.INS

```
ex1.dta          DATA FILE NAME
ex1.out          OUTPUT FILE NAME
5                NUMBER OF OBSERVATIONS
2                NUMBER OF OUTPUTS
3                NUMBER OF INPUTS
0                0=TORNQVIST AND 1=FISHER
0                0=NON-TRANSITIVE AND 1=TRANSITIVE
```

Table 4.3c, Listing of Output File, EX1.OUT

```
Results from TFPIP Version 1.0

Instruction file = ex1.ins
Data file        = ex1.dta

Tornqvist Index Numbers

These Indices are NOT Transitive


INDICES OF CHANGES REL. TO PREVIOUS OBSERVATION:

  obsn     output     input       TFP
     2     0.9986     1.1007     0.9073
     3     0.9974     1.0297     0.9686
     4     1.0877     1.0896     0.9983
     5     1.0586     1.0627     0.9962


CUMULATIVE INDICES:

  obsn     output     input       TFP
     1     1.0000     1.0000     1.0000
     2     0.9986     1.1007     0.9073
     3     0.9960     1.1333     0.8788
     4     1.0833     1.2348     0.8773
     5     1.1468     1.3122     0.8740
```

The output generated from the execution of TFPIP V1.0 is given in Table 4.3c. The output from the program lists output and input quantity index numbers as well as the resulting TFP index for each year, computed using the previous year as the base. These annual change index numbers are linked to provide chained (or cumulative) output, input and TFP indices with period 1 as the base period. Observe that the TFP index for this bus company has declined over the study period by almost 13%.

4.8.3 Transitivity and Multilateral TFP Indices

Routine application of the formulae in equation 4.27 to multilateral comparisons involving more than two enterprises leads to the problem of transitivity. Application of a binary TFP index formula yields inconsistent results. Following Caves, Christensen and Diewert (1982a), and the discussion in Section 4.7, the following formula is used if the Tornqvist index formula is preferred. The following index is derived by applying equation 4.15 to obtain a transitive CCD index, which is a multilateral generalisation of the Tornqvist index.

$$\ell n \ TFP_{st}^{*}$$

$$= \left[\tfrac{1}{2} \sum_{i=1}^{N} \left(\omega_{it} + \overline{\omega}_i \right) \left(\ln y_{it} - \overline{\ln y_i} \right) - \tfrac{1}{2} \sum_{i=1}^{N} \left(\omega_{is} + \overline{\omega}_i \right) \left(\ln y_{is} - \overline{\ln y_i} \right) \right]$$

$$- \left[\tfrac{1}{2} \sum_{j=1}^{K} \left(\upsilon_{jt} + \overline{\upsilon}_j \right) \left(\ln x_{jt} - \overline{\ln y_j} \right) - \tfrac{1}{2} \sum_{j=1}^{K} \left(\upsilon_{js} + \overline{\upsilon}_j \right) \left(\ln x_{js} - \overline{\ln y_j} \right) \right], \quad (4.29)$$

where TFP_{st}^{*} is a transitive TFP index and

$\overline{\omega}_i$ = arithmetic mean of output shares,

$\overline{\upsilon}_i$ = arithmetic mean of input shares

$$\overline{\ln y_i} = \tfrac{1}{M} \sum_{k=1}^{M} \ln y_{ik}, \ \text{and}$$

$$\overline{\ln x_j} = \tfrac{1}{M} \sum_{k=1}^{M} \ln x_{jk}$$

All averages are taken over the M enterprises or time periods or a combination of both.

The formula in equation 4.29 is computationally simple and employed in many empirical TFP studies. However, following the more general definition of a TFP index in equation 4.27, we can define alternative TFP formulae by using transitive output and input indices in the general multilateral TFP index given by

$$TFP_{st}^{*} = \frac{\text{Transitive output index}}{\text{Transitive input index}}. \quad (4.30)$$

It is feasible to use any output and input index numbers of our choice in equation 4.30. A suitable choice would be the multilateral generalisation of the Fisher index derived using the EKS procedure discussed in Section 4.7.

In concluding this discussion of multilateral TFP measurement, we note that transitivity is an important requirement for spatial comparisons, but it is not a major problem in the case of temporal comparisons, where the observations are in a naturally ordered sequence in which a simple chain-base index would be adequate.

4.8.4 Computation

We now return to the Billy's Bus Company example once more. The data set used in this example is the same as that in Table 4.3a above. The multilateral TFP index in equation 4.29, based on the Tornqvist index, is computed using TFPIP V1.0. The Instruction file for this computation is given below in Table 4.4a.

Table 4.4a Listing of Instruction File, EX2.INS

```
ex1.dta        DATA FILE NAME
ex2.out        OUTPUT FILE NAME
5              NUMBER OF OBSERVATIONS
2              NUMBER OF OUTPUTS
3              NUMBER OF INPUTS
0              0=TORNQVIST AND 1=FISHER
1              0=NON-TRANSITIVE AND 1=TRANSITIVE
```

Note from the listing above that the last instruction provides the option to derive a multilateral TFP index that is transitive. The second last line allows the choice between Tornqvist and Fisher indexes.

Table 4.5b lists the output derived using the instruction file above.

Table 4.4b Listing of Output File, EX2.OUT

```
Results from TFPIP Version 1.0

Instruction file = ex2.ins
Data file        = ex1.dta

Tornqvist Index Numbers

These Indices are Transitive


INDICES RELATIVE TO FIRST OBSERVATION:

  obsn     output      input        TFP
     1     1.0000     1.0000     1.0000
     2     0.9979     1.1003     0.9069
     3     0.9938     1.1333     0.8769
     4     1.0792     1.2347     0.8741
     5     1.1417     1.3129     0.8696
```

Since all the index numbers are transitive, only one set of index numbers with the base period equal to 1 is presented. If, however, we wish to compute an index for period 4 with period 3 as base, for example, we simply divide the index in the table above for year 4, 1.0792, by the index for period 3, 0.9938. The table shows a steady decline in the TFP over the five-year period.

4.9 Empirical Application: Australian National Railways

We now present a real example based on a study on the Australian National Railways undertaken by the Industry Commission (IC). The example is drawn from Industry Commission (1992), which reports a number of studies measuring the TFP of government trading agencies in Australia.[10] The IC report describes a number of case studies on various enterprises including: Australian National Railways; State Rail Authority of New South Wales; Melbourne Water; Port of Brisbane Authority; Pacific Power and Australia Post. We have selected the study on Australian National Railways for detailed discussion.

This is a study of TFP changes, at an aggregate level, over the period 1979/80 to 1990/91.[11] The main purpose of the study was to go beyond the usual partial productivity measures and construct a TFP index as a part of a set of key performance indicators.

The study covers a wide range of outputs and inputs. Three categories of outputs are distinguished. These are: mainland freight services, measured in net-tonne-kilometres (NTKs); Tasrail freight services,[12] measured in net-tonne-kilometres (NTKs); and passenger services, measured in passenger-train-kilometres (PTKs). The aggregated output data for the three categories along with the price data are presented in Table 4.5. These quantities are in themselves aggregates of distinctly different categories of output. For example, passenger output in kilometres ignores the class of travel as well as the terminal services provided. But the prices are also average prices, averaged over passenger travel of different kinds.

The study distinguishes between two types of inputs in computing the aggregate index: capital inputs and non-capital inputs. Capital inputs are further divided into: land, buildings/structures and perway; plant and equipment; and the rolling stock. The non-capital inputs are divided into: labour; fuel; and a composite "other inputs" category.

---

[10] The authors are grateful to the Industry Commission for publishing this report without copyright. The example presented here is a summary version of a more detailed presentation in Chapter 4 of Industry Commission (1992).

[11] Years here are of the form 1979-80 etc., reflecting the accounting year used in Australia which extends from 1 July to 30 June.

[12] Tasrail refers to railway operations in the island state of Tasmania.

Table 4.5: Output Data for the Australian National Railways Example

Quantities			Prices		
Mainland Freight ('000 NTKs)	Tasrail Freight ('000 NTKs)	Passenger ('000 PTKs)	Mainland Freight ($/NTK)	Tasrail Freight ($/NTK)	Passenger ($/PTK)
5235000	383000	2924	0.02	0.07	10
5331000	420000	3057	0.03	0.07	12
5356000	375000	2992	0.03	0.08	14
4967000	381000	2395	0.03	0.08	18
5511000	401000	2355	0.03	0.08	20
5867000	403000	2188	0.03	0.08	22
6679000	402000	2486	0.03	0.09	23
6445000	429000	2381	0.03	0.09	23
7192000	455000	2439	0.03	0.09	23
7618000	459000	2397	0.03	0.08	26
7699000	413000	2316	0.03	0.11	32
7420000	369000	1664	0.03	0.12	47

The labour input for the study is defined to be the amount of labour used during the year for operational and maintenance purposes. The quantity measure of labour refers to the level of full-time staff, as on 30 June. The study points out the need to refine the measure to capture the number of hours worked, as well as to make adjustments for the labour input used in producing capital stock. Labour input figures are shown in Table 4.6.

The second non-capital input used is the quantity of fuel used. The last of the inputs refers to the "other inputs" category, which is in the form of a series of *real expenditures* on this category. The price used for this item is the implicit price deflator for non-farm gross domestic product.

Table 4.6: Non-capital Input Data for the Australian National Railways Example

Quantities			Prices		
Labour (persons)	Fuel ('000 litres)	Other ($'000)ª	Labour ($/person)	Fuel ($/litre)	Other (index)
10481	77380	119113	13097	0.18	0.45
10071	80148	112939	14730	0.26	0.50
9941	77105	108263	16692	0.28	0.56
9575	72129	110210	18651	0.37	0.62
9252	85868	109292	20166	0.37	0.66
8799	89706	97594	21307	0.39	0.70
8127	96312	93178	24990	0.41	0.75
7838	92519	80054	26412	0.42	0.81
7198	96435	77716	28572	0.43	0.87
6648	101327	74147	32617	0.39	0.94
6432	98874	80826	34565	0.43	1.00
5965	96016	73172	35646	0.46	1.04

Note: a. These quantities are in 1989-90 values.

Data for the non-capital inputs are drawn mainly from annual reports. These reports also form the basis for the output series discussed earlier. Table 4.6 shows the input quantity series as well as the prices. A major feature of this input series is the significant reduction in labour input over the study period. Both labour and "other" inputs recorded a decrease while fuel recorded a steady increase until 1988/89.

The study explicitly recognises the importance of measuring capital input properly. Though the most appropriate input measure is the flow of capital services per period, a measure of capital stock is used in its place. The capital stock series for the three components were constructed using the Perpetual Inventory Method. The capital stock input used in the study refers to Australian National's own capital stock. Capital items leased were accounted for in the "other inputs" category. The price used for the capital items represents the economic rental price of capital. Capital inputs and the associated "prices" are shown in Table 4.7.

Table 4.8 shows the aggregate output and input indexes as well as the total factor productivity index derived using the TFPIP V1.0 program. The aggregate inputs index for the period has shown a steady decline, by about twenty five percent. A significant factor to consider here is that the input decline occurred at a time when output has shown an increasing trend.

Table 4.7 Capital Input Data for the Australian National Railways Example

Quantities			Prices		
Land, Building and Perway ($'000)[a]	Plant and Equipment ($'000)[a]	Rolling Stock ($'000)[a]	Land, Building and Perway (index)[b]	Plant and Equipment (index)[b]	Rolling Stock (index)[b]
1858038	94057	332307	10	50	50
2101035	93927	308491	20	80	80
2059365	89764	285626	30	120	120
2118357	93271	269265	30	100	100
2117625	91837	275134	70	140	140
2095680	90120	261495	70	160	160
2069494	89617	251588	50	90	90
2034867	88773	239736	70	120	120
2017626	89653	235834	80	200	200
1998345	98762	252514	80	240	240
2011753	100495	251850	80	190	190
2018802	107654	242662	130	200	200

Notes: a. These quantities are in 1989-90 values.
   b. These are indices of the rental price of capital.

The output data are combined using the Tornqvist index formula, to compute the output index presented in Table 4.8. These indices are also presented in Figure 4.1. Over the study period the output of Australian National has shown a steady increase, but with downturns in 1982/83 and also towards the end of the study period. The first of these downturns was associated with severe drought in rural Australia and the latter down turn shows the effects of the recent recession in the Australian economy.

Table 4.8 Indices of Output, Input and TFP for Australian National Railways

Year	Output	Input	TFP
79/80	1.0000	1.0000	1.0000
80/81	1.0343	0.9782	1.0573
81/82	1.0188	0.9515	1.0707
82/83	0.9304	0.9345	0.9956
83/84	1.0014	0.9316	1.0748
84/85	1.0311	0.8950	1.1521
85/86	1.1543	0.8596	1.3428
86/87	1.1268	0.8191	1.3756
87/88	1.2293	0.7885	1.5590
88/89	1.2766	0.7690	1.6600
89/90	1.2607	0.7684	1.6407
90/91	1.1283	0.7376	1.5296

Combining the input and output indices to derive the TFP index, we see that, apart from a decline during 1982/83 and then over the most recent period associated with recession in the Australian economy, TFP has shown a compound rate of growth of 4 per cent. This growth is significantly above the growth rate experienced in the whole economy.

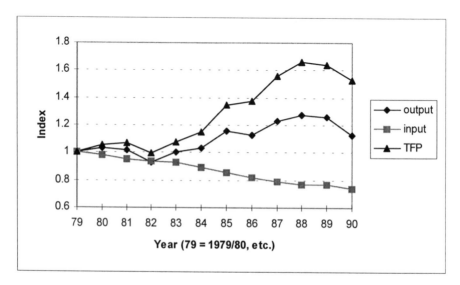

Figure 4.1 Indices of Output, Input and TFP for Australian National Railways

Industry commission (1992) provides some discussion of the TFP growth measures obtained for the Australian National Railways. This growth can be attributed to both *efficiency gains,* derived through labour reductions and internal reorganisation, as well as the effects of *technical progress*.

Given the aggregated nature of the data, it is not possible to measure these two components. The study speculated that efficiency gains were the main reason for the high compound growth rate of the TFP index. The Australian National Railways TFP growth study illustrates the various steps involved in the compilation of the TFP indices and also its shortcomings when it comes to final interpretation and use.

4.10 Conclusions

In this chapter, we have dealt with various index number formulae that are generally used in the construction of price and quantity index numbers. However, the main purpose of the chapter was to eventually lead to a measure of total factor productivity in the form of a TFP index. On an intuitive note, the TFP index provides a measure of output change over a given period net of input quantity use over the same period. The question now arises as the *real* meaning of the TFP index. What exactly does the TFP index measure? For a long period of time, and even now, some empirical economists interpret the TFP index as a measure of *technical change or progress* that has taken place over time. Is such an interpretation really justified? Could it be that firms had become more efficient in using the same technology? Or is it a combination of these and some other factors? To answer these and a few other questions it is necessary to look at the economic interpretation of these index numbers in terms of the production theory concepts discussed in Chapters 2 and 3. Notice how the present chapter has carefully avoided becoming entangled in the theoretical sophistication underlying productivity measurement. The exciting feature is that all the index numbers discussed in this chapter possess some useful economic theoretic properties, and it is indeed possible to use production theory concepts to place useful interpretation on the price, quantity (output and input), and total factor productivity indices described in this chapter. Chapter 5 attempts to provide a simple, non-rigorous, treatment of the production theory foundations of these various measures.

5. ECONOMIC THEORY AND INDEX NUMBERS

5.1 Introduction

This chapter is primarily devoted to a detailed examination of the economic-theoretic foundations of the various index numbers discussed in Chapter 4. Given the importance attached to index numbers in TFP measurement, it is hardly surprising that economic theory is extremely relevant in understanding what these index numbers actually measure and in making a proper application of the formulae described. This chapter is also important in that it provides a base from which we integrate the three principal approaches, viz., the index number, DEA and stochastic frontier approaches, in the context of productivity and efficiency measurement.

The economic-theoretic approach to index numbers is also known as the functional approach to index numbers, since the approach postulates a functional relationship between observed prices and quantities for inputs as well as outputs. In the case of productivity measurement, the economic theory relevant to production (i.e., the microeconomic theory of the firm) is even more relevant. The functional approach contrasts with the simple mathematical approach, usually known as the test (or axiomatic) approach (considered in Chapter 4) and its reliance on a range of well-defined properties or tests or axioms.

In this chapter we make use of the production theory and duality discussed in Chapters 2 and 3. It is inevitable that the approach explored here appears more involved and difficult, but we suggest that the reader focuses on the final results, their interpretation and their implications for the choice of a formula. A major feature of this chapter is that, despite the complexities of the theory involved, most discussions ultimately lead to or recommend the use of the Tornqvist or Fisher formulae for measuring price and quantity changes and in deriving a measure of total factor productivity. Thus, it is reassuring to note that these two formulae, which possess nice statistical properties, and which are computationally very simple, also possess some attractive economic-theoretic properties.

The approach we examine revolves around two basic indices proposed decades ago. All price index numbers, input as well as output price indices, are based on the famous Konus (1924) index and the approach discussed in Fisher and Shell (1972). The Konus index, in its original form, provided an analytical framework for measuring changes in consumer prices, i.e., the construction of cost of living index numbers. The input and output quantity index numbers, and productivity indices, are all based on the ideas of Malmquist and the distance function approach outlined in Malmquist (1953). No treatment of these aspects would be complete without reference to work by Diewert (1976, 1978, 1981), Caves, Christensen and Diewert (1982a and 1982b), Färe, Grosskopf and Lovell (1985, 1994), Färe and Primont (1995) and Balk (1997).

The plan for the chapter is as follows. Section 5.2 presents a simple case of one output and one input and uses it to examine the TFP index developed in Chapter 4 in more detail in conjunction with a production function. This section provides a simple decomposition of the TFP index from an economic-theoretic angle, and it helps in integrating the TFP index with some of the more recent work on efficiency and productivity measurement using Malmquist DEA and other techniques, when panel data are available. In Section 5.3 we examine the framework for defining input and output price index numbers, and see where the price index numbers defined in Chapter 4 fit into this approach. Section 5.4 focuses on input and output quantity index numbers, and Section 5.5 describes Malmquist productivity index numbers. The final section brings the various strands and approaches together, and provides a lead into the two principal frontier measurement techniques discussed in Chapters 6 to 9.

5.2 Decomposition of a Simple TFP Index

Let us consider the TFP index in the simplest case of a single input and a single output.[1] Let y_t, y_s and x_t, x_s represent observed quantities of outputs and inputs produced by a firm in periods t and s, respectively.[2] Suppose the production technologies in these two periods are represented by functions, $f_s(x)$ and $f_t(x)$.[3]

---

[1] The analysis here is based on Balk (1997), in which this simple case is used in making a case for direct and indirect quantity index numbers in productivity measurement.

[2] A similar analysis holds when s and t represent two firms, s and t, located in different geographic locations in a given time period.

[3] We assume that these functions possess characteristics associated with production functions derived from a production technology satisfying standard axioms, discussed in Chapter 3.

The TFP index in this simple case is the ratio of the ratio of the output ratio to the input ratio, for the two periods, namely

$$\text{TFP}_{st} = \frac{y_t / y_s}{x_t / x_s} \, . \tag{5.1}$$

If the firms were technically efficient in these two periods, then observed output levels would be the same as those implied by the production function. Otherwise we expect the outputs to be, for both t and s,

$$y_t = \lambda_t f_t(x_t) \qquad \text{, where } \ 0 \le \lambda_t \le 1 . \tag{5.2}$$

A value of λ_t less than unity implies that the firm is inefficient in that period. Substituting equation 5.2 in equation 5.1 we obtain

$$\text{TFP}_{st} = \frac{\lambda_t}{\lambda_s} \times \frac{f_t(x_t)/x_t}{f_s(x_s)/x_s} \, . \tag{5.3}$$

If the level of input usage in the two periods is the same, i.e., $x_t = x_s = x^*$, then equation 5.3 provides the following decomposition of the TFP index

$$\text{TFP}_{st} = \frac{\lambda_t}{\lambda_s} \times \frac{f_t(x^*)}{f_s(x^*)} \, . \tag{5.4}$$

The first ratio in equation 5.4 measures the change in technical efficiency; and the second ratio measures technical change, as it measures the output levels implied by the technologies in the two periods at the same input level, x^*. Consequently, if the firm is efficient in both periods, then the first ratio is equal to unity and the TFP measure, in fact, measures technical change. Since the level of inputs used is the same, scale issues do not arise in this context.

Now let us consider the case where the levels of input use are different. Since we are considering a single input case, we can write $x_t = \kappa \, x_s$. If the input quantity in period-t is larger (which is the case we consider here) then κ is greater than one. Further, assume that the production function is homogeneous of degree $\varepsilon(t)$, at x_t, in period-t. Then equation 5.3 can be written as

$$\text{TFP}_{st} = \frac{\lambda_t}{\lambda_s} \times \frac{f_t(\kappa \, x_s)/\kappa \, x_s}{f_s(x_s)/x_s}$$

$$\tag{5.5}$$

$$= \frac{\lambda_t}{\lambda_s} \times \kappa^{\varepsilon(t)-1} \times \frac{f_t(x_s)}{f_s(x_s)}$$

Equation 5.5 provides a complete decomposition of the TFP index. The first part, as discussed earlier, represents the change in technical efficiency, the last component measures technical change, and the middle component shows the effect of a change in the scale of operations. The scale effect is itself made up of two components, κ represents the scale of operations, and $\varepsilon(t)$ represents the returns to scale parameter. If we assume constant returns to scale (CRS) (locally or globally) then the scale effect becomes unity. Otherwise we need to know the magnitude of $\varepsilon(t)$ to be able to measure the scale effect within the TFP measure.

Notice that the derivations in equations 5.3 to 5.5 keep the period-s input levels fixed and manipulate the period-t input levels. We can repeat the exercise by letting $x_s = \mu x_t$, with μ less than unity if the period-t input usage is greater than the period-s input use. After some simple algebraic manipulation, we can show that

$$TFP_{st} = \frac{\lambda_t}{\lambda_s} \times \mu^{1-\varepsilon(s)} \times \frac{f_t(x_t)}{f_s(x_t)}, \tag{5.6}$$

where μ shows the scale of operations, and $\varepsilon(s)$ represents the local returns to scale parameter in period-s. If CRS prevails then the middle component in equation (5.6) once again becomes irrelevant.

The simple example allows us to draw a number of important conclusions and enables us to clarify some of the informal definitions introduced in Chapter 1.

1. From this discussion, it is quite clear that even for the simplest of cases we ever encounter, the case of single input and single output, it is still not possible to interpret TFP as a measure of pure technical change without knowledge of the production technologies in periods s and t, as represented by the respective production functions.

2. Even in this simple case, the measures of technical change, represented by the last components in equations 5.5 and 5.6, respectively, are not necessarily equal since these ratios are evaluated at x_s and x_t. These two measures of technical change coincide in the presence of global CRS (adequate in the single-input case) and input homotheticity[4] in the more general case of multi-input, multi-output production.

3. The index number approach to productivity measurement is usually applied when there are only two observations, one each for periods t and s. In such cases, without extraneous information, it is not possible to disentangle the efficiency, scale and technical change components of the TFP index. In much of the work on the economic-theoretic approach to productivity index numbers, assumptions are made to the effect that there are no technical inefficiencies in

---

[4] See Färe and Primont (1995) and Førsund (1997) for a definition and explanation of input homotheticity.

both periods, leading to the result that, under the CRS assumption, the TFP index does indeed measure technical change. If the CRS assumption does not hold, some adjustments need to be made for the presence of the scale effect in equations 5.5 and 5.6 for these to be measures of technical change.

4. A point that is worth mentioning here is that in deriving different expressions for TFP, we kept the denominator, the ratio of inputs in the two periods, untouched and worked only with the numerator. This approach is essentially an output-orientated approach, asking the question as to how much output can be produced under different technologies. It is just as easy to work with the inputs and deduce results based on an input-orientated approach using the inverse of the production function, $f^{-1}(y)$. Here $f^{-1}(y)$ shows the amount of input required to produce a given level of output, y. Subscripts, t and s, then show the differences in input requirements in periods t and s, under the respective technologies. A question that arises is, under what conditions do these measures of technical change and efficiency, based on input- and output-orientated approaches, lead to the same answers? If the technology is globally CRS, then these measures coincide (for the multi-input, multi-output case we also require input homotheticity).

5. In the presence of multiple outputs and multiple inputs, we need to replace the output and input changes in equation 5.1 by index numbers. Following the discussion on quantity index numbers in Chapter 4, we have a further choice as to whether we wish to use direct quantity index numbers or indirect quantity index numbers, derived as value changes deflated for price changes.

6. The issue of allocative efficiency also becomes important when we deal with multiple outputs and multiple inputs. As we note below, the assumption of allocative efficiency is utilised in the economic-theoretic justification for using Tornqvist and Fisher indices to measure input and output quantity changes. If this assumption does not hold, then the resulting TFP indices may also be confounded by the effects of allocative inefficiency.

Some of the points made above have been made earlier in different contexts and some of these concepts and conclusions have been illustrated graphically. This discussion is designed to reinforce the concepts. The remaining part of this chapter examines the economic-theoretic approach to index numbers with particular emphasis on the types of assumptions made in the derivation of various types of index numbers. We examine price, quantity and productivity index numbers in three separate sections.

5.3 The Economic-Theoretic Approach: Some Preliminaries

Before embarking on the economic-theoretic approach, we formally establish some of the tools used by theorists to derive various index numbers of interest. We consider the general case involving M outputs and K inputs. Let s and t represent two time periods or firms; p_{is} and p_{it} represent output prices for the i-th commodity in periods s and t, respectively; y_{is} and y_{it} represent output quantities in periods s and t, respectively (i = 1,2,...,M); w_{js} and w_{jt} represent input prices in periods s and t, respectively; and x_{js} and x_{jt} represent input quantities in periods s and t, respectively (j = 1,2,...,K). Further, let p_t, p_s, y_t, y_s, w_s, w_t, x_t and x_s represent vectors of non-negative real numbers of appropriate dimensions. Let S^s and S^t represent the production technologies in periods s and t, respectively.[5] A production technology consists of all feasible input and output combinations. Given the technology, it is possible to define input sets, $L^j(y)$, and output sets, $P^j(x)$, (j=t,s). $L^j(y)$ consists of all input vectors, x, which are capable of producing the given vector of outputs, y, using technology j. In contrast, $P^j(x)$ consists of all output vectors that can be produced using the input vector, x.

For period-t technology, these sets are defined as:[6]

$$L^t(y) = \left\{ x \mid (x,y) \in S^t \right\} \text{ for all } y,$$

and

$$P^t(x) = \left\{ y \mid (x,y) \in S^t \right\} \text{ for all } x.$$

These input and output sets are assumed to satisfy some basic axioms. We refer the reader to Section 3.4. Making use of the description of the production technology and various assumptions/axioms associated with the technology, we now examine how economic theory is used in measuring changes in output and input prices, changes in quantities of inputs and outputs, and, finally, derive measures of productivity changes. In deriving each of these index numbers we make use of revenue and cost functions, and the input and output distance functions discussed in Chapter 3.

The results presented in the ensuing sections are drawn from Caves, Christensen and Diewert (1982b), Diewert (1983), Diewert (1992), Färe and Primont (1995), Färe, Grosskopf and Roos (1997) and Balk (1997). The foundations for some of this work, in fact, dates back to Diewert (1976) where the ideas of *exact* and *superlative* index numbers were first introduced. The exposition presented here is not meant to be exhaustive in its coverage, rather it is to provide the reader with a flavour of what is on offer.

---

[5] In the presence of multiple outputs, it is not possible to express the production technology in the form of a simple production function since the production function is a "real-valued function" showing the maximum level of output that can be produced with a given level of inputs. As a result, we use sets to represent the technology. Alternatively we could use a transformation function.

[6] Some of the definitions below are also given in Section 3.4, where output and input distance functions are introduced.

An important point to keep in mind is that *the economic-theoretic approach to index numbers assumes that the firms observed in periods s and t are both technically and allocatively efficient.*[7] This means that observed output and input data are assumed to represent optimising behaviour involving revenue maximisation and cost minimisation, or in some cases constrained optimisation involving revenue maximisation with cost constraints, and so on. A compensating factor in lieu of these somewhat restrictive assumptions is that we are able to derive various index numbers of interest with just two observations on prices and quantities for the two periods, s and t. We now examine different classes of index numbers derived using this approach.

5.4 Output Price Indices

For a given level of inputs, x, let the (maximum) revenue function be defined, for technology in period-t, as

$$R^t(p,x) = \max_y \{py: (y,x) \text{ is feasible in } S^t\} \tag{5.7}$$

We can illustrate this function by looking at the production possibility curve and iso-revenue line (for the case of two outputs) plotted in Figure 5.1. Recall that these concepts are discussed in Section 3.4.1. The point of tangency between the production possibility curve and the iso-revenue line indicates the combination of the two outputs (y_1 and y_2) that maximise revenue, given the input vector x, the output price vector, p_t, and the technology, S^t.

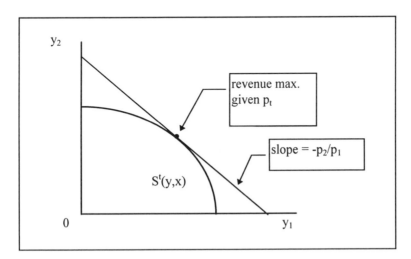

Figure 5.1 Revenue Maximisation

---

[7] Recent work of Balk (1997) relaxes the assumption of technical efficiency in deriving various index numbers. However, for purposes of this section we maintain the assumption of allocative efficiency.

The output price index, due to Fisher and Shell (1972) and Diewert (1980), based on period-t technology, is defined as

$$P_o^{\,t}(p_s,p_t,x) = \frac{R^t(p_t,x)}{R^t(p_s,x)}.$$ (5.8)

This index is the ratio of the maximum revenues possible with the two price vectors, p_s and p_t, using a fixed level of inputs, x, and period-t technology. This is illustrated in Figure 5.2, where we observe the revenue maximising points associated with the two price vectors, p_t and p_s.

The output price index in equation 5.8 can also be defined using period-s technology leading to

$$P_o^{\,s}(p_s,p_t,x) = \frac{R^s(p_t,x)}{R^s(p_s,x)}.$$ (5.9)

Some basic features of the two output price index numbers in equations 5.8 and 5.9 can be noted. These indices depend upon the state of technology, whether it is the period-t or period-s (or, for that matter any other period) technology involved, and then on the input vector, x, at which the index is calculated. It is then useful to ask the question: under what conditions are these indices independent of these two factors?

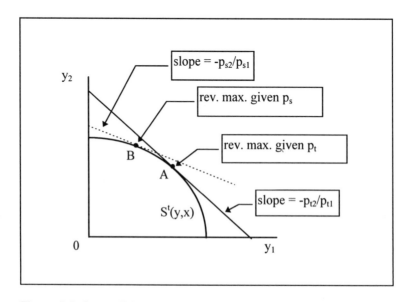

Figure 5.2 Output Price Index

These indices are independent of x if and only if the technology is output homothetic. Following Färe and Primont (1995, p. 68), a production technology is output homothetic if the output sets P(x) depend upon the output set for the unit input vector (input quantities equal to one for all inputs) and a real valued function, G(x), of x. In simple terms, the production possibility curves in Figures 5.1 and 5.2, for different input vectors, x, are all parallel shifts of the production possibility curve for the unit-input vector.

In a similar vein, it can be shown that if the technology exhibits implicit output neutrality then the indices are independent of which period's technology is used in the derivation.

The output price index numbers in equations 5.8 and 5.9 satisfy a number of standard properties. For example, these indices satisfy monotonicity, linear homogeneity; identity; proportionality, independence of units of measurement, transitivity for fixed t and x, and time-reversal properties.[8]

Since x_t and x_s are the actual input levels used in periods t and s, we can define the indices in equations 5.8 and 5.9 using the actual input levels, leading to two natural output price index numbers:

$$P_o^t(p_s, p_t, x_t) = \frac{R^t(p_t, x_t)}{R^t(p_s, x_t)} \tag{5.10}$$

$$P_o^s(p_s, p_t, x_t) = \frac{R^s(p_t, x_t)}{R^s(p_s, x_t)} \tag{5.11}$$

While the indexes defined here have intuitive appeal, computing them requires the knowledge of the functional form of the revenue functions as well as the numerical values of the parameters underlying the functions. In essence, we need to have a complete description of the technology, which is a hopeless task since we are trying to measure these changes based only on observed prices and quantities in these two periods. The following results illustrate how we can get close to the theoretically defined index numbers in equations 5.10 and 5.11.

Result 5.1: Under the assumptions of optimal behaviour (allocative and technical efficiency) and regularity conditions on the production technologies, the two index numbers in equations 5.10 and 5.11 are, respectively, bounded by the Laspeyres and Paasche indexes defined in Chapter 4. That is,

---

[8] Most of these properties can be established using simple logic and, in some cases, using the properties of the revenue function that flow from the basic assumptions on the production technology discussed in Section 3.4.

$$\text{Laspeyres Price Index} = \frac{\sum\limits_{i=1}^{M} p_{it} y_{is}}{\sum\limits_{i=1}^{M} p_{is} y_{is}} \leq P_o^s\left(p_s, p_t, x_s\right)$$

$$\text{Paasche Price Index} = \frac{\sum\limits_{i=1}^{M} p_{it} y_{it}}{\sum\limits_{i=1}^{M} p_{is} y_{it}} \geq P_o^t\left(p_s, p_t, x_s\right).$$

Proofs of these results are obtained by recalling that we have assumed that y_t is optimal for x_t at price p_t and y_s is optimal for x_s at price p_s. For example, in the case of the Paasche index, this implies that the revenue produced at the point A in Figure 5.2 must be equal to $\sum_i p_{it} y_{it}$ and we also know that the revenue produced at the point B in Figure 5.2 must be at least as large as $\sum_i p_{is} y_{it}$ (because that revenue is associated with a y vector which produces maximum revenue for the given p_s). Hence we find that the Paasche index is at least as large as $P^t(p_s,p_t,x_s)$. A similar argument is involved for the Laspeyres index.

The main point to note from Result 5.1 is that the Laspeyres and Paasche indices, which were defined on a heuristic basis (within the atomistic approach), provide lower and upper bounds for theoretical output price indices defined using production technologies and optimising behaviour. The following two results show that even though the two indices in equations 5.10 and 5.11 cannot be individually determined, the geometric mean of these two indices can be reasonably well approximated.

Result 5.2: A reasonable approximation to the geometric mean of the two indices in equations 5.10 and 5.11 is provided by the Fisher output price index number. That is,

$$[P_o^t(p_s, p_t, x_t) \times P_o^s(p_s, p_t, x_s)]^{1/2} \cong \left[\frac{\sum\limits_{i=1}^{M} p_{it} y_{is}}{\sum\limits_{i=1}^{M} p_{is} y_{is}} \times \frac{\sum\limits_{i=1}^{M} p_{it} y_{it}}{\sum\limits_{i=1}^{M} p_{is} y_{it}} \right]^{1/2}$$

$$= \text{Fisher Price Index.}$$

The accuracy of this approximation relies on how symmetric the Laspeyres and Paasche index numbers are, relative to the respective economic-theoretic index numbers in equations 5.10 and 5.11.

Suppose we now assume that the revenue functions have the translog form.[9] This assumption is essentially in line with the fact that the translog function is a flexible form and provides a second-order approximation to the unknown revenue function.[10] It should be noted, however, that alternative specifications such as the normalised quadratic, generalised Leontief and the generalised McFadden functions are also available. See Diewert and Wales (1987) for a discussion on the properties of various flexible functional forms.

The translog revenue function is given by[11]

$$\ln R^t(x,p) = \alpha_{0t} + \sum_{i=1}^{K} \alpha_{it} \ln x_i + \sum_{j=1}^{M} \beta_{it} \ln p_j + \frac{1}{2} \sum_{i=1}^{K} \sum_{j=1}^{K} \alpha_{ijt} \ln x_i \ln x_j +$$

$$\frac{1}{2} \sum_{i=1}^{M} \sum_{j=1}^{M} \beta_{ijt} \ln p_i \ln p_j + \frac{1}{2} \sum_{i=1}^{K} \sum_{j=1}^{M} \gamma_{ijt} \ln x_i \ln p_j$$

where $\alpha_{ijt} = \alpha_{jit}$ and $\beta_{ijt} = \beta_{jit}$ and $\gamma_{ijt} = \gamma_{jit}$. The following result uses a translog specification for the revenue function.

Result 5.3: If the revenue functions for periods s and t are represented by translog functions, with second-order coefficients being equal for periods s and t ($\alpha_{ijt} = \alpha_{ijs}$, $\beta_{ijt} = \beta_{ijs}$, $\gamma_{ijt} = \gamma_{ijs}$) then the geometric mean of the two price indices in equations 5.10 and 5.11 is equal to the Tornqvist output price index

$$\left[P_o^s(p_s, p_t, x_s) \times P_o^t(p_s, p_t, x_t) \right]^{1/2} = \prod_{i=1}^{M} \left(\frac{p_{it}}{p_{is}} \right)^{\frac{\upsilon_{it} + \upsilon_{is}}{2}}, \qquad (5.12)$$

where $\upsilon_{it} = \dfrac{p_{it} y_{it}}{\sum_{i=1}^{M} p_{it} y_{it}}$ and $\upsilon_{is} = \dfrac{p_{is} y_{is}}{\sum_{i=1}^{M} p_{is} y_{is}}$ are the value shares in periods s and t respectively. A proof of this result is in Diewert (1983).

Some comments on these results are in order. The importance of this result is that even though the theoretical indices in equations 5.10 and 5.11 require the knowledge of the parameters of the revenue function, their geometric mean is equal to the Tornqvist index and the index can be computed from the observed price and quantity data. No knowledge of the parameters of the translog functions is necessary.

---

[9] Examples of translog functions were given in equations 3.37 and 3.40 in Chapter 3 for the case of two inputs and a single output.

[10] The same translog functional form can be used in approximating any unknown function. We also make use of the translog form to approximate input cost functions, input and output distance functions as well as profit functions. Note that in each case we use different variables depending upon which function is involved.

[11] Note that some restrictions on the β- and γ-parameters need to be imposed to make the function satisfy linear homogeneity in output prices. We will not provide detailed translog specifications of each of the functions we come across in the remainder of this chapter.

If the translog function is replaced by a quadratic function then the Fisher index can be shown to be equal to the geometric mean on the left-hand side of equation 5.12 in Result 5.3 (proof in Diewert, 1992).

The Tornqvist index is considered to be *exact* for the translog revenue function, and it is considered *superlative* since the translog function is a flexible functional form (i.e., provides a second-order approximation to any arbitrary function). The Fisher index is *exact* for a quadratic function and hence is also *superlative*. A more detailed exposition of exact and superlative index numbers is available in the original paper on this subject by Diewert (1976).

5.5 Input Price Indices

The following framework for input price index numbers is essentially adapted from the Konus (1924) cost-of-living index which measures the changes in the cost of maintaining certain utility levels at different sets of prices. Extending this concept we can measure input price index numbers by comparing costs of producing a certain vector of outputs, given different input price vectors. In this process we need to define a cost function, associated with a given production technology, for a given output level, y, namely

$$C^t(w, y) = \min_x \{wx \mid (x, y) \in S^t\}. \tag{5.13}$$

The cost function, $C^t(w,y)$, is the minimum cost of producing y, given period-t technology, using input price vector, w.

It is easy to check that the cost function, $C^t(w,y)$, is linearly homogeneous in w^{12} and it is non-decreasing in the output vector, y. We can use the cost function to define input price index numbers. Given the input prices, w_t and w_s, in periods t and s, we can define the input price index as the ratio of the minimum costs of producing a given output vector y using an arbitrarily selected production technology, S^j (j=s,t). Then the index is given by

$$P_i^{\,j}(w_s, w_t, y) = \frac{C^j(w_t, y \mid S)}{C^j(w_s, y \mid S)}, \tag{5.14}$$

where the cost functions are defined using technology set, S. The cost elements in equation 5.14 can be seen from Figure 5.3 below. Let the isoquant under technology, S^s, for a given output level, y, be represented by Isoq(y)-S^s. The two sets of input prices, w_s and w_t can be represented by isocost lines AA′ and BB′, respectively. Minimum-cost combinations of inputs, producing output vector, y, for

---

[12] This implies that if all the input prices are multiplied by a common factor, λ, then the cost associated with the new prices is λ times the original cost.

these two input price vectors are given by the points, x* and x**. These points are obtained by shifting lines AA′ and BB′ to aa′ and bb′, respectively, where they are tangential to Isoq(y)-S^s. The input price index number in equation 5.14 for this two input case is then given by the ratio of the costs at points, x* and x**.

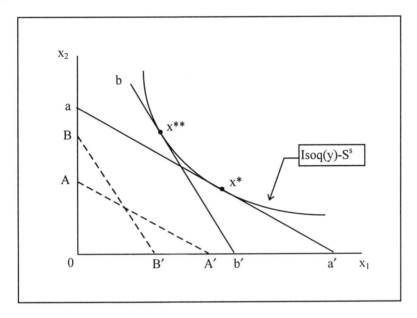

Figure 5.3 Input Price Index

The input price index defined above can be shown to satisfy many useful properties, including: monotonicity, linear homogeneity in input prices, independent of units of measurement, proportionality and transitivity (for fixed y and technology). These properties follow from duality theory and the fact that the cost function, $C^j(w,y)$, is associated with a production technology, S^j, with certain characteristics.[13]

In order to be able to actually compute the input price index in equation 5.14 we need to specify the technology and also the output level, y, at which we wish to compute the index. Two points can be made here. First, the price index is independent of which period technology we use if and only if the technology exhibits implicit Hicks input neutrality. Second, the index $P_i(w_t, w_s, y)$, for a given technology, is independent of the output level, y, if and only if the technology exhibits input homotheticity (see Färe and Primont, 1995).

If the technology does not satisfy these conditions, then we can define many input price index numbers using alternative specifications for technology, S, and the

---

[13] Refer to the section on duality in Chapter 3 for a discussion of these properties.

output vector, y. Two natural specifications are to use the period-s and period-t technologies, along with the output vectors, y_s and y_t. These result in the following input price index numbers[14]

$$P_i^s(w_s, w_t, y_s) = \frac{C^s(w_t, y_s)}{C^s(w_s, y_s)},$$

(5.15)

and

$$P_i^t(w_s, w_t, y_t) = \frac{C^t(w_t, y_t)}{C^t(w_s, y_t)}.$$

(5.16)

Observe that under the assumptions of allocative and technical efficiency, the observed input costs, $w_s x_s$ and $w_t x_t$, are equal to $C^s(w_s, y_s)$ and $C^t(w_t, x_t)$, respectively. We now state the following two results without proofs. Proof of Result 5.4 is fairly straightforward, while the proof of Result 5.5 is a bit more involved.

Result 5.4: Under our assumptions on the production technologies in periods, t and s, and given the optimal behaviour of the firm in these periods, the Laspeyres and Paasche indices provide upper and lower bounds to the economic-theoretic index numbers in equations 5.15 and 5.16. Also the geometric mean of these indices can be approximated by the Fisher price index numbers for input prices.

The next result is based on the assumption that the cost function, $C(w,y)$, has a translog form,[15] along with appropriate restrictions on the parameters of the cost function to ensure linear homogeneity in input prices.

Result 5.5: If the technologies in periods t and s are represented by the translog cost function, with the additional assumption that the second order coefficients are identical in these periods, then, under the assumption of technical and allocative efficiency the geometric mean of the two input price index numbers in equations 5.15 and 5.16 is given by the Tornqvist price index number applied to input prices and quantities. That is

$$\left[P_i^s(w_s, w_t, y_s) \times P_i^t(w_s, w_t, y_t)\right]^{1/2} = \prod_{i=1}^K \left(\frac{w_{it}}{w_{is}}\right)^{\frac{\omega_{it} + \omega_{is}}{2}},$$

(5.17)

where ω_{it} and ω_{is} are the input expenditure shares of i-th input in periods t and s, respectively. The right-hand side of equation 5.17 is the Tornqvist price index defined in Chapter 4.

---

[14] These indices correspond to the usual Laspeyres and Paasche-type index numbers because they rely on the base- and current-period technologies and output vectors.

[15] Note here that we made a similar assumption in the context of output price index number where the *revenue function* was assumed to be a translog form. However, due to the non-dual nature of the translog function, one assumption does not imply the other. The translog functional form is assumed for input and output distance functions that are used in the next two subsections.

Results 5.4 and 5.5 imply that the Fisher and Tornqvist indices, discussed in Chapter 4, can be applied in measuring changes in input prices and at the same time have a proper economic-theoretic framework to support their use. These results also illustrate that, under certain assumptions, it is not necessary to know the numerical values of the parameters of the cost or revenue function or the underlying production technology: it is sufficient to have the observed input price and quantity data to measure changes in input prices.

Result 5.5 shows that the Tornqvist input price index is *exact* for the geometric mean of the two theoretical indices, when the underlying cost function is translog and hence can also be considered *superlative*. Diewert (1983) shows that the Fisher input price index, while it provides an approximation as in Result 5.4, is also *exact* for a quadratic cost function. Diewert (1992) introduces yet another specification for the cost function under which the Fisher input price index can be shown to be exact.

An important point to note here is that much of the recent emphasis and popularity enjoyed by the Tornqvist and Fisher indices owe a great deal to the work of Diewert (1976, 1981, 1983 and 1992) and Caves, Christensen and Diewert (1982b). However, it is important to be aware of the assumptions underlying these results.

5.6 Output Quantity Indices

This section deals with the theoretical approach used in deriving output quantity index numbers. It is at this point, we make use of the distance functions introduced in Chapter 3. Use of distance functions in defining quantity (both output and input) index numbers is based on the work of Malmquist (1953).

Unlike the case of price index numbers, three possible strategies can be followed in deriving theoretically sound quantity index numbers. These are discussed below. We describe the first two approaches only briefly and then focus mainly on the Malmquist index defined using the distance function.

5.6.1 The Method of Deflation

This approach is discussed in Fisher and Shell (1972) and follows closely the indirect quantity index numbers discussed in Chapter 4. The approach here is to divide the value index by the output price index. Using period-t technology, at input level x_t, the output quantity index is given by

$$Q_o^t(p_s, p_t, x_t, y_s, y_t) = \frac{\sum_{i=1}^{M} p_{it} y_{it}}{\sum_{i=1}^{M} p_{is} y_{is}} \bigg/ P^t(p_s, p_t, x_t) \qquad (5.18)$$

This equation provides a quantity index which is a generalisation of equation 4.11, obtained by deflating the value index by a theoretically meaningful index of output prices. Equation 5.18 makes use of period-t technology and input vector, x_t. An index similar to equation 5.18 can be defined using period-s technology and input vector, x_s.

It is necessary to make a choice about which formula we use in measuring the output price changes. Either Tornqvist or Fisher output price index numbers could be used in equation 5.18. As we observed in Section 5.4, the final choice depends upon the functional form of the revenue function we are prepared to assume.

5.6.2   The Samuelson and Swamy Approach

In this section, we briefly describe the approach suggested by Samuelson and Swamy (1974) for measuring changes in output levels. Their approach uses the revenue function, $R(x,p)$, associated with an output price vector, p, and input vector, x, under a given production technology.

Under this approach the quantity index is defined as the ratio of the revenue functions derived from the inputs x_s and x_t, in periods s and t, at some arbitrarily defined price vector, p, namely

$$Q_o^{SS}\left(x_s, x_t, p\right) = \frac{R^t\left(p, x_t\right)}{R^s\left(p, x_s\right)}$$

$$= \frac{R^t\left(p, x_t\right)}{R^s\left(p, x_t\right)} \times \frac{R^s\left(p, x_t\right)}{R^s\left(p, x_s\right)}.$$

(5.19)

It is possible to interpret the first ratio on the right hand-side of the last line of equation 5.19 as a measure of the technical change from periods to period t, and the second component as a measure of output change, as measured from revenue changes, due to change in input use under the period-s technology.

5.6.3   The Malmquist Approach

The Malmquist approach is the most commonly used approach for output comparisons. This approach is based on the output distance function concept discussed in Section 3.4.2.

For period-t technology, the output distance function for a given output vector, y, and input vector, x, is defined as:

$$d_o^t(x, y) = \min \left\{ \delta : (y / \delta, x) \in S^t \right\}$$ (5.20)

$$= \min \left\{ \delta : (y / \delta) \in P^t(x) \right\}.$$ (5.21)

The distance here represents the smallest factor, δ, by which output needs to be deflated so as to be feasible or producible with a given input vector, x, under period-t technology. Distance functions associated with two output vectors y and y* are illustrated in Figure 5.4. In this figure, we have illustrated cases where the observation may lie above or below the technology.[16] Note that δ is greater than unity for y and less than unity for y*, both with respect to the same input vector, x. This means that we need to deflate y to bring it onto the surface of the production possibility set, P(x), associated with x. However, y* needs to be inflated. We also note that the distance function depends upon the choice of reference input vector, x.

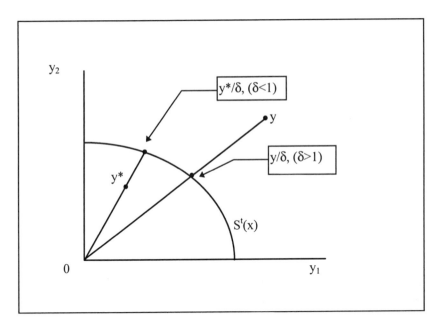

Figure 5.4 Output Distance Function

Using the distance functions defined above, the Malmquist output index, based on technology in period-t, is defined as

---

[16] Such situations do not arise when we measure efficiency of firms operating under a given frontier. However, when we are comparing levels of output in two periods, it is possible that observed output levels may be larger than what is feasible under the reference input vector, x, used in the distance function definition.

$$Q_o^t(y_s, y_t, x) = \frac{d_o^t(x, y_t)}{d_o^t(x, y_s)},$$

(5.22)

for an arbitrarily selected input vector, x.

A similar Malmquist index can be defined using period-s technology. In fact, we can also define many alternative indices using different levels of x. As before, the index defined in equation 5.22 is independent of the technology involved, if and only if the technology exhibits Hicks output neutrality. The quantity index is independent of the input level, x, if and only if the technology is output homothetic. Even in the cases where these assumptions hold, we still need to know the functional form of the distance function as well as numerical values of all the parameters involved. The index number approach attempts to bypass this problem by providing approximations to the index in equation 5.22 when we are not sure of the functional form, or do not have adequate information to estimate the parameters of the distance function, even when we know the form of the function.[17]

If we consider output quantity indices based on technology in periods s and t, along with the inputs used in these periods, we have two possible measures of output change, given by $Q_o^s(y_t, y_s, x_s)$ and $Q_o^t(y_t, y_s, x_t)$. There are many standard results of interest[18] that relate these indices to the standard Laspeyres and Paasche quantity index numbers, defined in Chapter 4. A result of particular interest is that the Fisher index provides an approximation to the geometric average of these two indices (see Diewert, 1981, 1983; and Balk, 1997). The following result establishes the economic-theoretic properties of the Tornqvist output index and shows why the index is considered to be an *exact* and a *superlative* index.

Result 5.6: If the distance functions for periods s and t are both represented by translog functions with identical second-order parameters, then a geometric average of the Malmquist output indices in equation 5.22, based on technologies of periods s and t, with corresponding input vectors x_s and x_t, is equivalent to the Tornqvist output quantity index. That is,

$$\left[Q_o^s(y_s, y_t, x_s) \times Q_o^t(y_s, y_t, x_t)\right]^{1/2} = \text{Tornqvist output index.}$$

(5.23)

This result implies that the Tornqvist index is *exact* for the geometric mean of the period-t and period-s theoretical output index numbers when the technology is represented by a translog output distance function. Since the translog functional

---

[17] Such estimation requires considerable panel data. These issues are further considered in the discussion of data envelopment analysis and stochastic frontiers in the following chapters. At this point, the strength of the index number approach lies in the fact that we can measure output changes without a lot of data.

[18] These results are very similar to Results 5.1 to 5.3, stated in the context of output price index numbers, and Results 5.4 and 5.5, stated for input price index numbers. It is easy to restate these results for output quantity index numbers incorporating appropriate modifications.

form is *flexible* (i.e., it provides a second-order approximation to an arbitrary, twice continuously differentiable, functional form), the Tornqvist index is also consider to be *superlative*.

If the translog functions are replaced by quadratic functions, with appropriate normalisation and restrictions, to represent the output distance function, then the left-hand side of equation 5.23 can be shown to be equal to the Fisher output quantity index number, which in turn establishes the *exact* and *superlative* nature of the Fisher output quantity index.

It should also be noted that if the Laspeyres or Paasche indices are used to calculate output (or input) indices, then this would imply an underlying linear technology for the production structure. If we cast our minds back to the "S-shaped" production functions, discussed in Chapter 1, it is obvious that a linear technology would be a simplifying assumption. It would imply constant returns to scale and constant marginal products throughout, together with other restrictive properties.

In terms of the choice between the three alternative measures of quantity change discussed in this subsection, the Malmquist index is the only index that satisfies the homogeneity property which states that, if $y_t = \lambda y_s$, then $Q_o^t(y_s, y_t, x) = Q_o^t(y_s, \lambda y_s, x) = \lambda$. This property does not hold for the Fisher-Shell and Samuelson-Swamy approaches. Diewert (1983) states some necessary and sufficient conditions under which all the three approaches are equivalent. Mainly these conditions revolve around homotheticity. Some practical issues arising out of practical applications of direct versus implicit quantity index numbers are discussed in Allen and Diewert (1981). These practical issues are discussed in Chapter 4.[19]

5.7 Input Quantity Indices

We now turn to the measurement of change in the input use by a firm over two time periods, t and s. An obvious strategy, which we are not going to pursue any further, is to measure input change by deflating the change in expenditure on inputs over periods s and t, by the input price index number defined in Section 5.5. In this section we describe the input quantity index number, derived using the Malmquist distance measure.

The input distance function defines the distance between a given output vector, y, and an input vector, x, as the maximum value of a scalar, ρ, such that the scaled input vector, x/ρ, remains (or becomes) feasible. If $d_i^t(x,y)$ denotes the distance function, then it is given by

---

[19] Balk (1997) recommends the use of Fisher-Shell approach when productivity measures are derived, given the assumption of economic behaviour of the firm under cost or revenue restrictions. These results suggest that quantity index numbers derived under constrained optimisation behaviour are in the form of values deflated by the respective price index numbers.

$$d_i^t(x, y) = \max\{\rho: (y, x/\rho) \in S^t\} \qquad (5.24)$$
$$= \max\{\rho: (x/\rho) \in L^t(y)\}.$$

Refer to Section 3.4.3 for further discussion of the input distance function.

Using the concept of the input distance function, we can now define the input quantity index. Along the same lines as the output index, we can compare the levels of input vectors x_t and x_s, by measuring their respective distances from a given output vector, for a given state of the production technology.

The input quantity index, based on the Malmquist input distance function, is defined for input vectors, x_s and x_t, with base period-s and using period-t technology, is given by

$$Q_i^t(x_s, x_t, y) = \frac{d_i^t(x_t, y)}{d_i^t(x_s, y)}. \qquad (5.25)$$

It is easy to see that the quantity index could have been defined with reference to the production technology of any other period. The two distance functions involved are illustrated in Figure 5.5 below.

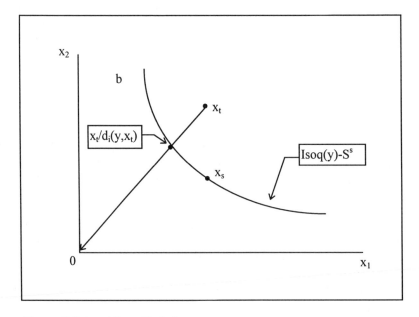

Figure 5.5 Input Quantity Index

In Figure 5.5, the points x_t and x_s represent the two input vectors. Then the Malmquist input distances are measured along the radial lines to these two points. Note that, for purposes of input quantity measurement it is not necessary that the input vectors are above the isoquant in order for equation 5.25 to hold.

As in the case of other index numbers we have defined before, the input quantity index in equation 5.25 satisfies monotonocity, linear homogeneity in the input vector x_t, and it is invariant to scalar multiplication of the input vectors, ie., if both input vectors are multiplied by a constant, κ, then the index remains unchanged. In addition, the index is independent of units of measurement. Proofs of these results follow from the properties of the input distance function, which can be derived using the axioms of the production technology.

Following the same approach as in the previous sections, we note that the input quantity index depends upon the output level, y, we choose, as well as the production technology. If we use period-s technology in defining the input distance functions, then we get the following index

$$Q_i^s(x_s, x_t, y) = \frac{d_i^s(x_t, y)}{d_i^s(x_s, y)} . \tag{5.26}$$

The input indices defined in equations 5.25 and 5.26 are usually different. These two coincide and, in fact, are independent of which technology we choose, if the technologies in these periods exhibit implicit Hicks input neutrality (see Färe and Primont, 1995). These indices are independent of the reference output vector, y, used in the definitions above if and only if the technology exhibits input homotheticity.

Our main purpose is to relate this Malmquist input quantity index number to the input index number derived using some of the formulae in Chapter 4. The input index in equation 5.26, defined using base period-s technology is bounded from above by the Laspeyres quantity index. Further, the index in equation 5.25, defined on current period-t technology, is bounded from below by the Paasche quantity index. Therefore, the Fisher input quantity index provides an approximation to the geometric mean of the indices, $Q_i^s(x_t, x_s, y)$ and $Q_i^t(x_t, x_s, y)$.

If we wish to go further we need to know the functional form of the input distance functions in equations 5.25 and 5.26. If we assume a quadratic function, then the Fisher input quantity index can be shown to be equal to the geometric average of the two indices. However, if the distances functions are of the translog form,[20] if the distances functions in periods t and s have identical second-order

---

[20] This does not imply or follow from the results concerning the translog form we obtained in Section 5.7 when dealing with output quantity index numbers.

coefficients satisfying the usual restrictions on the parameters of the translog form, and if the assumption of allocative and technical efficiency holds, then

$$\left[Q_i^s(x_s,x_t,y)\times Q_o^t(x_s,x_t,y)\right]^{1/2} = \text{Tornqvist Input quantity index}$$

$$= \prod_{i=1}^{K}\left[\frac{x_{it}}{x_{is}}\right]^{(\omega_{it}+\omega_{is})/2}, \qquad (5.27)$$

where ω_{it} and ω_{is} are input cost-shares in periods t and s, respectively. This result shows that the Tornqvist index is *exact* and *superlative* for the geometric mean of Malmquist input index numbers based on the technologies of periods t and s.

In this section, we have concluded our discussion of the economic-theoretic framework for index numbers measuring changes in prices and quantities. We now turn our attention to the measurement of productivity and the role of index numbers in deriving theoretically meaningful measures of productivity.

5.8 Productivity Indices

The output quantity index numbers, discussed in Section 5.6, simply measure growth in output but do not distinguish between the contribution due to growth in inputs and the contribution due to technical change or changes in efficiency. Thus, real output may grow a great deal between period s and period t but this may be due to growth in the use of the inputs. We wish to examine the role of index numbers in measuring growth in outputs that is net of input growth.

This section is primarily based on the seminal paper by Caves, Christensen and Diewert (1982b) which provided a theoretical framework for the measurement of productivity. We also draw upon more recent work by Diewert (1992), Färe, Grosskopf and Roos (1997), Førsund (1997) and Balk (1997). The main purpose of this section is to provide a simple guide to the main concepts and results and to also point towards techniques such as Data Envelopment Analysis and Stochastic Frontiers for measuring changes in efficiency and technology.

We distinguish between two theoretical approaches to measuring productivity change. The first approach is what Diewert (1992), termed the "Hicks-Moorsteen" approach, which is essentially the TFP measure we discuss in Chapter 4. The second approach is the more standard approach discussed in Caves, Christensen and Diewert (CCD) (1982b) which forms the basis for what has come to be known as the Malmquist productivity index number approach.

Under the CCD approach, one way to measure the change in productivity is to see how much more output has been produced, using a given level of inputs and the present state of the technology, relative to what could be produced under a given reference technology using the same level of inputs. An alternative is to measure change in productivity by examining the reduction in input use which is feasible given the need to produce a given level of output under a reference technology. These two approaches are referred to as the *output-orientated* and *input-orientated* measures of change in productivity.

A simple illustration of how the Malmquist index approach works is as follows. Suppose a firm produced 30 units of output using 20 units of input in period-s, using the technology available in that period efficiently. In period t, suppose the firm produces 50 units of output using 25 units of input using period-t technology efficiently. The output index in this case indicates an increase in output of 67 percent, and this is associated with a 25 per cent increase in input use. Therefore, if we use the Hicks-Moorsteen approach, we obtain a productivity index of 1.33 implying a productivity increase of 33 percent. If we follow the CCD approach, and ask the question as to what could have been produced with 25 units of input, using period-s technology, and if the answer is 40 units then the CCD (output-orientated) measure of productivity is 50/40, or 1.25, which is a bit lower than that given by the Hicks-Moorsteen index.[21]

5.8.1 Hicks-Moorsteen Productivity Indices

The approach we discuss here is attributed to Hicks (1961) and Moorsteen (1961) by Diewert (1992), and also discussed in Bjurek (1996), in which the index is referred to as the Malmquist Total Factor Productivity Index. Productivity indices here are defined as the ratio of output index numbers to input index numbers, where the respective indices are all defined using the Malmquist approach discussed in Sections 5.6 and 5.7.

Using the notation introduced at the beginning of the chapter, the observed input-output vectors that were actually produced using technologies S^s and S^t are represented by (x_t, y_t) and (x_s, y_s), respectively. Subscripts, s and t, could refer to a single firm in periods s and t or to firms s and t in the same period, but using different technologies.

The Hicks-Moorsteen productivity index,[22] denoted by $HM(x_s, y_s, x_t, y_t)$ is defined as

$$HM^t(x_t, y_t, x_s, y_s) = \frac{Q_o^t(y_s, y_t, x_t)}{Q_i^t(x_s, x_t, y_t)}.$$

(5.28)

---

[21] A few questions can be asked at this stage. For example, are there situations where these two approaches lead to the same productivity index? What exactly are these indices measuring? These questions are briefly discussed in the ensuing sections.

[22] As before, all the indices discussed here are for period t, with period s as the base or reference.

Notice that the HM index in equation 5.28 is defined using Malmquist indices based on period-t. Using the definitions of these indices from Sections 4.6 and 4.7, we have

$$HM^t(x_t, y_t, x_s, y_s) = \frac{d_o{}^t(y_t, x_t) / d_o{}^t(y_s, x_t)}{d_i{}^t(y_t, x_t) / d_i{}^t(y_s, x_t)}.$$ (5.29)

We can similarly define a period-s HM index. If we are interested in the geometric mean of the period-t and period-s HM indices, then we can use the results in Sections 5.6 and 5.7, along with the assumptions made regarding the functional form of the respective distance functions, we can use either

$$\left[HM^t(.)HM^s(.)\right]^{1/2} = \frac{\text{Fisher Output Index}}{\text{Fisher Input Index}},$$

or define it using the Tornqvist indices based on translog distance functions as,

$$\left[HM^t(.)HM^s(.)\right]^{1/2} = \frac{\text{Tornqvist Output Index}}{\text{Tornqvist Input Index}}.$$

It is easy to notice the similarity between the H-M indices defined here with the TFP measure discussed in Chapter 4. We now turn to the more standard approach in the productivity measurement literature.

5.8.2 Malmquist Productivity Indices

Malmquist index numbers can be defined using either the output-orientated approach or the input-orientated approach. These are discussed in the following two subsections.

Output-Orientated Indices

The output-orientated productivity measures focus on the maximum level of outputs that could be produced using a given input vector and a given production technology relative to the observed level of outputs. This is achieved using the output distance functions we defined in Chapter 3. For purposes of exposition, let us concentrate on the period-s Malmquist productivity index. This is given by

$$m_o{}^s(y_s, y_t, x_s, x_t) = \frac{d_o{}^s(y_t, x_t)}{d_o{}^s(y_s, x_s)}.$$ (5.30)

Since we assume throughout this chapter that the firm is *technically* efficient in both periods, we have $d_o^s(y_s, x_s) = 1$. Then[23]

$$m_o^s(y_s, y_t, x_s, x_t) = d_o^s(y_t, x_t).$$ (5.31)

Equation 5.30 shows that $m_o^s(y_t, y_s, x_t, x_s)$ is the minimal output deflation factor, such that the deflated output vector for the firm in period-t, $y_t/[m_o^s(.)]$, and the input vector, x_t, are just on the production surface of the technology in period-s. If firm t has a higher level of productivity than is implied by the period-s technology then $m_o^s(\cdot) > 1$.

We can similarly define an output-orientated Malmquist productivity index based on period-t technology

$$m_o^t(y_s, y_t, x_s, x_t) = \frac{d_o^t(y_t, x_t)}{d_o^t(y_s, x_s)} = \frac{1}{d_o^t(y_s, x_s)}.$$ (5.32)

The second equality in equation 5.32 follows from the fact that the firm is technically efficient in period-t, and therefore $d_o^t(y_t, x_t) = 1$.

As before, we encounter problems in making these productivity indices operational. That is, in order to compute these indices we need to know the functional form, as well as the numerical values of the relevant parameters, of the output distance functions in the two periods. It is here the results in Caves, Christensen and Diewert (1982) become significant. We state the following result without proof.

Result 5.7: If the Malmquist output distance functions for periods s and t have a translog functional form with identical second-order terms, then under the assumption of technical and allocative efficiency of the firm in the two periods, the geometric average of the two output-based Malmquist productivity indices in equations 5.28 and 5.30 is given by

$$m_o(y_s, y_t, x_s, x_t) = \left[m_o^t(y_s, y_t, x_s, x_t) \times m_o^s(y_s, y_t, x_s, x_t) \right]^{1/2}$$

$$= \frac{\text{Tornqvist output index}}{\text{Tornqvist input index}} \times \prod_{i=1}^K \left(\frac{x_{it}}{x_{is}} \right)^{\omega_i^*/2}$$ (5.33)

---

[23] Equation 5.30 shows that the Malmquist productivity index in this case is simply the output distance function defined with respect to period s technology.

where $\omega_i^* = \omega_{it}(1-\varepsilon_t) + \omega_{is}(1-\varepsilon_s)$, and ε_t and ε_s are local returns to scale in periods t and s, at the observed input and output levels, respectively.

Result 5.7 is again an extremely useful result. A few remarks are in order.

- First, it shows that, even when we do not know the exact nature of the output distance functions, we can define an exact measure of the geometric average of the Malmquist output-orientated productivity indices, based on the technologies of periods s and t.

- If we have constant returns to scale in both periods ($\varepsilon_t = \varepsilon_s = 1$), then

$$\text{Malmquist productivity index} = \frac{\text{Tornqvist output index}}{\text{Tornqvist input index}}.$$

This is the total factor productivity measure used in most empirical studies, and in the TFP measure we discussed in Chapter 4.

- Under decreasing returns to scale, using duality results and a profit-maximisation assumption, Caves, Christensen and Diewert (1982b) show that the returns to scale parameters can be measured using the observed price and quantity data as:

$$\varepsilon_j = \frac{\text{value of output in period j}}{\text{value of input in period j}}, \quad j = t,s.$$

In the case of increasing returns to scale observed costs and revenues cannot be used to compute returns to scale parameters.

- Equation 5.33 shows that the second factor on the right hand side depends, not only upon the local returns to scale parameters, ε_t and ε_s, but also upon the relative input levels in periods t and s. If the input use has not changed over the two periods, then returns to scale issues do not arise in productivity change calculations. This case is similar to that discussed in Section 5.2.

- Result 5.7 provides an economic-theoretic justification for the use of the standard measure of total factor productivity (TFP), defined as a ratio of Tornqvist indices of output and inputs. Such a justification holds when the underlying technologies exhibit constant returns to scale.

Input-Orientated Indices

The input-orientated productivity measure compares the input requirements for producing output level, y_t, produced under period-t technology, with the input that would have been required if the production technology was the same as that in period-s. This means the input orientated input index essentially compares x_t with what would have been required under technology s. This leads to the period-s based input-orientated Malmquist productivity index. Formally, we define this as:

$$m_i{}^s\left(y_s, y_t, x_s, x_t\right) = \frac{d_i{}^s\left(y_t, x_t\right)}{d_i{}^s\left(y_s, x_s\right)}. \tag{5.34}$$

Since we assume throughout this chapter that the firm is *technically* efficient, in both periods, we have $d_i{}^s(y_s, x_s) = 1$. Then

$$m_i{}^s\left(y_s, y_t, x_s, x_t\right) = d_i{}^s\left(y_t, x_t\right). \tag{5.35}$$

In cases where the firm in period-t has a higher productivity level, we observe that $d_i{}^s(y_t, x_t)$ is greater than unity.

We can similarly define the input-orientated Malmquist productivity index, based on period-t technology, as

$$m_i{}^t\left(y_s, y_t, x_s, x_t\right) = \frac{d_i{}^t\left(y_t, x_t\right)}{d_i{}^t\left(y_s, x_s\right)} = \frac{1}{d_i{}^t\left(y_s, x_s\right)}. \tag{5.36}$$

The second equality in equation 5.34 follows from the fact that the firm is technically efficient in period-t and therefore $d_i{}^t(y_t, x_t) = 1$.

Now we state a result similar to Result 5.6 for the Malmquist input-orientated productivity indices when the input distance functions are characterised by translog functions.

Result 5.8: If the Malmquist input distance functions for periods s and t have a translog functional form with identical second-order terms, then under the assumption of technical and allocative efficiency of the firm in the two periods, the geometric average of the two input-orientated Malmquist productivity indices in equations 5.34 and 5.36 is

$$m_i\left(y_s, y_t, x_s, x_t\right) = \left[m_i{}^t\left(y_s, y_t, x_s, x_t\right) \times m_i{}^s\left(y_s, y_t, x_s, x_t\right)\right]^{1/2}$$

$$= \frac{\text{Tornqvist output index}}{\text{Tornqvist input index}} \times \prod_{j=1}^{M}\left(\frac{y_{jt}}{y_{jss}}\right)^{v_j{}^{*}/2}, \tag{5.37}$$

where $\upsilon_j* = \left[(\varepsilon^s)^{-1} - 1\right]\upsilon_j{}^s + \left[(\varepsilon^t)^{-1} - 1\right]\upsilon_j{}^t$, and ε^t and ε^s are local output returns to scale in periods t and s, at the observed input and output vectors, respectively.

As before, we can examine a few points regarding this result. The first is that if the local returns to scale parameters are equal to 1, then the Malmquist input-oriented productivity index is identical to the usual TFP index, defined similarly to the Hicks-Moorsteen index. Even if the returns to scale parameters are different from unity, if the output levels are the same, then we still end up with the same measure of productivity as the usual TFP index.

Further, the output-oriented and input-oriented Malmquist measures of productivity are in general different, but if the technologies of both periods exhibit constant returns to scale then both indices will provide the same measure of productivity change over the two periods considered.

A recent paper by Färe, Grosskopf and Roos (1996) shows that the Hicks-Moorsteen productivity index and the CCD-based Malmquist productivity index are equal if and only if the technologies involved are *inversely homothetic* and exhibit constant returns to scale.

5.9 The Malmquist Productivity Index: Some Additional Issues

So far we have been concerned with the basic theoretical framework for measuring changes in input and output prices and quantities and changes in productivity. In this section we briefly discuss a number of related aspects of productivity measurement. Suppose we find, after whatever empirical route we take, that the Malmquist productivity index (MPI) for a given firm, over periods s and t, is 1.30. What exactly does this mean? Can we interpret this as being a measure of technical change? What if some of the assumptions necessary to make the Malmquist productivity index operational, as in Results 5.7 and 5.8, are violated, or if the firms are known to have a different behavioural pattern (such as revenue maximisation with cost constraints)? We cannot provide comprehensive answers to these issues in this introductory textbook, but in this section we hope to provide some appreciation of what is involved and, at the same time, offer some useful references to recent work in this area.

5.9.1 The MPI and Various Assumptions

The basic definition of the Malmquist productivity index, itself, does not require any assumptions, except that the production technology satisfies standard axioms, including weak disposability. But in order to be able to compute the MPI, we essentially followed the CCD approach and assumed that each firm is technically and allocatively efficient. Given this assumption, and adding the assumption of a constant returns to scale technology, Results 5.7 and 5.8 show that the MPI can be computed by simply using the TFP index defined in Chapter 4, using the Tornqvist index number formula to measure output and quantity changes.

Under this scenario, recalling the simple example we discussed in Section 5.2, we can interpret the MPI as a measure of *pure technical change*.[24] However, if any of the assumptions do not hold, then the MPI is a compound measure of productivity change that can be attributable to various other factors, such as changes in *technical efficiency, allocative efficiency or scale efficiency*. Chapter 10 is devoted to the decomposition of the MPI into various components when panel data are available. In the spirit of the issues raised here, Grifell-Tatje and Lovell (1995) attempt to provide a generalisation of the Malmquist productivity index that accounts for scale efficiency.

But more important are the assumptions that require the existence of competitive markets, that encourage a firm to use efficient strategies. In practice, most firms operate under an institutional environment which may not be conducive to competition.

An even more serious factor to consider here is that the formula derived under the Caves, Christensen and Diewert (1982b) approach assumes that the firm is the decision making unit involved in revenue maximisation or cost minimisation. However, in many applications, the TFP index is calculated for an *industry as a whole* or a *sector*. In such cases, any economic theory that is applicable to the firm may not be applicable since the industry is not a decision making unit. We may have to impose very restrictive conditions if we want to extend the same interpretation to industry- or sectoral-level productivity measures.

5.9.2 The MPI and Technical Inefficiency

In this section, we observe that the definition of the MPI does not, in itself, require any assumptions of optimal behaviour on the part of the firm. Caves, Christensen and Diewert (1982b) required the assumptions that firms were technically and allocatively efficient to show that it is possible to use Tornqvist index numbers to derive an MPI from just two observations on prices and quantities (for both inputs and outputs). In this section, we observe that if we have sufficient observations in each period, so that we are able to estimate the technology in each period (e.g., using mathematical programming or econometric methods), then we do not require the assumptions of technical and allocative efficiency to be able to calculate the MPI.

The output-orientated MPI is the geometric mean of the indices based on period-s and period-t technologies, given in equations 5.29 and 5.30. We have

---

[24] In fact, we have assumed away any other possible sources to productivity change.

$$m_o\left(y_s, y_t, x_s, x_t\right) = \left[m_o{}^s\left(y_s, y_t, x_s, x_t\right) m_o{}^t\left(y_s, y_t, x_s, x_t\right)\right]^{1/2}$$

$$= \left[\frac{d_o^s\left(x_t, y_t\right)}{d_o^s\left(x_s, y_s\right)} \times \frac{d_o^t\left(x_t, y_t\right)}{d_o^t\left(x_s, y_s\right)}\right]^{1/2} . \qquad (5.38)$$

Under the CCD setup, we assumed no technical inefficiency and hence that $d_o{}^s(x_s, y_s) = d_o{}^t(x_t, y_t) = 1$. However, it is common to observe some degree of inefficiency in the operations of most firms. Hence, assuming that $d_o{}^s(x_s, y_s) \leq 1$ and $d_o{}^t(x_t, y_t) \leq 1$ is likely to be more realistic. Where technical inefficiency is present, the Malmquist (output-orientated) productivity index, defined in equation 5.38, can be rewritten as:

$$m_o\left(y_s, y_t, x_s, x_t\right) = \frac{d_o^t\left(y_t, x_t\right)}{d_o^s\left(y_s, x_s\right)} \left[\frac{d_o^s\left(y_t, x_t\right)}{d_o^t\left(y_t, x_t\right)} \times \frac{d_o^s\left(y_s, x_s\right)}{d_o^t\left(y_s, x_s\right)}\right]^{1/2}, \qquad (5.39)$$

where the ratio outside the square brackets measures the change in the output-orientated measure of technical efficiency between years, s and t, and the geometric mean of the two ratios inside the square brackets captures the shift in technology between the two periods, evaluated at x_s and x_t.

Observe that equation 5.39 is a generalisation of the simple single input, single output example, presented in equation 5.4. Given that suitable panel data are available, the various distance functions in equation 5.39 can be directly calculated. Two methods (DEA and stochastic frontiers) that may be used to calculate these distance functions are discussed in some detail in Chapter 10. These two techniques form the subject matter for the next four chapters.

5.9.3 MPI under Constrained Optimisation

Throughout this chapter, we have made several assumptions regarding the behaviour of the firm. In deriving the output price index numbers, we used the assumption of revenue maximisation, and in the case of input price index numbers, we assumed cost minimising behaviour. In deriving the quantity index numbers, we have used the input and output distance functions, derived *directly* from the production technology.

Following Färe and Primont (1995) and Balk (1997), we recognise that the firm may be actually optimising under constraints. For example, a firm may be maximising revenue subject to a constraint that input costs are to be kept below a specified level (perhaps due to a credit constraint). In such cases, the firm's behaviour can be modelled using a *cost-indirect revenue function*.

It is also possible to model firms which seek to minimise input costs subject to generating a minimum revenue. The firm under consideration may be a branch of a parent firm which stipulates that, for the firm to be viable, it is constrained to generate a minimum amount of revenue. The resulting cost function is usually referred to as a *revenue-indirect cost function*.

The constrained optimisation scenarios in the previous paragraphs can also be used in defining input and output distance functions which are referred to as *cost- or revenue- indirect input and output distance functions*.

We can then apply the conceptual framework for various index numbers discussed in Sections 5.3 to 5.8 and derive various index numbers of interest. We refer the interested reader to Balk (1997). The use of indirect cost, revenue or distance functions usually means that we replace the direct quantity index numbers (input and output) by indirect quantity index numbers, defined as the costs or revenues deflated by appropriate price index numbers.

The most important conclusion to be drawn from this discussion is that, *if we have reason to believe that the firm under consideration operates under constraints, then it is theoretically more meaningful to derive the quantity changes through the indirect method of deflating the value figures by the respective price index numbers.* This point adds to some of the arguments made in Chapter 4 regarding the choice between direct and indirect quantity index numbers. Much of the discussion in Chapter 4 centred on the availability and reliability of price and quantity data, but in this section we see that the choice between direct and indirect measures could be influenced by the economic behaviour of the firms under consideration.

5.9.4 The MPI and Transitivity

The issue of transitivity has received some attention (see Färe, 1993; Althin, 1995; and Balk and Althin, 1996). Since much of the work on productivity change is based on time-series data, the issue of transitivity has not been a problem. Most studies are content with measuring productivity changes over consecutive years. However, if we are interested in computing productivity indexes on cross-sectional elements, such as firms within an industry over a number of years, or even for a given firm over time, then it is necessary to ensure some internal consistency in the results.

Consider the simple scenario where we measure productivity change from period t to period t+1 and then also from period t+1 to period t+2. These productivity indexes can be chained to yield a comparison between periods t and t+2. Would this index be the same as obtained if we compared period-t directly with period t+2? The answer is generally in the negative, both from an analytical perspective, as well as from a computational point of view, we use a Fisher or a Tornqvist index to compute the Malmquist productivity index. That is, in general,

$$MPI\ (t,\ t+2) \neq MPI\ (t,t+1) \times MPI\ (t+1,\ t+2).$$

The main reason for this possible inconsistency is due to the nature of the underlying production technology. Refer to the Malmquist productivity index in equation 5.39.

It is easy to see that the technical efficiency change measure, the first component in this equation, is transitive. But the second component is not transitive unless technological change over time is neutral. Under non-neutral technical change, the output- (or input-) orientated productivity indices depend on the technology under which the various distance functions are derived.

The problem is compounded when panel data sets are used. Balk and Althin (1996) examine the issue of transitivity and propose a transitive index for multilateral comparisons which, as a by-product, also provides a measure of non-neutrality of the production technology.

The derivation of transitive index numbers is discussed in Chapter 4, where we discussed the EKS method, which generates transitive index numbers from non-transitive bilateral comparisons. So it is feasible to generate transitive multilateral Malmquist productivity indexes from bilateral indexes using the EKS procedure. Even the procedure of Balk and Althin (1996) is somewhat mechanical in its approach. Further work is needed for generating a theoretically meaningful transitive multilateral Malmquist productivity index numbers.

5.10 Conclusions

Now that we have completed a discussion of the theoretical and practical issues associated with index numbers in general, and productivity indexes in particular, it is important to point out that the theoretical framework discussed above clearly brings out various assumptions and data requirements of the index number approach.

In Section 5.9 we examined a number of important points relating to the various assumptions involved. Despite some of the limitations imposed by the basic assumptions required for the use of index numbers, the results in the last few sections show that the index number approach requires only a minimal amount of data: just price and quantity data for two periods or for two firms. In practice, it is not even necessary to have the price data: it is adequate if we have data on the value shares; revenue shares of various output commodities; and cost shares associated with various input commodities. As is noted in subsequent chapters, most of the frontier methods are much more data intensive. In Chapter 11 we provide a simple assessment of various methods for productivity measurement and list their merits and disadvantages.

If the preceding sections have created sufficient interest, there are a number of excellent books and journal articles on the economic-theoretic approach which could be consulted. For economic-theoretic approaches, the published works of Diewert (1976, 1978, 1981, 1983 and 1990) are recommended. The two papers by Caves, Christensen and Diewert (1982a, 1982b) are quite important. Some recent work on duality and Malmquist indexes can be found in Färe and Primont (1995), Russell (1997), Färe, Grosskopf and Russell (1997) and Balk (1997). Be warned, however, that these papers do use some involved mathematics.

6. EFFICIENCY MEASUREMENT USING DATA ENVELOPMENT ANALYSIS (DEA)

6.1 Introduction

This chapter is a pivotal chapter in this book. We now begin to explicitly consider the issue of inefficiency. In the previous four chapters we have discussed least squares econometric methods and index number methods, which implicitly assume that all firms are fully efficient. In the remaining chapters, we relax this assumption and describe methods which may be used to estimate frontier functions and measure the efficiencies of firms relative to these estimated frontiers.

Frontiers have been estimated using many different methods over the past 40 years. Lovell (1993) provides an excellent introduction to this literature. The two principal methods that have been used are data envelopment analysis (DEA) and stochastic frontiers, which involve mathematical programming and econometric methods, respectively. This chapter and the next are concerned with the DEA method, while Chapters 8 and 9 discuss stochastic frontiers.

The chapter is divided into several sections. Section 6.2 provides a brief introduction to the efficiency concepts developed by Farrell (1957); Färe, Grosskopf and Lovell (1985, 1994), and others. We then introduce the basic DEA models, namely the constant returns to scale (CRS) and variable returns to scale (VRS) DEA models. Input-orientated versions of these two models are discussed in Section 6.3 and 6.4, respectively, and output-orientated versions are presented in Section 6.5.

The final section contains some concluding comments which point us towards Chapter 7 in which a number of additional DEA models are discussed.

6.2 Efficiency Measurement Concepts

The primary purpose of this section is to outline a number of commonly used efficiency measures and to discuss how they may be calculated relative to a given technology, which is generally represented by some form of frontier function.

The discussion in this section provides a very brief introduction to modern efficiency measurement. A more detailed treatment is provided by Färe, Grosskopf and Lovell (1985, 1994) and Lovell (1993). Our discussion of efficiency measurement begins with Farrell (1957), who drew upon the work of Debreu (1951) and Koopmans (1951) to define a simple measure of firm efficiency which could account for multiple inputs. Farrell (1957) proposed that the efficiency of a firm consists of two components: *technical efficiency*, which reflects the ability of a firm to obtain maximal output from a given set of inputs, and *allocative efficiency*, which reflects the ability of a firm to use the inputs in optimal proportions, given their respective prices and the production technology. These two measures are then combined to provide a measure of total *economic efficiency*.[1]

The following discussion begins with Farrell's original ideas which were illustrated in input/input space and, hence, had an input-reducing focus. These are usually termed *input-orientated* measures.

6.2.1 Input-Orientated Measures

Farrell illustrated his ideas using a simple example involving firms which use two inputs (x_1 and x_2) to produce a single output (y), under the assumption of constant returns to scale.[2] Knowledge of the unit isoquant of *fully efficient firms*,[3] represented by SS′ in Figure 6.1, permits the measurement of technical efficiency. If a given firm uses quantities of inputs, defined by the point P, to produce a unit of output, the technical inefficiency of that firm could be represented by the distance QP, which is the amount by which all inputs could be proportionally reduced without a reduction in output. This is usually expressed in percentage terms by the ratio QP/0P, which represents the percentage by which all inputs need to be reduced to achieve technically efficient production. The technical efficiency (TE) of a firm is most commonly measured by the ratio

---

[1] Some of Farrell's terminology differed from that which is used here. He used the term *price efficiency* instead of *allocative efficiency* and the term *overall efficiency* instead of *economic efficiency*. The terminology used in this book conforms with that which has been used most often in recent literature.

[2] The assumption of constant returns to scale allows the technology to be represented using the unit isoquant. Farrell also discussed the extension of his method so as to accommodate more than two inputs, multiple outputs, and non-constant returns to scale.

[3] The production frontier of fully efficient firms is not known in practice, and thus must be estimated from observations on a sample of firms in the industry concerned. In this chapter we consider the use of DEA to estimate this frontier.

$$TE_i = 0Q/0P, \tag{6.1}$$

which is equal to one minus $QP/0P$.[4] It will take a value between zero and one, and hence provides an indicator of the degree of technical inefficiency of the firm. A value of one indicates the firm is fully technically efficient. For example, the point Q is technically efficient because it lies on the efficient isoquant.

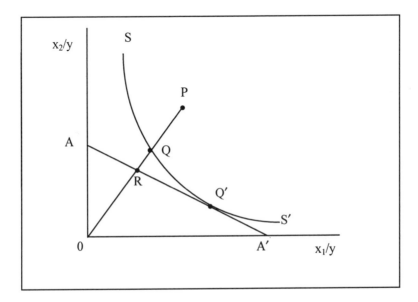

Figure 6.1 Technical and Allocative Efficiencies

If the input price ratio, represented by the slope of the isocost line, AA′, in Figure 6.1, is also known, allocative efficiency may also be calculated. The *allocative efficiency (AE)* of the firm operating at P is defined to be the ratio

$$AE_i = 0R/0Q, \tag{6.2}$$

since the distance RQ represents the reduction in production costs that would occur if production were to occur at the allocatively (and technically) efficient point Q′, instead of at the technically efficient, but allocatively inefficient, point Q.[5]

The total *economic efficiency (EE)* is defined to be the ratio

---

[4] The subscript "i" is used on TE to indicate that it is an input-orientated measure. Output-orientated measures are defined below.

[5] One could illustrate this by drawing two isocost lines through Q and Q′. Irrespective of the slope of these two parallel lines (which is determined by the input price ratio) the ratio RQ/0Q represents the proportional reduction in costs of production associated with movement from Q to Q′.

$$EE_i = 0R/0P, \qquad (6.3)$$

where the distance RP can also be interpreted in terms of a cost reduction. Note that the product of the technical and allocative efficiency measures provides the measure of overall economic efficiency

$$TE_i \times AE_i = (0Q/0P) \times (0R/0Q) = (0R/0P) = EE_i. \qquad (6.4)$$

Note also that all three measures are bounded by zero and one.

These efficiency measures assume the production function is known. In practice, this is not the case, and the efficient isoquant must be estimated from the sample data. Farrell (1957) suggested the use of either (a) a non-parametric piece-wise-linear convex isoquant, constructed such that no observed point lies to the left or below it (refer to Figure 6.2); or (b) a parametric function, such as the Cobb-Douglas form, fitted to the data, again such that no observed point lies to the left or below it. Farrell provided an illustration of his methods using agricultural data for the 48 continental states of the US.

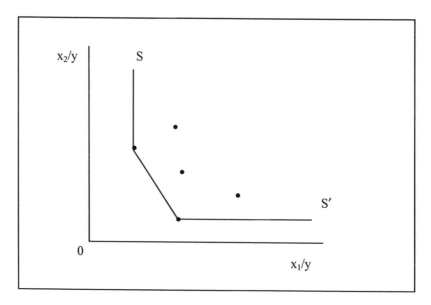

Figure 6.2 Piece-wise Linear Convex Unit Isoquant

The above efficiency measures are defined in the context of a constant returns to scale technology. These measures can be equivalently defined for the non-constant returns case. To illustrate this we could adjust Figure 6.1 by changing the axes labels to x_1 and x_2 and assuming that the isoquant represents the lower bound of the input set associated with the production of a particular level of output.   The efficiency measures are then defined analogously to those above.

Observe that the technical efficiency measure defined above is exactly equal to the inverse of the input distance function defined in Chapter 3 and also that the concept of allocative efficiency is dealt with in Chapter 2 in the discussion of optimal input choices under cost minimisation.

6.2.2 Output-Orientated Measures

The above input-orientated technical efficiency measures address the question: "By how much can input quantities be proportionally reduced without changing the output quantities produced?". One could alternatively ask the question: "By how much can output quantities be proportionally expanded without altering the input quantities used?". This gives output-orientated measures as opposed to the input-oriented measure discussed above. The difference between the output- and input-orientated measures can be illustrated using a simple example involving one input, x, and one output ,y. This is depicted in Figure 6.3(a) where we have a decreasing returns to scale technology, represented by f(x), and an inefficient firm operating at the point P. The Farrell input-orientated measure of TE would be equal to the ratio AB/AP, while the output-orientated measure of TE would be CP/CD. The output- and input-orientated measures are equivalent measures of technical efficiency only when constant returns to scale exist (Färe and Lovell, 1978). The constant returns to scale (CRS) case is depicted in Figure 6.3(b), where we observe that AB/AP=CP/CD, for the inefficient firm operating at point P.

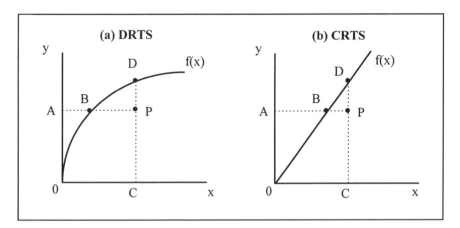

Figure 6.3 Input- and Output-Orientated Technical Efficiency Measures and Returns to Scale

One can illustrate output-orientated measures by considering the case where production involves two outputs (y_1 and y_2) and a single input (x_1). If we hold the input quantity fixed at a particular level, we can represent the technology by a production possibility curve in two dimensions. This example is depicted in Figure 6.4 where the line ZZ′ is the production possibility curve and the point A corresponds to an inefficient firm. Note that an inefficient firm operating at point A, lies *below* the curve, because ZZ′ represents the upper bound of production possibilities.

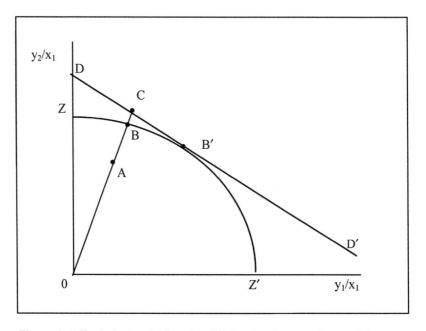

Figure 6.4 Technical and Allocative Efficiencies from an Output Orientation

The Farrell output-orientated efficiency measures (see Färe, Grosskopf and Lovell, 1985, 1994) are defined as follows. In Figure 6.4, the distance AB represents technical inefficiency. That is, the amount by which outputs could be increased without requiring extra input. Hence a measure of output-orientated technical efficiency is the ratio

$$TE_o = 0A/0B. \tag{6.5}$$

If we have price information then we can draw the isorevenue line, DD′, and define the allocative efficiency to be

$$AE_o = 0B/0C \tag{6.6}$$

which has a revenue increasing interpretation (similar to the cost reducing interpretation of allocative inefficiency in the input-orientated case). Furthermore, we define overall economic efficiency as the product of these two measures

$$EE_o = (0A/0C) = (0A/0B) \times (0B/0C) = TE_o \times AE_o. \tag{6.7}$$

Again, we note that all of these three measures are bounded by zero and one. We also observe that the output-orientated technical efficiency measure is exactly equal to the output distance function, introduced in Chapter 3, and the output allocative efficiency concept was dealt with in the brief discussion of revenue maximisation in Chapter 3.

Before we conclude this section, we note three points about the efficiency measures we have defined. First, technical efficiency has been measured along a ray from the origin to the observed production point. Hence these measures hold the relative proportions of inputs (or outputs) constant. One advantage of these *radial* efficiency measures is that they are *units invariant*. That is, changing the units of measurement (e.g., measuring quantity of labour in person hours instead of person years) does not change the value of the efficiency measure. A non-radial measure, such as the shortest distance from the production point to the production surface, seems intuitively appealing, but such a measure is not invariant to the units of measurement. Changing the units of measurement in this case could result in the identification of a different "nearest" point.[6]

Secondly, you will note that we have discussed allocative efficiency from a cost minimising perspective and from a revenue maximising perspective, but not from a profit maximising perspective (where both cost minimisation and revenue maximisation are assumed). Profit maximisation can be accommodated in a number of ways. The principal difficulty is associated with the selection of the orientation in which to measure technical efficiency (input, output or both). One suggestion is presented in Färe, Grosskopf and Lovell (1994), in which DEA is used to measure profit efficiency along with a hyperbolic measure of technical efficiency (which considers simultaneous expansion of outputs and contraction of inputs). The difference between the two measures is then interpreted as allocative efficiency.[7] An alternative approach is suggested by Kumbhakar (1987) in a stochastic frontier framework, and involves the decomposition of profit efficiency into three components: input-allocative efficiency, output-allocative efficiency and input-orientated technical efficiency. No particular profit efficiency methodology has become widely used to date. The references suggested above provide a reasonable starting point for researchers who may wish to explore this issue.

---

[6] A number of alternative non-radial efficiency measures have been proposed which sacrifice units-invariance but have other desirable properties. For example, see Färe and Lovell (1978) and Kopp (1981).
[7] A related suggestion has recently been proposed which involves the use of newly developed *directional distance functions* which also involve simultaneous expansion of outputs and reduction in inputs. Refer to Färe and Grosskopf and Weber (1997) for more on this method.

Finally, we repeat our observations that the Farrell input- and output-orientated technical efficiency measures are equivalent to the input and output distance functions, discussed in Shephard (1970) and Färe and Primont (1995).[8] This observation is especially important when we discuss the use of DEA methods in calculating Malmquist indices of TFP change in Chapter 10.

6.3 The Constant Returns to Scale (CRS) DEA Model

Data envelopment analysis (DEA) involves the use of linear programming methods to construct a non-parametric piece-wise surface (or frontier) over the data. Efficiency measures are then calculated relative to this surface. Comprehensive reviews of the methodology are presented by Seiford and Thrall (1990), Lovell (1993), Ali and Seiford (1993), Lovell (1994), Charnes et al (1995) and Seiford (1996).

The piece-wise-linear convex hull approach to frontier estimation, proposed by Farrell (1957), was considered by only a few authors in the two decades following Farrell's paper.   Boles (1966) and Afriat (1972) suggested mathematical programming methods which could achieve the task, but the method did not receive wide attention until the paper by Charnes, Cooper and Rhodes (1978), in which the term *data envelopment analysis* (DEA) was first used. Since then there has been a large number of papers which have extended and applied the DEA methodology.

Charnes, Cooper and Rhodes (1978) proposed a model which had an input orientation and assumed constant returns to scale (CRS).[9] Subsequent papers have considered alternative sets of assumptions, such as Banker, Charnes and Cooper (1984), in which a variable returns to scale (VRS) model is proposed.   Our discussion of DEA begins with a description of the input-orientated CRS model because this model was the first to be widely applied.

We first define some notation. Assume there are data on K inputs and M outputs for each of N firms. For the i-th firm these are represented by the column vectors x_i and y_i, respectively. The K×N input matrix, X, and the M×N output matrix, Y, represent the data for all N firms.

An intuitive way to introduce DEA is via the *ratio* form. For each firm, we would like to obtain a measure of the ratio of all outputs over all inputs, such as $u'y_i/v'x_i$, where u is an M×1 vector of output weights and v is a K×1 vector of input weights.   The optimal weights are obtained by solving the mathematical programming problem:

---

[8]In fact, as they are defined in this book, the input-orientated technical efficiency measure is equal to the inverse of the input distance function.

[9] Note that we use CRS to refer to constant returns to scale rather than CRTS. Most economics texts use the latter, while most DEA papers use the former.

$$\max_{u,v} (u'y_i/v'x_i),$$
$$\text{st}^{10} \quad u'y_j/v'x_j \leq 1, \quad j=1,2,...,N,$$
$$u, v \geq 0. \tag{6.8}$$

This involves finding values for u and v, such that the efficiency measure for the i-th firm is maximised, subject to the constraints that all efficiency measures must be less than or equal to one. One problem with this particular ratio formulation is that it has an infinite number of solutions.[11] To avoid this, one can impose the constraint $v'x_i = 1$, which provides:

$$\max_{\mu,v} (\mu'y_i),$$
$$\text{st} \quad v'x_i = 1,$$
$$\mu'y_j - v'x_j \leq 0, \quad j=1,2,...,N,$$
$$\mu, v \geq 0, \tag{6.9}$$

where the change of notation from u and v to μ and v is used to stress that this is a different linear programming problem. The form in equation 6.9 is known as the *multiplier* form of the DEA linear programming problem.

Using the duality in linear programming, one can derive an equivalent *envelopment* form of this problem:

$$\min_{\theta,\lambda} \theta,$$
$$\text{st} \quad -y_i + Y\lambda \geq 0,$$
$$\theta x_i - X\lambda \geq 0,$$
$$\lambda \geq 0, \tag{6.10}$$

where θ is a scalar and λ is a Nx1 vector of constants. This envelopment form involves fewer constraints than the multiplier form (K+M < N+1), and hence is generally the preferred form to solve.[12] The value of θ obtained will be the efficiency score for the i-th firm. It will satisfy: $\theta \leq 1$, with a value of 1 indicating a point on the frontier and hence a technically efficient firm, according to the Farrell (1957) definition. Note that the linear programming problem must be solved N times, once for each firm in the sample. A value of θ is then obtained for each firm.

---

[10] The notation "st" stands for "subject to".

[11] That is, if (u*,v*) is a solution, then (αu*,αv*) is another solution, etc.

[12] The forms defined by equations 6.8 and 6.9 are introduced here for expository purposes. They are not used again in the remainder of this chapter. The multiplier form has, however, been utilised in a number of studies. The μ and v weights provide extra information in that they can be interpreted as normalised shadow prices. The multiplier form can also be used to determine returns to scale properties in variable returns to scale (VRS) DEA models. For a discussion of these issues, see Lovell (1994).

The DEA problem in equation 6.10 has a nice intuitive interpretation. Essentially, the problem takes the i-th firm and then seeks to radially contract the input vector, x_i, as much as possible, while still remaining within the feasible input set. The inner-boundary of this set is a piece-wise linear isoquant (refer to Figure 6.2), determined by the observed data points (i.e., all the firms in the sample). The radial contraction of the input vector, x_i, produces a projected point, $(X\lambda, Y\lambda)$, on the surface of this technology. This projected point is a linear combination of these observed data points. The constraints in equation 6.10 ensure that this projected point cannot lie outside the feasible set.

Slacks

The piece-wise linear form of the non-parametric frontier in DEA can cause a few difficulties in efficiency measurement. The problem arises because of the sections of the piece-wise linear frontier which run parallel to the axes (refer the Figure 6.2) which do not occur in most parametric functions.[13] To illustrate the problem, refer to Figure 6.5 where the firms using input combinations C and D are the two efficient firms which define the frontier, and firms A and B are inefficient firms. The Farrell (1957) measure of technical efficiency gives the efficiency of firms A and B as 0A'/0A and 0B'/0B, respectively. However, it is questionable as to whether the point A' is an efficient point since one could reduce the amount of input x_2 used (by the amount CA') and still produce the same output. This is known as *input slack* in the literature.[14] Once one considers a case involving more inputs and/or multiple outputs, the diagrams are no longer as simple, and the possibility of the related concept of *output slack* also occurs.[15] Some authors argue that both the Farrell measure of technical efficiency (θ) and any non-zero input or output slacks should be reported to provide an accurate indication of technical efficiency of a firm in a DEA analysis.[16]

Now it can be stated that, for the i-th firm, the output slacks will be equal to zero if and only if $Y\lambda - y_i = 0$ and the input slacks will be equal to zero if and only if $\theta x_i - X\lambda = 0$ (for the given optimal values of θ and λ). However, we should note that the converse does not necessarily apply when one uses equation 6.10 to solve the DEA problem. That is, the slacks reported by the linear program in equation 6.10 need not identify all (inefficiency) slacks. This can occur whenever there are two or more optimal λ-vectors for a particular firm. Hence, if one wishes to be sure to identify all efficiency slacks one must solve additional linear programs. For more on this

---

[13]From Figure 6.5 we can see that the technology defined by equation 6.10 has the property of strong disposability. This ensures that the isoquant does not "bend back" and display input congestion. The DEA model can be modified to allow for weak disposability. This is discussed in Chapter 7.

[14] Some authors use the term *input excess*.

[15] Output slack is illustrated later (see Figure 6.8).

[16] Farrell (1957) defined technical inefficiency in terms of the radial reduction in inputs that is possible. Koopmans (1951) provides a more strict definition of technical efficiency which is equivalent to stating that a firm is only technically efficient if it operates on the frontier and furthermore that all associated slacks are zero.

issue, see the discussion of slacks in Chapter 7. For the remainder of this chapter, however, we avoid the issue by only considering simple empirical examples in which all efficiency slacks are identified by the LP in equation 6.10. However, as we argue in the next chapter, the importance of slacks can be overstated for a variety of reasons.

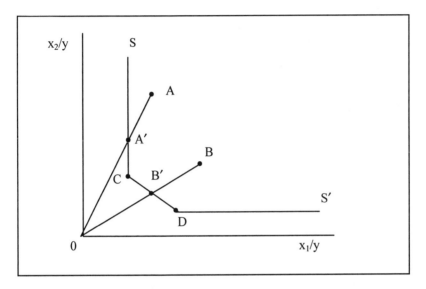

Figure 6.5 Efficiency Measurement and Input Slacks

A Simple Numerical Example

We illustrate CRS input-orientated DEA using a simple example involving observations on five firms which use two inputs to produce a single output. The data are as follows:

Table 6.1 Example Data for CRS DEA Example

firm	y	x_1	x_2	x_1/y	x_2/y
1	1	2	5	2	5
2	2	2	4	1	2
3	3	6	6	2	2
4	1	3	2	3	2
5	2	6	2	3	1

The input/output ratios for this example are plotted in Figure 6.6, along with the DEA frontier corresponding to the solution of the DEA model defined in equation 6.10. You should keep in mind, however, that this DEA frontier is the result of running five linear programming problems - one for each of the five firms. For example, for firm 3, we could rewrite equation 6.10 as

$$\min_{\theta, \lambda} \theta,$$
$$\text{st} \quad -y_3 + (y_1\lambda_1 + y_2\lambda_2 + y_3\lambda_3 + y_4\lambda_4 + y_5\lambda_5) \geq 0,$$
$$\theta x_{13} - (x_{11}\lambda_1 + x_{12}\lambda_2 + x_{13}\lambda_3 + x_{14}\lambda_4 + x_{15}\lambda_5) \geq 0,$$
$$\theta x_{23} - (x_{21}\lambda_1 + x_{22}\lambda_2 + x_{23}\lambda_3 + x_{24}\lambda_4 + x_{25}\lambda_5) \geq 0,$$
$$\lambda \geq 0, \quad\quad\quad\quad\quad\quad\quad\quad\quad\quad\quad\quad\quad\quad\quad\quad (6.11)$$

where $\lambda = (\lambda_1, \lambda_2, \lambda_3, \lambda_4, \lambda_5)'$.

The values of θ and λ which provide a minimum value for θ are listed in row 3 of Table 6.2. We note that the TE of firm 3 is 0.833. That is, firm 3 could possibly reduce the consumption of all inputs by 16.7% without reducing output. This implies production at the point denoted 3' in Figure 6.6. This projected point, 3', lies on a line joining points 2 and 5. Firms 2 and 5 are therefore usually referred to as the *peers* of firm 3. They define where the relevant part of the frontier is (i.e., relevant to firm 3) and hence define efficient production for firm 3. Point 3' is a linear combination of points 2 and 5, where the weights in this linear combination are the λs in row 3 of Table 6.2.

Many DEA studies also talk about *targets* as well as peers. The targets of firm 3 are the coordinates of the efficient projection point 3'. These are equal to $0.833 \times (2,2) = (1.666, 1.666)$. Thus firm 3 should aim to produce its 3 units of output with $3 \times (1.666, 1.666) = (5,5)$ units of the two inputs.

One could go through a similar discussion of the other two inefficient firms. Firm 4 has TE = 0.714 and has the same peers as firm 3. Firm 1 has TE = 0.5 and has firm 2 as its peer. You will also note that the projected point for firm 1 (i.e., the point 1') lies upon part of the frontier which is parallel to the x_2 axis. Thus it does not represent an efficient point (according to Koopmans' definition) because we could decrease the use of the input x_2 by 0.5 units (thus producing at the point 2) and still produce the same output. Thus firm 1 is said to be radially inefficient in input usage by a factor of 50% plus it has (non-radial) input slack of 0.5 units of x_2. The targets of firm 1 would therefore be to reduce usage of both inputs by 50% and also to reduce the use of x_2 by a further 0.5 units. This would result in targets of ($x_1=1$, $x_2=2$), which are the coordinates of point 2.

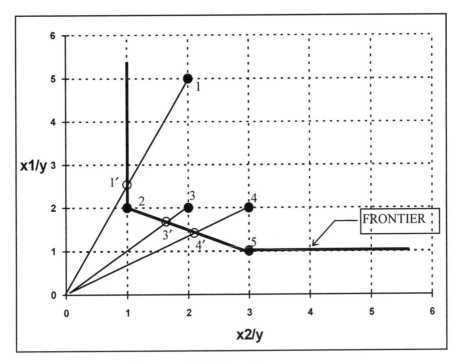

Figure 6.6 CRS Input-Orientated DEA Example

Table 6.2 CRS Input-Orientated DEA Results

firm	θ	λ₁	λ₂	λ₃	λ₄	λ₅	IS₁	IS₂	OS
1	0.5	-	0.5	-	-	-	-	0.5	-
2	1.0	-	1.0	-	-	-	-	-	-
3	0.833	-	1.0	-	-	0.5	-	-	-
4	0.714	-	0.214	-	-	0.286	-	-	-
5	1.0	-	-	-	-	1.0	-	-	-

A quick glance at Table 6.2 shows that firms 2 and 5 have TE values of 1.0 and that their peers are themselves. This is as one would expect for the efficient points which define the frontier.

DEA Calculations using the Computer

DEA calculations can be conducted using a number of different computer programs. If you are familiar with linear programming (LP), then all you need is access to computer software that can conduct LP. For example, one could use spreadsheet software such as Excel or statistical software such as SAS or SHAZAM. There are also a few specialist DEA computer packages available, such as IDEAS, Frontier Analyst, WDEA and DEAP. We use DEAP Version 2.1 in this book. A brief description of the DEAP computer program is provided in the Appendix.

The DEAP computer program has a similar structure to the TFPIP computer program introduced in Chapter 4. To calculate the above simple numerical example using DEAP the user must construct a data file and an instruction file. Note that all data, instruction and output files are text files. The data file for this example, EG1.DTA, (refer to Table 6.7a) contains five observations on one output and two inputs. The output quantities are listed in the first column and the inputs in the next two columns. This data is identical to that listed in Table 6.1.

The instruction file, EG1.INS, is listed in Table 6.3b. The purpose of the majority of entries in the file should be self explanatory, due to the comments on the right-hand side of the file.[17] The first two lines of the file contain the name of the data file (EG1.DTA) and an output file name (here we have used EG1.OUT). Then on the next four lines we specify the number of firms (5); number of time periods (1);[18] number of outputs (1); and number of inputs (2). On the last three lines, we specify a "0" to indicate CRS; a "0" to indicate an input orientation; and a "0" to indicate that we wish to estimate a standard DEA model.[19]

Table 6.3a Listing of Data File, EG1.DTA

```
1  2  5
2  2  4
3  6  6
1  3  2
2  6  2
```

Finally, we execute DEAP and type in the name of the instruction file (EG1.INS). The program sends the output to the file (EG1.OUT). This file is reproduced in Table 6.3c. The information presented in this output file should be self explanatory given the preceding discussion. Note that the results are identical to those presented in Table 6.2.

---

[17] The comments in this instruction file are not read by the program.

[18] Note that the number of time periods must be equal to 1 unless the Malmquist DEA option is selected.

[19] Note that by specifying "0" on the final line we are asking that slacks be calculated using the multi-stage method. If we wished the 1-stage or 2-stage methods to be used we would have used a "3" or a "4", respectively. These different methods for the calculation of slacks are discussed further in the following chapter.

Table 6.3b Listing of Instruction File, EG1.INS

```
eg1.dta          DATA FILE NAME
eg1.out          OUTPUT FILE NAME
5                NUMBER OF FIRMS
1                NUMBER OF TIME PERIODS
1                NUMBER OF OUTPUTS
2                NUMBER OF INPUTS
0                0=INPUT AND 1=OUTPUT ORIENTATED
0                0=CRS AND 1=VRS
0                0=DEA(MULTI-STAGE), 1=COST-DEA, 2=MALMQUIST-DEA,
                    3=DEA(1-STAGE), 4=DEA(2-STAGE)
```

Table 6.3c Listing of Output File, EG1.OUT

```
Results from DEAP Version 2.1

Instruction file = eg1.ins
Data file        = eg1.dta

Input orientated DEA

Scale assumption: CRS

Slacks calculated using multi-stage method


EFFICIENCY SUMMARY:

 firm      te
    1   0.500
    2   1.000
    3   0.833
    4   0.714
    5   1.000

mean   0.810


SUMMARY OF OUTPUT SLACKS:

 firm  output:           1
    1               0.000
    2               0.000
    3               0.000
    4               0.000
    5               0.000

mean               0.000


SUMMARY OF INPUT SLACKS:

 firm  input:           1             2
```

```
        1                    0.000          0.500
        2                    0.000          0.000
        3                    0.000          0.000
        4                    0.000          0.000
        5                    0.000          0.000

mean                         0.000          0.100
```

SUMMARY OF PEERS:

```
firm   peers:
    1       2
    2       2
    3       5      2
    4       5      2
    5       5
```

SUMMARY OF PEER WEIGHTS:
  (in same order as above)

```
firm   peer weights:
    1    0.500
    2    1.000
    3    0.500 1.000
    4    0.286 0.214
    5    1.000
```

PEER COUNT SUMMARY:
  (i.e., no. times each firm is a peer for another)

```
firm   peer count:
    1       0
    2       3
    3       0
    4       0
    5       2
```

SUMMARY OF OUTPUT TARGETS:

```
firm   output:           1
    1                 1.000
    2                 2.000
    3                 3.000
    4                 1.000
    5                 2.000
```

SUMMARY OF INPUT TARGETS:

```
firm   input:            1              2
    1                 1.000          2.000
    2                 2.000          4.000
    3                 5.000          5.000
    4                 2.143          1.429
    5                 6.000          2.000
```

FIRM BY FIRM RESULTS:

```
Results for firm:      1
Technical efficiency = 0.500
PROJECTION SUMMARY:
  variable          original       radial         slack       projected
                      value       movement       movement        value
  output    1         1.000         0.000         0.000          1.000
  input     1         2.000        -1.000         0.000          1.000
  input     2         5.000        -2.500        -0.500          2.000
LISTING OF PEERS:
  peer    lambda weight
    2       0.500


Results for firm:      2
Technical efficiency = 1.000
PROJECTION SUMMARY:
  variable          original       radial         slack       projected
                      value       movement       movement        value
  output    1         2.000         0.000         0.000          2.000
  input     1         2.000         0.000         0.000          2.000
  input     2         4.000         0.000         0.000          4.000
LISTING OF PEERS:
  peer    lambda weight
    2       1.000


Results for firm:      3
Technical efficiency = 0.833
PROJECTION SUMMARY:
  variable          original       radial         slack       projected
                      value       movement       movement        value
  output    1         3.000         0.000         0.000          3.000
  input     1         6.000        -1.000         0.000          5.000
  input     2         6.000        -1.000         0.000          5.000
LISTING OF PEERS:
  peer    lambda weight
    5       0.500
    2       1.000


Results for firm:      4
Technical efficiency = 0.714
PROJECTION SUMMARY:
  variable          original       radial         slack       projected
                      value       movement       movement        value
  output    1         1.000         0.000         0.000          1.000
  input     1         3.000        -0.857         0.000          2.143
  input     2         2.000        -0.571         0.000          1.429
LISTING OF PEERS:
  peer    lambda weight
    5       0.286
    2       0.214


Results for firm:      5
Technical efficiency = 1.000
PROJECTION SUMMARY:
  variable          original       radial         slack       projected
                      value       movement       movement        value
  output    1         2.000         0.000         0.000          2.000
  input     1         6.000         0.000         0.000          6.000
  input     2         2.000         0.000         0.000          2.000
```

```
LISTING OF PEERS:
  peer    lambda weight
    5        1.000
```

6.4 The Variable Returns to Scale (VRS) Model and Scale Efficiencies

The CRS assumption is only appropriate when all firms are operating at an optimal scale. Imperfect competition, constraints on finance, etc., may cause a firm to be not operating at optimal scale. Banker, Charnes and Cooper (1984) suggested an extension of the CRS DEA model to account for variable returns to scale (VRS) situations. The use of the CRS specification when not all firms are operating at the optimal scale, results in measures of TE which are confounded by *scale efficiencies* (SE). The use of the VRS specification permits the calculation of TE devoid of these SE effects.

The CRS linear programming problem can be easily modified to account for VRS by adding the convexity constraint: $N1'\lambda=1$ to equation 6.10 to provide:

$$\min_{\theta,\lambda} \theta,$$
$$\text{st} \quad -y_i + Y\lambda \geq 0,$$
$$\theta x_i - X\lambda \geq 0,$$
$$N1'\lambda=1$$
$$\lambda \geq 0, \tag{6.12}$$

where N1 is an N×1 vector of ones. This approach forms a convex hull of intersecting planes which envelope the data points more tightly than the CRS conical hull and thus provides technical efficiency scores which are greater than or equal to those obtained using the CRS model. The VRS specification has been the most commonly used specification in the 1990s.

Note that the convexity constraint ($N1'\lambda=1$), essentially ensures that an inefficient firm is only "benchmarked" against firms of a similar size. That is, the projected point (for that firm) on the DEA frontier will be a *convex* combination of observed firms. This convexity restriction is not imposed in the CRS case. Hence, in a CRS DEA, a firm may be benchmarked against firms which are substantially larger (smaller) than it. In this instance the λ-weights will sum to a value greater than (less than) one.

Calculation of Scale Efficiencies

Given that one believes that the technology is VRS, one may then obtain a scale efficiency measure for each firm. This is done by conducting both a CRS and a VRS DEA. One then decomposes the TE scores obtained from the CRS DEA into two components, one due to scale inefficiency and one due to "pure" technical inefficiency. If there is a difference in the CRS and VRS TE scores for a particular firm, then this indicates that the firm has scale inefficiency, and that the scale inefficiency can be calculated from the difference between the VRS and CRS TE scores.

In Figure 6.7, we illustrate scale inefficiency using a one-input, one-output example. The CRS and VRS DEA frontiers are indicated in the figure. Under CRS, the input-orientated technical inefficiency of the point P is the distance PP_C. However, under VRS, the technical inefficiency would only be PP_V. The difference between these two TE measures, P_CP_V, is due to scale inefficiency. These concepts can be expressed in ratio efficiency measures as:

$$TE_{CRS} = AP_C/AP$$

$$TE_{VRS} = AP_V/AP$$

$$SE = AP_C/AP_V$$

where all of these measures are bounded by zero and one. We also note that

$$TE_{CRS} = TE_{VRS} \times SE$$

because

$$AP_C/AP = (AP_V/AP) \times (AP_C/AP_V).$$

Thus, the CRS technical efficiency measure is decomposed into "pure" technical efficiency and scale efficiency. This scale efficiency measure can be roughly interpreted as the ratio of the average product of a firm operating at the point P_V to the average product of the point operating at a point of (technically) optimal scale (point R).

One shortcoming of this measure of scale efficiency is that the value does not indicate whether the firm is operating in an area of increasing or decreasing returns to scale. This latter issue can be determined by running an additional DEA problem with non-increasing returns to scale (NIRS) imposed. This is done by altering the DEA model in equation 6.12 by substituting the $N1'\lambda = 1$ restriction with $N1'\lambda \leq 1$, to provide:

$$
\begin{aligned}
&\min_{\theta,\lambda} \theta, \\
&\text{st} \quad -y_i + Y\lambda \geq 0, \\
&\quad\quad \theta x_i - X\lambda \geq 0, \\
&\quad\quad N1'\lambda \leq 1 \\
&\quad\quad \lambda \geq 0.
\end{aligned}
\tag{6.13}
$$

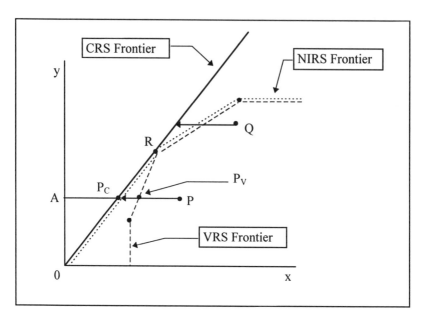

Figure 6.7 Calculation of Scale Economies in DEA

The NIRS DEA frontier is also plotted in Figure 6.7. The nature of the scale inefficiencies (i.e., due to increasing or decreasing returns to scale) for a particular firm can be determined by seeing whether the NIRS TE score is equal to the VRS TE score. If they are unequal (as is the case for the point P in Figure 6.7) then increasing returns to scale exist for that firm. If they are equal (as is the case for point Q in Figure 6.7) then decreasing returns to scale apply.[20] Examples of this approach applied to international airlines and electricity are provided in Bureau of Industry Economics (1994) and Färe, Grosskopf and Logan (1985), respectively.

Note that the constraint: $N1'\lambda \leq 1$, ensures that the i-th firm will not be "benchmarked" against firms which are substantially larger than it, but may be compared with firms smaller than it.

Example 2

This is a simple numerical example involving five firms which produce a single output using a single input. The data are listed in Table 6.4 and the VRS and CRS input-orientated DEA results are plotted in Figure 6.8 and listed in Table 6.5. Given that we are using an input orientation, the efficiencies are measured horizontally across Figure 6.8. We observe that firm 3 is the only efficient firm (i.e., on the DEA

---

[20] Note that if $TE_{CRS}=TE_{VRS}$, then by definition, the firm is operating under CRS.

frontier) when CRS is assumed, but that firms 1, 3 and 5 are efficient when VRS is assumed.

Table 6.4 Example Data for VRS DEA

Firm	y	x
1	1	2
2	2	4
3	3	3
4	5	5
5	5	6

The calculation of the various efficiency measures can be illustrated using firm 2 which is inefficient under both CRS and VRS technologies. The CRS technical efficiency (TE) is equal to 2/4=0.5; the VRS TE is 2.5/4=0.625 and the scale efficiency is equal to the ratio of the CRS TE to the VRS TE which is 0.5/0.625=0.8. We also observe that firm 2 is on the increasing returns to scale (IRS) portion of the VRS frontier.

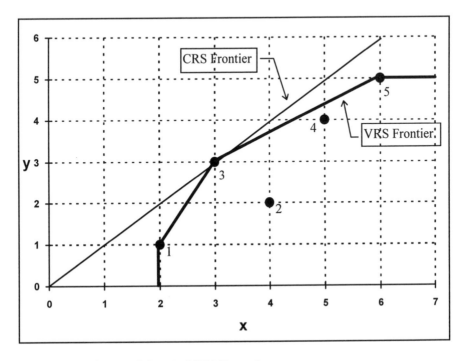

Figure 6.8 VRS Input-Orientated DEA Example

Table 6.5 VRS Input-Orientated DEA Results

Firm	CRS TE	VRS TE	Scale	
1	0.500	1.000	0.500	irs
2	0.500	0.625	0.800	irs
3	1.000	1.000	1.000	-
4	0.800	0.900	0.889	drs
5	0.833	1.000	0.833	drs
mean	**0.727**	**0.905**	**0.804**	

We now illustrate these calculations using the DEAP computer program. The data file for this example, EG2.DTA (refer to Table 6.6a), contains five observations on one output and one input. The output quantities are listed in the first column and the inputs in the second column. These data are identical to those listed in Table 6.4.

The DEAP instruction file, EG2.INS, is listed in Table 6.6b. The only changes relative to EG1.INS are that:

- the input and output file names are different;

- the number of inputs is reduced to 1; and

- there is a "1" entered on the 2nd last line to indicate that VRS is required.

The output file, EG1.OUT, is reproduced in Table 6.6c. These results are identical to those presented in Table 6.5. Note that when the VRS option is specified, the DEAP program conducts VRS, CRS and NIRS DEA and calculates scale efficiencies as well as technical efficiencies.

Table 6.6a Listing of Data File, EG2.DTA

```
1 2
2 4
3 3
4 5
5 6
```

Table 6.6b Listing of Instruction File, EG2.INS

```
eg2.dta        DATA FILE NAME
eg2.out        OUTPUT FILE NAME
5              NUMBER OF FIRMS
1              NUMBER OF TIME PERIODS
1              NUMBER OF OUTPUTS
1              NUMBER OF INPUTS
0              0=INPUT AND 1=OUTPUT ORIENTATED
1              0=CRS AND 1=VRS
0              0=DEA(MULTI-STAGE), 1=COST-DEA, 2=MALMQUIST-DEA,
                  3=DEA(1-STAGE), 4=DEA(2-STAGE)
```

Table 6.6c Listing of Output File, EG2.OUT

```
Results from DEAP Version 2.1

Instruction file = eg2.ins
Data file        = eg2.dta

Input orientated DEA

Scale assumption: VRS

Slacks calculated using multi-stage method


EFFICIENCY SUMMARY:

 firm  crste  vrste  scale

    1  0.500  1.000  0.500 irs
    2  0.500  0.625  0.800 irs
    3  1.000  1.000  1.000  -
    4  0.800  0.900  0.889 drs
    5  0.833  1.000  0.833 drs

mean  0.727  0.905  0.804

Note: crste = technical efficiency from CRS DEA
      vrste = technical efficiency from VRS DEA
      scale = scale efficiency = crste/vrste


Note also that all subsequent tables refer to VRS results


SUMMARY OF OUTPUT SLACKS:

 firm  output:        1
    1               0.000
    2               0.000
    3               0.000
    4               0.000
    5               0.000
```

```
mean                    0.000


SUMMARY OF INPUT SLACKS:

  firm  input:                1
    1                     0.000
    2                     0.000
    3                     0.000
    4                     0.000
    5                     0.000

mean                    0.000


SUMMARY OF PEERS:

  firm  peers:
    1      1
    2      1    3
    3      3
    4      3    5
    5      5


SUMMARY OF PEER WEIGHTS:
  (in same order as above)

  firm  peer weights:
    1    1.000
    2    0.500 0.500
    3    1.000
    4    0.500 0.500
    5    1.000


PEER COUNT SUMMARY:
  (i.e., no. times each firm is a peer for another)

  firm  peer count:
    1      1
    2      0
    3      2
    4      0
    5      1



SUMMARY OF OUTPUT TARGETS:

  firm  output:                1
    1                     1.000
    2                     2.000
    3                     3.000
    4                     4.000
    5                     5.000


SUMMARY OF INPUT TARGETS:

  firm  input:                1
    1                     2.000
    2                     2.500
```

```
3                    3.000
4                    4.500
5                    6.000


FIRM BY FIRM RESULTS:


Results for firm:      1
Technical efficiency = 1.000
Scale efficiency     = 0.500   (irs)
PROJECTION SUMMARY:
   variable           original        radial          slack      projected
                         value      movement       movement         value
   output    1          1.000         0.000          0.000         1.000
   input     1          2.000         0.000          0.000         2.000
LISTING OF PEERS:
  peer    lambda weight
    1        1.000


Results for firm:      2
Technical efficiency = 0.625
Scale efficiency     = 0.800   (irs)
PROJECTION SUMMARY:
   variable           original        radial          slack      projected
                         value      movement       movement         value
   output    1          2.000         0.000          0.000         2.000
   input     1          4.000        -1.500          0.000         2.500
LISTING OF PEERS:
  peer    lambda weight
    1        0.500
    3        0.500


Results for firm:      3
Technical efficiency = 1.000
Scale efficiency     = 1.000   (crs)
PROJECTION SUMMARY:
   variable           original        radial          slack      projected
                         value      movement       movement         value
   output    1          3.000         0.000          0.000         3.000
   input     1          3.000         0.000          0.000         3.000
LISTING OF PEERS:
  peer    lambda weight
    3        1.000


Results for firm:      4
Technical efficiency = 0.900
Scale efficiency     = 0.889   (drs)
PROJECTION SUMMARY:
   variable           original        radial          slack      projected
                         value      movement       movement         value
   output    1          4.000         0.000          0.000         4.000
   input     1          5.000        -0.500          0.000         4.500
LISTING OF PEERS:
  peer    lambda weight
    3        0.500
    5        0.500


Results for firm:      5
```

```
Technical efficiency = 1.000
Scale efficiency     = 0.833   (drs)
PROJECTION SUMMARY:
   variable          original        radial         slack       projected
                        value       movement      movement         value
   output   1          5.000         0.000         0.000          5.000
   input    1          6.000         0.000         0.000          6.000
LISTING OF PEERS:
   peer    lambda weight
     5         1.000
```

6.5 Input and Output Orientations

In the preceding input-orientated models, discussed in Sections 6.3 and 6.4, the method sought to identify technical inefficiency as a proportional reduction in input usage, with output levels held constant. This corresponds to Farrell's input-based measure of technical inefficiency. As discussed in Section 6.2, it is also possible to measure technical inefficiency as a proportional increase in output production, with input levels held fixed. The two measures provide the same value under CRS but are unequal when VRS is assumed (see Figure 6.3). Given that linear programming does not suffer from such statistical problems as simultaneous equation bias, the choice of an appropriate orientation is not as crucial as it is in the case of econometric estimation. In a number of studies, analysts have tended to select input-orientated models because many firms have particular orders to fill (e.g., as in electricity generation) and hence the input quantities appear to be the primary decision variables, although this argument may not be as strong in all industries. In some industries, the firms may be given a fixed quantity of resources and asked to produce as much output as possible. In this case, an output orientation would be more appropriate. Essentially, one should select the orientation according to which quantities (inputs or outputs) the managers have most control over. Furthermore, in many instances, the choice of orientation has only a minor influence upon the scores obtained (e.g., see Coelli and Perelman, 1996b).

The output-orientated DEA models are very similar to their input-orientated counterparts. Consider the example of the following output-orientated VRS model:

$$\max_{\phi,\lambda} \phi,$$
$$\text{st} \quad -\phi y_i + Y\lambda \geq 0,$$
$$x_i - X\lambda \geq 0,$$
$$N1'\lambda = 1$$
$$\lambda \geq 0, \tag{6.14}$$

where $1 \leq \phi < \infty$, and $\phi-1$ is the proportional increase in outputs that could be achieved by the i-th firm, with input quantities held constant.[21] Note that $1/\phi$ defines

---

[21] An output-orientated CRS model is defined in a similar way, but it is not presented here for brevity.

a TE score which varies between zero and one (and that this is the output-orientated TE score reported by DEAP).

A two-output example of an output-orientated DEA could be represented by a piece-wise linear production possibility curve, such as that depicted in Figure 6.9. Note that the observations lie *below* this curve, and that the sections of the curve which are at right angles to the axes result in output slack being calculated when a production point is projected onto those parts of the curve by a radial expansion in outputs. For example, the point P is projected to the point P′ which is on the frontier but not on the *efficient frontier*, because the production of y_1 could be increased by the amount AP′ without using any more inputs. Thus there is output slack in this case of AP′ in output y_1.

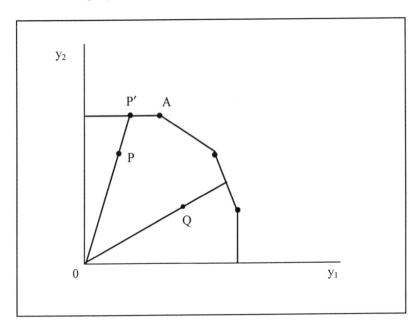

Figure 6.9 Output-Orientated DEA

One point of importance is that *the output- and input-orientated models will estimate exactly the same frontier and therefore, by definition, identify the same set of firms as being efficient. It is only the efficiency measures associated with the inefficient firms that may differ between the two methods.* The two types of measures are illustrated in Section 6.2 using Figure 6.3, where we observe that the two measures provide equivalent values only under constant returns to scale.

6.6 Conclusions

In this chapter, we provide a brief introduction to the basic DEA models. Namely, the input- and output-orientated CRS and VRS models. We discuss how these models can be used to measure technical and scale efficiencies and how one can use NIRS DEA to help identify the nature of scale economies. Terminology, such as peers, targets and slacks, are also introduced.

In the following chapter we discuss some of the ways in which these basic DEA models can be extended. We discuss allocative efficiency, environmental variables, non-discretionary variables, the treatment of slacks, and a variety of other issues.

7. ADDITIONAL TOPICS ON DATA ENVELOPMENT ANALYSIS

7.1 Introduction

This chapter continues the discussion of data envelopment analysis (DEA) which began in the previous chapter. In the previous chapter, we introduced the efficiency measurement concepts of Farrell (1957) and described how they could be implemented using the linear programming approach known as DEA. We discussed the basic constant returns to scale (CRS) and variable returns to scale (VRS) DEA models from both the input- and output-orientations.

In this chapter we discuss some popular extensions of these basic DEA models. The extensions we consider involve allocative efficiency, environmental variables, non-discretionary variables, the treatment of slacks and congestion efficiency. We also provide an empirical example using data on Australian universities.

7.2 Price Information and Allocative Efficiency

If price information is available and a behavioural objective, such as cost minimisation or revenue or profit maximisation, is appropriate, then it is possible to measure allocative efficiencies as well as technical efficiencies. To achieve this, two sets of linear programs are required; one to measure technical efficiency and the other to measure economic efficiency. The allocative efficiency measure is then obtained residually as described in the previous chapter. We now illustrate this procedure using the cost minimisation case.

7.2.1 Cost Minimisation

For the case of VRS cost minimisation, the input-orientated DEA model, defined in equation 6.12, is conducted to obtain technical efficiencies (TE). The next step requires the solution of the following cost minimisation DEA:

$$\min_{\lambda, xi*} \ w_i'x_i^*,$$
$$\text{st} \quad -y_i + Y\lambda \geq 0,$$
$$x_i^* - X\lambda \geq 0,$$
$$N1'\lambda = 1$$
$$\lambda \geq 0, \tag{7.1}$$

where w_i is a vector of input prices for the i-th firm and x_i^* (which is calculated by the LP) is the cost-minimising vector of input quantities for the i-th firm, given the input prices w_i and the output levels y_i. The total cost efficiency or economic efficiency (EE)of the i-th firm is calculated as

$$EE = w_i'x_i^*/ \ w_i'x_i.$$

That is, EE is the ratio of minimum cost to observed cost, for the i-th firm.

The allocative efficiency is calculated residually by

$$AE = CE/TE.$$

Note that this procedure implicitly includes any slacks into the allocative efficiency measure. This is often justified on the grounds that slacks reflects inappropriate input mixes (see Ferrier and Lovell, 1990, p.235).

7.2.2 Revenue Maximisation

If revenue maximisation is a more appropriate behavioural assumption, then allocative inefficiency in output mix selection can be accounted for in a similar manner. For the case of VRS revenue maximisation, technical efficiencies are calculated by solving the output-orientated DEA model, defined in equation 6.14. The following revenue maximisation DEA problem is then solved,

$$\max_{\lambda, yi*} \ p_i'y_i^*,$$
$$\text{st} \quad -y_i^* + Y\lambda \geq 0,$$
$$x_i - X\lambda \geq 0,$$
$$N1'\lambda = 1$$
$$\lambda \geq 0, \tag{7.2}$$

where p_i is a vector of input prices for the i-th firm and y_i^* (which is calculated by the LP) is the revenue-maximising vector of output quantities for the i-th firm, given the output prices p_i and the input levels x_i. The total revenue efficiency or economic efficiency (EE) of the i-th firm is calculated as

$$EE = p_i'y_i / p_i'y_i^*$$

That is, EE is the ratio of observed revenue to maximum revenue. The (output) allocative efficiency measure is obtained residually using equation 6.4 (AE = EE/TE).

Cost minimisation and revenue maximisation together imply profit maximisation. Only a handful of studies have considered profit efficiency using DEA methods. Färe, Grosskopf and Weber (1997) suggest solving two sets of linear programs. The first involves a profit maximising DEA to measure profit efficiency and the second DEA is one in which technical efficiency is measured as a simultaneous reduction in the input vector and expansion of the output vector. This technical efficiency measure uses what are known as *directional distance functions*. For more on this recently proposed approach, see Färe, Grosskopf and Weber (1997).

7.2.3 A CRS Cost Efficiency DEA Example

In this example, we take the data from the two-input, one-output, input-orientated DEA example in Table 6.1 and add the information that all firms face the same prices, which are 1 and 3 for inputs 1 and 2, respectively. The solution of this CRS cost efficiency DEA problem is illustrated in Figure 7.1. This figure is equivalent to Figure 6.6 except that the isocost line with a slope of -1/3 is also drawn so that it is tangential to the isoquant. From this diagram, we observe that firm 5 is the only cost efficient firm and that all other firms have some allocative inefficiency. The various cost efficiencies and allocative efficiencies are listed in Table 7.1.

The calculation of these efficiencies can be illustrated using firm 3. We noted in Chapter 6 that the technical efficiency of firm 3 is measured along the ray from the origin (0) to the point 3 and that it is equal to the ratio of the distance from 0 to the point 3′ over the distance from 0 to the point 3 and that this is equal to 0.833. The allocative efficiency is equal to the ratio of the distances 0 to 3″ over 0 to 3′, which is equal to 0.9. The cost efficiency is the ratio of distances 0 to 3″ over 0 to 3, which is equal to 0.75. We also note that 0.833×0.9=0.750.

The DEAP instructions needed to calculate the technical, allocative and cost efficiency measures, reported in Table 7.1, are minor variants of those presented in the previous chapter. The data file, EG3.DTA (refer to Table 7.2a), contains the same data as EG1.DTA plus two additional columns. Recall that there are five observations on one output and two inputs. The output quantities are listed in the first column and the input quantities in the next two columns. In addition to this, two columns containing input price data are listed to the right of these. In this particular example we assume all firms face the same prices and that these prices are 1 and 3 for inputs 1 and 2, respectively.

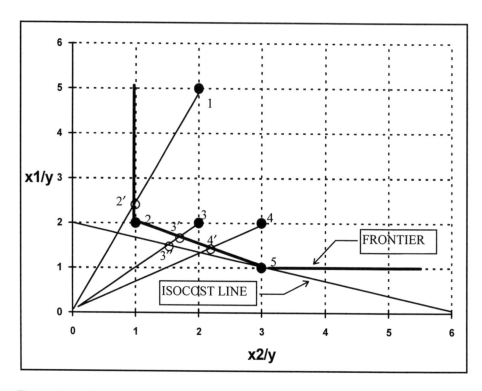

Figure 7.1: CRS Cost Efficiency DEA Example

Table 7.1: CRS Cost Efficiency DEA Results

firm	technical efficiency	allocative efficiency	cost efficiency
1	0.500	0.706	0.353
2	1.000	0.857	0.857
3	0.833	0.900	0.750
4	0.714	0.933	0.667
5	1.000	1.000	1.000
mean	**0.810**	**0.879**	**0.725**

The EG3.INS file is listed in Table 7.2b. The only changes in this instruction file relative to the EG1.INS file, presented in Table 6.3b, are that:

- the input and output file names are different;
- there is a "1" entered on the last line to indicate that a cost efficiency DEA is required.

The output file, EG3.OUT, is reproduced in Table 7.2c. The technical efficiency results are identical to those listed in EG1.OUT in Table 6.3c. However, the allocative and cost efficiencies are now also listed. Furthermore, a table of input quantities for minimum cost production are now also listed. Note that all of the optimal input quantities are used in the same ratio (3:1) because each firm faces the same relative input prices. If the prices differed for different firms the optimal input ratios are then likely to differ.

Table 7.2a: Listing of Data File, EG3.DTA

```
1 2 5 1 3
2 2 4 1 3
3 6 6 1 3
1 3 2 1 3
2 6 2 1 3
```

Table 7.2b Listing of Instruction File, EG3.INS

```
eg3.dta        DATA FILE NAME
eg3.out        OUTPUT FILE NAME
5              NUMBER OF FIRMS
1              NUMBER OF TIME PERIODS
1              NUMBER OF OUTPUTS
2              NUMBER OF INPUTS
0              0=INPUT AND 1=OUTPUT ORIENTATED
0              0=CRS AND 1=VRS
1              0=DEA(MULTI-STAGE), 1=COST-DEA, 2=MALMQUIST-DEA,
                 3=DEA(1-STAGE), 4=DEA(2-STAGE)
```

Table 7.2c: Listing of Output File, EG3.OUT

```
Results from DEAP Version 2.1

Instruction file = eg3.ins
Data file        = eg3.dta
```

```
Cost efficiency DEA

Scale assumption: CRS


EFFICIENCY SUMMARY:

firm       te       ae       ce
   1    0.500    0.706    0.353
   2    1.000    0.857    0.857
   3    0.833    0.900    0.750
   4    0.714    0.933    0.667
   5    1.000    1.000    1.000

mean    0.810    0.879    0.725

Note: te = technical efficiency
      ae = allocative efficiency = ce/te
      ce = cost efficiency


SUMMARY OF COST MINIMISING INPUT QUANTITIES:

firm   input:          1             2
   1                3.000         1.000
   2                6.000         2.000
   3                9.000         3.000
   4                3.000         1.000
   5                6.000         2.000
```

7.3 Adjusting for Environment

Here we use the term *environment* to describe factors which could influence the efficiency of a firm, where such factors are not traditional inputs and are assumed not under the control of the manager. Some examples of environmental variables include (see Fried, Schmidt and Yaisawarng, 1995):

1. ownership differences, such as public/private or corporate/non-corporate;

2. location characteristics, such as:

    -   coal-fired electric power stations influenced by coal quality;

    -   electric power distribution networks influenced by population density and average customer size;

    -   schools influenced by socio-economic status of children and city/country location; etc.

3. labour union power; and

4. government regulations.

There are a number of ways in which environmental variables can be accommodated in a DEA analysis. Some possible methods are discussed below.

Method 1

If the values of the environmental variable can be ordered from the least to the most detrimental effect upon efficiency, then the approach of Banker and Morey (1986a) can be followed. In this approach the efficiency of the i-th firm is compared with those firms in the sample which have a value of the environmental variable which is less than or equal to that of the i-th firm. For example, consider the case where an analyst is studying hamburger restaurants and the analyst believes that the type of location has an influence upon production. The analyst has information on whether the restaurant is located in a city centre, the suburbs or in a country area, and believes that the city is the most favourable location and that the country is the least favourable. In this instance the analyst would restrict the comparison set to be: (i) only country restaurants for a country restaurant; (ii) only country and suburban restaurants for a suburban restaurant; and (iii) all restaurants for a city restaurant. This would ensure that no restaurant is compared with another restaurant which has a more favourable environment.

Method 2

If there is no natural ordering of the environmental variable (e.g., public versus private ownership) then one can use a method proposed by Charnes, Cooper and Rhodes (1981). This method involves three stages:

1. divide the sample into public/private sub-samples and solve DEAs for each sub-sample;

2. project all observed data points onto their respective frontiers; and

3. solve a single DEA using the projected points and assess any difference in the mean efficiency of the two sub-samples.

Note that one problem with Methods 1 and 2 is that the comparison set can be greatly reduced, resulting in many firms being found to be efficient and thus reducing the discriminating power of the analysis. Another problem is that only one environmental variable can be considered by these two methods. Method 2 has the additional problem that it requires that the environmental variable be a categorical variable, while Method 1 suffers from the problem that it requires that the direction of the influence of the environmental variable (upon efficiency) be known *a priori*. In fact, in many instances the direction of influence is not known. For example, in an analysis of electricity utilities, we may be primarily interested in *determining* the influence of ownership status (public versus private) upon efficiency, and hence not wish to impose any prior judgement.

Method 3

Another possible method is to include the environmental variable(s) directly into the LP formulation.[1] The environmental variable(s) may be included either as an input, an output, or as a neutral variable, and may be assumed to be discretionary (under the control of the manager) or not. These different possibilities can be classified into three cases:

3a) non-discretionary, neutral variable;

3b) discretionary input; and

3c) non-discretionary input.

We ignore the case where the environmental variable can be included as an "output" because a similar effect can be achieved by inverting the environmental "output" and including it as an "input" (more on this later).

Method 3a:

If one is unsure as to the direction of the influence of the environmental variables, then the variables can be included in the LP problem in an equality form. For example, consider the VRS input-orientated LP problem in equation 6.12, and assume we have L environmental variables to add to our model, and these are denoted by the L×1 vector z_i for the i-th firm and by the L×N matrix Z for the full sample. The input-orientated CRS DEA in equation 6.12 would become:

$$\min_{\theta, \lambda} \theta,$$
$$\text{st} \quad -y_i + Y\lambda \geq 0,$$
$$\theta x_i - X\lambda \geq 0,$$
$$z_i - Z\lambda = 0,$$
$$N1'\lambda = 1$$
$$\lambda \geq 0. \tag{7.3}$$

This formulation ensures the i-th firm is only compared to a (theoretical) frontier firm which has the same environment. Two points can be made here. Firstly, that this restriction can greatly reduce the reference set and hence inflate the efficiency scores. Secondly, that in some cases it may be unacceptable (unfair?) to compare the i-th firm with another firm which has a more favourable environment. Note that the linear combination, $Z\lambda$, which represents the environment of the theoretical firm, may involve a number of peers, some of which have more favourable environments

---

[1] For example, see Bessent and Bessent (1980) and Ferrier and Lovell (1990).

and some have less favourable environments. For example, consider the influence of population density in an analysis of electric power distribution companies. If the i-th firm operates in a geographical region which has a particular population density, then is it fair to use one or more firms which enjoy higher population densities in assessing the performance of the i-th firm?[2]

Method 3b:

The environmental variables can be included as (discretionary) inputs, in which case equation 7.3 becomes:

$$\min_{\theta,\lambda} \theta,$$
$$\text{st} \quad -y_i + Y\lambda \geq 0,$$
$$\theta x_i - X\lambda \geq 0,$$
$$\theta z_i - Z\lambda \geq 0,$$
$$N1'\lambda = 1$$
$$\lambda \geq 0. \tag{7.4}$$

This approach treats the environmental variables as regular inputs. One advantage of this approach is that the i-th firm is only compared with a theoretical firm which has an environment which is no better than that of the i-th firm. One disadvantage is that the method requires that the direction of the influence of the environmental variable be known in advance which is not always the case. An additional point is that the method assumes the environmental variables can be radially reduced (by θ) just like a regular input. In some instances this may not be possible. Consider the case of electric power plants which face differing coal qualities. A power plant is often forced to use the local coal reserves and hence must accept the coal quality. Thus, in some cases, it may be better to treat the environmental variables as fixed variables (i.e., non-discretionary).

Method 3c:

When the environmental variables are included as non-discretionary inputs, equation 7.4 becomes:

$$\min_{\theta,\lambda} \theta,$$
$$\text{st} \quad -y_i + Y\lambda \geq 0,$$
$$\theta x_i - X\lambda \geq 0,$$
$$z_i - Z\lambda \geq 0,$$
$$N1'\lambda = 1$$
$$\lambda \geq 0. \tag{7.5}$$

---

[2] It should be noted that the signs on the dual variables associated with the Z's indicate whether a variable has a favourable or unfavourable effect upon production.

In this case, the θ is removed from the line involving Z. Again, the i-th firm is compared with a theoretical firm which has an environment which is no better than that of the i-th firm. However, this time we are not assuming the firms can alter their environment, and hence we do not include these environmental variables in the calculation of the efficiency score (even though the Z-restriction limits the comparison set).

Two disadvantages of Methods 3a to 3c are to be noted. Firstly, the environmental variables must be continuous variables, they cannot be categorical. If there are categorical environmental (or input) variables, then the more complicated mixed integer LP models, suggested by Banker and Morey (1986b), can be used.[3]

The second disadvantage of Methods 3b and 3c is that one must decide *a priori* whether the environmental variable has a positive or a negative influence upon efficiency. If we believe it has a negative effect we can invert the measure before including it in the Z matrix (alternatively we could include it as an "output" by using a restriction of the form $-z_i + Z\lambda \geq 0$).[4] In many cases we may not know what the direction of the influence is likely to be, and may, in fact, wish to determine the direction of this influence. In this case a two-stage procedure could be used.

Method 4

The two-stage method involves solving a DEA problem in a first-stage analysis, involving only the traditional inputs and outputs. In the second stage, the efficiency scores from the first stage are regressed upon the environmental variables. The sign of the coefficients of the environmental variables indicate the direction of the influence, and standard hypothesis tests can be used to assess the strength of the relationship. The second-stage regression can be used to "correct" the efficiency scores for environmental factors by using the estimated regression coefficients to adjust all efficiency scores to correspond to a common level of environment (e.g., the sample means).

This method accommodates both continuous and categorical variables. It also has the advantage of being easy to calculate. All that is needed is a basic DEA program and a package which can conduct ordinary least squares (OLS) regression (e.g. Excel, SHAZAM, SAS, Minitab). It should be noted, however, that frequently a significant proportion of the efficiency scores are equal to one, and that the OLS regression could predict scores greater than one. It is thus recommended that the Tobit regression method be used, because it can account for truncated data.[5]

---

[3] See also Kamakura (1988) and Rousseau and Semple (1993) for further comments on mixed integer LP models.

[4] The inclusion of variables into DEA LPs which are not traditional inputs or outputs can introduce some difficulties involving the issue of translation invariance. The way in which these non-traditional variables are defined can have a significant influence upon results. See Lovell and Pastor (1995) for some discussion of translation invariance in various DEA models.

[5] For example, see McCarty and Yaisawarng (1993).

Econometrics packages such as SHAZAM, SAS and Limdep have commands for Tobit regression.

One disadvantage of the two-stage method is that if the variables used in the first stage are highly correlated with the second-stage variables then the results are likely to be biased.

Another criticism that is sometimes levelled against the two-stage approach is that it only considers radial inefficiency and ignores the slacks. A possible solution to this is suggested by Fried, Schmidt and Yaisawarng (1995), which involves a four-stage approach which includes estimating an SUR system of equations for the slacks. A good review of alternative approaches to dealing with environmental variables is also presented in that paper.

Also note that some authors use the above two-stage method to determine the direction of influence of the environmental variables, and then use this information to formulate a single-stage model such as that specified in Method 3c.

Concluding Points on Environmental Variables

We have considered a number of possible approaches to the consideration of environmental variables. We recommend the two-stage approach in most cases. It has the advantages that:

- it can accommodate more than one variable;

- it can accommodate both continuous and categorical variables;

- it does not make prior assumptions regarding the direction of the influence of the categorical variable;

- one can conduct hypothesis tests to see if the variables have a significant influence upon efficiencies;

- it is easy to calculate; and

- the method is simple and therefore transparent.

The two-stage approach can also be used to assess the influence of various management factors upon efficiency. For example, the effects upon efficiency of the age, experience, education and training of the manager(s) can be estimated by including these factors in the second-stage regression.

7.4 Non-Discretionary Variables

In our input- (output-) orientated DEA models we have assumed that all inputs (outputs) can be radially reduced (expanded). That is, that the manager is able to alter the quantities of all the inputs (outputs). In some instances, the manager may not be able to alter all inputs (outputs). For example, consider an input-orientated

DEA problem, where the manager may not be able to alter some input quantities in the short run. For example, a factory manager may not be able to adjust the quantity of capital employed in the short run, but is likely to be able to adjust quantities of labour and materials

We can formulate a model in which we only seek radial reduction in the inputs over which the manager has discretionary control. In this case, we divide the inputs into discretionary and non-discretionary sets (denoted by X^D and X^{ND}, respectively) and rewrite equation 6.12 (for the VRS case) as:

$$
\begin{aligned}
&\min_{\theta,\lambda} \ \theta, \\
&\text{st} \quad -y_i + Y\lambda \geq 0, \\
&\qquad \theta x_i^D - X^D\lambda \geq 0, \\
&\qquad x_i^{ND} - X^{ND}\lambda \geq 0, \\
&\qquad N1'\lambda = 1 \\
&\qquad \lambda \geq 0,
\end{aligned} \tag{7.6}
$$

In the above DEA problem the θ-parameter is only associated with the discretionary inputs and hence the problem only seeks radial reduction in this subset of the inputs. This approach may be visualised in the two input case by looking at Figure 6.5, and assuming that the capital input is on the vertical axis and labour is on the horizontal axis. If our discretionary set involved labour and our non-discretionary set involved capital, then the linear program in 7.6 would seek a radial contraction in the labour input only. For example, in the case of the firm operating at the point B in Figure 6.5, it would seek contraction in a horizontal direction (to the left) until the isoquant was reached. This will reduce the quantity of labour used, while holding the input quantity fixed. For more on this approach, see Banker and Morey (1986a) and Kopp (1981)..

7.5 Input Congestion

In our discussion in Chapter 2, it was stated that an isoquant may "bend backwards" and obtain a positive slope at some point. This was explained as being due to congestion in the use of an input, to the extent that it begins to have a negative marginal product (i.e., corresponding to the declining part of the TP curve). Some DEA studies have allowed the DEA input isoquant to have segments with a positive slope to account for this possibility. It is usually argued that the excess input use is due to constraints which are not under the control of the firm. Examples include: labour unions preventing a reduction in staff, or government controls setting the levels of various inputs.[6]

---

[6] We are hesitant to recommend this approach because the method can identify "congestion inefficiencies" which may be simply due to one not having sufficient data points at the extremities of the isoquants. We have included this section on congestion because of the number of publications (e.g., Färe, Grosskopf and Lovell, 1985 and 1994) which have considered congestion efficiency.

The standard DEA models discussed in the previous chapter implicitly assume strong disposability in inputs (and outputs). That is, we assume that a firm can always costlessly dispose of unwanted inputs (and outputs). A DEA model that accounts for input congestion relaxes the strong disposability in inputs assumption. In this section we replace the strong disposability in inputs assumption with a weak disposability in inputs assumption.[7]

Following Färe, Grosskopf and Lovell (1985, 1994), input congestion is accounted for in the input orientated VRS DEA problem in equation 6.12 by changing the inequalities in the input restrictions to equalities and by introducing a δ parameter in the input restrictions. Thus, equation 6.12 becomes:

$$\min_{\theta, \lambda, \delta} \theta,$$
$$\text{st} \quad -y_i + Y\lambda \geq 0,$$
$$\delta\theta x_i - X\lambda = 0,$$
$$N1'\lambda = 1$$
$$\lambda \geq 0, 0 < \delta \leq 1. \tag{7.7}$$

The technical efficiency scores obtained from this weak disposability VRS DEA are greater than or equal to the strong disposability VRS DEA scores obtained from the LP in equation 6.12. This is because the effects of congestion inefficiency have been removed from the technical efficiency measure.

Recall that in Chapter 6 we decomposed CRS technical efficiency into "pure" (VRS) technical efficiency and scale efficiency by solving separate VRS and CRS DEA models. In a similar manner, we can solve a strong disposability and a weak disposability DEA and identify input congestion efficiency (CE) from the differences in the TE scores from the two models. This is illustrated in Figure 7.2 where we have a frontier constructed assuming strong disposability (SS_S) and one assuming weak disposability (SS_W). The latter curve has "bent back" to pass through the point A. The congestion inefficiency for the firm producing at P is equal to $P_W P_S$. In ratio terms an input congestion efficiency measure is expressed as

$$CE = 0P_S/0P_W,$$

The TE measure under strong disposability (TE_S) is equal to the product of the TE measure under weak disposability (TE_W) and the input congestion efficiency (CE). That is,

$$0P_S/0P = (0P_S/0P_W) \times (0P_W/0P)$$
or

---

[7] Recall from Chapter 3 that weak disposability of inputs implies that if a vector of inputs, x, can produce an output vector, y, then κx (where $\kappa \geq 1$ is a scalar) can also produce y. Note that analogous output disposability assumptions can also be defined.

$TE_S = CE \times TE_W$.

Thus by solving the strong and weak disposability DEA models we can identify CE by the ratio of TE_S to TE_W.

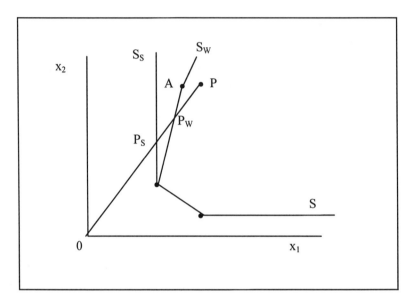

Figure 7.2: Efficiency Measurement and Input Disposability
(Congestion)

In fact, as shown in Bureau of Industry Economics (1994) and Färe, Grosskopf and Logan (1985), the technical efficiency scores calculated from a CRS DEA can be decomposed into congestion inefficiency, scale inefficiency and "pure" technical efficiency by solving three DEA models: a CRS assuming strong disposability; a VRS assuming strong disposability; and a VRS assuming weak disposability.

Weak disposability in outputs can also be considered. This would permit the existence of a positively sloped portion of the production possibility curve, implying a negative shadow price for a particular output. This would allow one to explicitly include unwanted outputs such as pollutants in a DEA model. For example, see Färe, Grosskopf, Lovell and Pasurka (1989) and Färe, Grosskopf and Lovell (1985, 1994).

Note that weak disposability in both inputs and outputs can be imposed together. Furthermore, one could alternatively impose weak disposability upon a subset of the inputs and/or outputs. For example, one may have a strong reason to believe that some rail companies may have been required to invest in excess capital because of political directives. In that instance one may decide to impose weak disposability in the capital input and allow strong disposability in all other inputs. However, it should be stressed again that unless one has a strong reason for suspecting congestion one should not go looking for it because one will often find it whether or not it actually exists.

7.6 Treatment of Slacks

It was noted in Chapter 6 that the LP's discussed in that chapter may not always identify all (efficiency) slacks. Some authors (e.g., Ali and Seiford, 1993) have suggested the use of a second-stage linear programming problem to ensure the identification of an efficient frontier point by maximising the sum of slacks required to move from the first-stage projected point (such as A′ in Figure 6.5) to a Koopmans efficient frontier point (such as point C in Figure 6.5). This second-stage linear programming problem is defined by:

$$\min_{\lambda,OS,IS} -(M1'OS + K1'IS),$$
$$\text{st} \quad -y_i + Y\lambda - OS = 0,$$
$$\theta x_i - X\lambda - IS = 0,$$
$$\lambda \geq 0, OS \geq 0, IS \geq 0, \tag{7.8}$$

where OS is an M×1 vector of output slacks, IS is a K×1 vector of input slacks, and M1 and K1 are M×1 and K×1 vectors of ones, respectively. Note that in this second-stage linear program, θ is not a variable, its value is taken from the first-stage results. Furthermore, note that this second-stage linear program must be solved for each of the N firms involved.[8]

There are two major problems associated with this second-stage LP. The first and most obvious problem is that the sum of slacks is *maximised* rather than *minimised*. Hence it identifies not the *nearest* efficient point but the *furthest* efficient point. The second major problem associated with the above second-stage approach is that it is not invariant to units of measurement. The alteration of the units of measurement, say for a labour input from days to hours (while leaving other units of measurement unchanged), could result in the identification of different efficient boundary points and hence different slack and λ-values.[9]

However, these two issues are not a problem in the simple example presented in Figure 6.5 because there is only one efficient point to choose from on the vertical facet. However, if slack occurs in two or more dimensions (which is often the case)

---

[8] This method is used in DEA software, such as WDEA and IDEAS.
[9] Charnes, Cooper, Rousseau and Semple (1987) suggest a units invariant model where the unit worth of a slack is made inversely proportional to the quantity of that input or output used by the i-th firm. This does solve the immediate problem, but does create another, in that there is no obvious reason for the slacks to be weighted in this way.

then the above mentioned problems are relevant. Coelli (1997) suggests using a multi-stage DEA method to avoid the problems inherent in the two-stage method. This multi-stage method involves a sequence of radial DEA models and hence is more computationally demanding that the other two methods. However, the benefits of the approach are that it identifies efficient projected points which have input and output mixes as similar as possible to those of the inefficient points, and that it is also invariant to units of measurement. Hence, we recommend the use of the multi-stage method over other alternatives. For more on the multi-stage method, see Coelli (1997).

In the DEAP software, the user is given three choices regarding the treatment of slacks. These are:

- One-stage DEA, in which the first-stage LP in equation 6.12 is solved and slacks are calculated residually;

- Two-stage DEA, which involves the solution of the LP's in equations 6.12 and 7.8; and

- Multi-stage DEA, which involves the solution of a sequence of radial LP's.

Having devoted some space to the issue of slacks we would like to conclude this discussion by observing that the importance of slacks can be overstated. Slacks may be viewed as being an artefact of the frontier construction method chosen (DEA) and the use of finite sample sizes. If an infinite sample size were available and/or if an alternative frontier construction method was used, which involved a smooth function surface, the slack issue would disappear. In addition to this observation it also seems quite reasonable to accept the arguments of Ferrier and Lovell (1990) that slacks may essentially be viewed as allocative inefficiency. Hence we believe that an analysis of technical efficiency can reasonably concentrate upon the radial Farrell efficiency score provided in the first stage DEA LP (refer to equation 6.12). However, if one insists on identifying Koopmans-efficient projected points then we would strongly recommend the use of the multi-stage method in preference to the two-stage method for the reasons outlined above.

7.7 Empirical Application: Australian Universities

In 1996 senior management at the University of New England (UNE) formed a committee to look at the performance of UNE relative to other universities in Australia. Of particular concern to management was some evidence that suggested that UNE's administration sector appeared to be larger than some comparable universities. This committee commissioned a DEA study (see Coelli, 1996d) which looked at the relative performance of Australia's 36 universities. The study involved the construction of three separate models: one for the administration sectors; one for the academic sectors; and one for universities as a whole. To conserve space in this section we restrict our discussion of this study to the model for the administration sectors of Australian universities.

The data used in this analysis is for 36 Australian universities for the 1994 calendar year. An input-orientated VRS DEA model is used in the analysis. CRS and NIRS models are also run to investigate scale issues. An input orientation is chosen because we believe that, in 1994, universities had greater control over input quantities relative to output quantities (in particular we note that the vast majority of student load was fixed by government quotas). However, one could also argue the converse, so we also ran our models assuming an output-orientation and observed that orientation had little influence on the efficiency scores obtained in this instance.

Because of the limited number of observations available we attempted to restrict the total number of input and output variables in the analysis to ensure some degree of discretionary power remained. The model hence involved only two inputs and two outputs. The two inputs used were *expenditure on administrative staff* and *other administrative costs*. We would have preferred to use physical quantity measures but these were not available for the labour input and would be too difficult to measure in the case of the *other inputs* variable. We hypothesise that the use of the value measures are unlikely to introduce much bias in our measures because the wage levels and the prices of other administrative inputs did not vary significantly across Australian universities in 1994.

The specification of the outputs of a university administration was a challenging task. The principle role of a university administration is to keep records on staff and students. With regard to university staff, the administration is principally involved in activities such as recruitment, payroll, study leave, and keeping financial records associated with departmental budgets and research grant budgets. With regard to the students, the administration is involved in promotion, enrolment, record keeping for fees and charges, examination records, and so on. It was hence decided that the outputs of the university administrations would be proxied by two measures: the total number of students (measured in equivalent full time student units (EFTSU)) and the total number of staff (again in full-time equivalent units).

The above two-input, two-output model of university administration is an obvious simplification of reality. The variable specifications can be criticised from many angles. In an attempt to head off some of the potential criticisms we ran the model using some different variable definitions so as to assess the sensitivity of our results to different specifications. We considered three alternative models.

1. We noted that the use of EFTSU measures may underestimate the output of an administration at a university where there are a large number of part-time students. We attempt to deal with this issue by using total enrolments instead of EFTSU. This measure, however, is likely to overstate the output of those universities (like UNE) with a large part-time student population

because part-time students do fewer units per year and hence involve less record keeping.

2. There was some concern that the *total staff* output variable does not properly reflect the extra administration load that results when the academic staff at a university apply for and attract a lot of research money. In an attempt to address this issue we replaced the *total staff* output variable with a *total research grants* variable. This variable would be appropriate if the majority of service provided by the administration staff to the staff of the university involved assisting academic staff apply for grants and the administration of grant monies obtained. This is unlikely to be true, but we conducted this sensitivity to address the above criticism.

3. We ran an additional model where the above two changes were simultaneously imposed.

The DEA results of the (base-run) university administration model are listed in Table 7.3. We observe that UNE achieves a (VRS) technical efficiency score of 0.713 which ranks it 31st in 36 universities. This result appears to confirm the suspicions of the UNE management. The average technical efficiency score in the sample is 0.818 with the lowest technical efficiency score being 0.404 for Newcastle. The UNE scale efficiency score is 0.991 which indicates that UNE is operating quite close to optimal scale. From the computer printout (which is not listed) we observe that UNE's peers are Flinders, Tasmania, Ballarat and Australian National University (ANU), in order of importance. The relative weights of these peers are: 0.49, 0.41, 0.09 and 0.01, respectively. Hence Flinders and Tasmania provide 90% of the peer weighting. This information is reassuring because Flinders and Tasmania are quite similar in structure to UNE.

The three alternative DEA model specifications discussed above were also run to test the robustness of our results. The results did improve slightly for UNE (because the changes were particularly structured to do so) but it was still apparent that even under these favourable assumptions the UNE administration was still observed to have significant room for improvement.

UNE is one of the principal providers of distance education in Australia. It enrols approximately 5,000 on-campus students and 14,000 off-campus (distance education) students each year. Some observers argue that distance education students are more costly in terms of administrative requirements. In an attempt to address this issue we applied the two-stage method described in Section 7.3 to this analysis. We conducted a second-stage Tobit regression in which the VRS technical efficiency scores from our base model were regressed upon the percentage of external enrolments in each university and the average unit load of students (measured by the ratio of EFTSU to total enrolments). The results suggested that neither of these factors had a significant influence upon the efficiency scores, with the Tobit regression equation explaining less than 3% of the total variation in the technical efficiency scores.

Much more information on this analysis is provided in Coelli (1996). The additional two DEA models which looked at academic sectors and universities as a whole found that UNE was located on the frontier in these cases. This may suggest that academics have been working extra hard at UNE - a conclusion that the authors of this book are quite comfortable with!

Table 7.3 DEA Results for the Australian Universities Study

University	VRS TE	CRS TE	scale eff.	
Australian Catholic University	0.757	0.806	0.938	irs
Australian National University	1.000	1.000	1.000	-
Central Queensland University	0.499	0.557	0.896	irs
Charles Sturt University	1.000	1.000	1.000	-
Curtin University of Technology	0.700	0.702	0.997	drs
Deakin University	0.786	0.800	0.982	drs
Edith Cowan University	0.784	0.861	0.911	drs
Flinders University of South Australia	1.000	1.000	1.000	-
Griffith University	0.720	0.738	0.975	drs
James Cook University	0.725	0.757	0.958	irs
La Trobe University	0.930	0.947	0.982	drs
Macquarie University	0.770	0.778	0.990	irs
Monash University	0.728	1.000	0.728	drs
Murdoch University	0.779	0.824	0.946	irs
Northern Territory University	0.662	0.980	0.676	irs
Queensland University of Technology	0.978	1.000	0.978	drs
Royal Melbourne Institute of Tech.	0.739	0.786	0.939	drs
Southern Cross University	0.950	1.000	0.950	irs
Swinburne University of Technology	0.876	0.925	0.947	irs
University of Adelaide	0.653	0.665	0.982	drs
University of Ballarat	0.867	1.000	0.867	irs
University of Canberra	1.000	1.000	1.000	-
University of Melbourne	0.838	1.000	0.838	drs
University of New England	**0.707**	**0.713**	**0.991**	**irs**
University of New South Wales	0.745	0.930	0.801	drs
University of Newcastle	0.404	0.404	1.000	-
University of Queensland	1.000	1.000	1.000	-
University of South Australia	1.000	1.000	1.000	-
University of Southern Queensland	0.798	0.826	0.967	irs
University of Sydney	0.765	1.000	0.765	drs
University of Tasmania	1.000	1.000	1.000	-
University of Technology, Sydney	1.000	1.000	1.000	-
University of Western Australia	0.865	0.870	0.995	irs
University of Western Sydney	0.622	0.625	0.995	drs
University of Wollongong	0.882	0.892	0.989	irs
Victoria University of Technology	0.904	0.918	0.985	irs
Mean	**0.818**	**0.870**	**0.944**	

7.8 Conclusions

In this chapter we have discussed a limited number of extensions to the basic DEA models outlined in Chapter 6. A discussion of all the extensions that have been proposed in the literature would fill a number of volumes. Some additional model extensions that readers may wish to pursue include: the stochastic DEA models proposed by Land, Lovell and Sten (1993) and Olsen and Petersen (1995); the additive model proposed by Charnes, Cooper, Golany, Seiford and Stutz (1985); the DEA models in which restrictions are placed upon the shadow prices in Dyson and Thanassoulis (1988) and Wong and Beasley (1990); the attempts at developing statistical inference in DEA models which have been recently discussed in Banker (1996), Grosskopf (1996) and Simar (1996); the *Flexible Disposable Hull* (FDH) approach of Deprins, Simar and Tulkens (1984) which relaxes convexity assumptions; and the development of panel data methods, such as the window analysis method proposed by Charnes, Clark, Cooper and Golany (1985) and the Malmquist index approach of Färe, Grosskopf, Norris and Zhang (1994). The Malmquist method is discussed in some detail in Chapter 10.

For those people who wish to do further reading on DEA there are a number of useful books available. These include Färe, Grosskopf and Lovell (1985, 1994), Ganley and Cubbin (1992), Fried, Lovell and Schmidt (1993) and Charnes, Cooper, Lewin and Seiford (1995).

Before finishing with DEA it is important to quickly point out a few of the limitations and possible problems that one may encounter in conducting a DEA. These include:

- Measurement error and other noise may influence the shape and position of the frontier.

- Outliers may influence the results.

- The exclusion of an important input or output can result in biased results.

- The efficiency scores obtained are only relative to the best firms in the sample. The inclusion of extra firms (e.g., from overseas) may reduce efficiency scores.

- Be careful when comparing the mean efficiency scores from two studies. They only reflect the dispersion of efficiencies within each sample - they say nothing about the efficiency of one sample relative to the other.

- The addition of an extra firm in a DEA analysis cannot result in an increase in the TE scores of the existing firms.

- The addition of an extra input or output in a DEA model cannot result in a reduction in the TE scores.

- When one has few observations and many inputs and/or outputs many of the firms will appear on the DEA frontier.[10]

- Treating inputs and/or outputs as homogenous commodities when they are heterogenous may bias results.

- Not accounting for environmental differences may give misleading indications of relative managerial competence.

- Standard DEA does not account for multi-period optimisation nor risk in management decision making.

It should also be stressed that all of these issues are also applicable (in varying degrees) to the stochastic frontier method discussed in the following chapters. The relative merits of the two approaches are discussed at the end of Chapter 9.

---

[10] This point and the previous two points are related. One implication is that if an investigator wished to make an industry look good, he/she could reduce the sample size and increase the number of inputs and outputs in order to increase the TE scores.

8. EFFICIENCY MEASUREMENT USING STOCHASTIC FRONTIERS

8.1 Introduction

DEA and stochastic frontiers are two alternative methods for estimating frontier functions and thereby measuring efficiency of production. DEA involves the use of linear programming whereas stochastic frontiers involve the use of econometric methods.

The following literature review of stochastic frontier modelling and efficiency measurement is brief. The purpose of this chapter is to provide an introduction to the method without burdening the reader with excessive notation and technical detail. More detailed reviews are found in Førsund, Lovell and Schmidt (1980), Schmidt (1986), Bauer (1990), Battese (1992), Lovell (1993) and Greene (1993).

We begin by recalling that Farrell (1957) proposed a measure of the efficiency of a firm that consists of two components: *technical efficiency*, which reflects the ability of a firm to obtain maximal output from a given set of inputs, and *allocative efficiency*, which reflects the ability of a firm to use the inputs in optimal proportions, given their respective prices. These two measures are then combined to provide a measure of total *economic efficiency*. Formal definitions of these measures, both from an input- and an output-orientation, are presented in Chapter 6.

The above efficiency measures assume that the production function of fully efficient firms is known. Since the production function is never known in practice, Farrell (1957) suggested that the function be estimated from sample data using either a non-parametric piece-wise-linear technology or a parametric function, such as the

Cobb-Douglas form. The first suggestion was taken up by Charnes, Cooper and others, resulting in the development of the DEA approach (discussed in Chapters 6 and 7). The latter parametric approach was taken up by Aigner and others, subsequently resulting in the development of the stochastic frontier model.

Aigner and Chu (1968) considered the estimation of a parametric frontier production function of Cobb-Douglas form, using data on a sample of N firms. The model is defined by

$$\ln(y_i) = x_i\beta - u_i \qquad , i=1,2,...,N, \qquad (8.1)$$

where $\ln(y_i)$ is the logarithm of the (scalar) output for the i-th firm;

x_i is a (K+1)-row vector, whose first element is "1" and the remaining elements are the logarithms of the K-input quantities used by the i-th firm;

$\beta=(\beta_0, \beta_1, ..., \beta_K)'$ is a (K+1)-column vector of unknown parameters to be estimated; and

u_i is a non-negative random variable, associated with technical inefficiency in production of firms in the industry involved.

The ratio of the observed output for the i-th firm, relative to the potential output, defined by the frontier function, given the input vector, x_i, is used to define the technical efficiency of the i-th firm:

$$TE_i = \frac{y_i}{\exp(x_i\beta)} = \frac{\exp(x_i\beta - u_i)}{\exp(x_i\beta)} = \exp(-u_i). \qquad (8.2)$$

This measure is an output-orientated Farrell measure of technical efficiency, which takes a value between zero and one. It indicates the magnitude of the output of the i-th firm relative to the output that could be produced by a fully-efficient firm using the same input vector. The technical efficiency, defined by equation 8.2, can be estimated by the ratio of the observed output, y_i, to the estimated value of the frontier output, $\exp(x_i\beta)$, obtained by estimating β using linear programming, where $\sum_{i=1}^{N} u_i$ is minimised, subject to the constraints that $u_i \geq 0$, i=1,2,...,N.[1]

Afriat (1972) specified a model similar to that of equation 8.1, except that the u_is were assumed to have a gamma distribution and the parameters of the model were estimated using the *maximum-likelihood* (ML) method. Richmond (1974) noted that the parameters of Afriat's model could also be estimated using a method that has become known as *corrected ordinary least-squares* (COLS). This method uses the

---

[1] Aigner and Chu (1968) also suggested the use of quadratic programming to estimate β.

ordinary least-squares (OLS) estimators, which are unbiased for the slope parameters, but the (negatively biased) OLS estimator of the intercept parameter, β_0, is adjusted up, using the sample moments of the error distribution, obtained from the OLS residuals.   Schmidt (1976) pointed out that the linear and quadratic programming estimators, proposed by Aigner and Chu (1968), are ML estimators if the u_is are distributed as exponential or half-normal random variables, respectively.

One of the primary criticisms of the above *deterministic*[2] frontier model is that no account is taken of the possible influence of measurement errors and other noise upon the frontier. All deviations from the frontier are assumed to be the result of technical inefficiency. Timmer (1971) adopted the suggestion of Aigner and Chu (1968) of deleting a percentage of the sample firms closest to the estimated frontier, and re-estimated the frontier using the reduced sample. The arbitrary nature of the selection of a percentage of observations to delete, has meant that this so-called *probabilistic* frontier approach has not been widely followed.   An alternative approach to the solution of the 'noise' problem has, however, been widely adopted. This is the method known as the stochastic frontier approach.

8.2 The Stochastic Frontier Production Function

Aigner, Lovell and Schmidt (1977) and Meeusen and van den Broeck (1977) independently proposed the stochastic frontier production function, in which an additional random error, v_i, is added to the non-negative random variable, u_i, in equation 8.1 to provide:

$$\ln(y_i) = x_i\beta + v_i - u_i \qquad , i=1,2,...,N. \qquad (8.3)$$

The random error, v_i, accounts for measurement error and other random factors, such as the effects of weather, strikes, luck, etc., on the value of the output variable, together with the combined effects of unspecified input variables in the production function. Aigner, Lovell and Schmidt (1977) assumed that the v_is were independent and identically distributed (i.i.d.) normal random variables with mean zero and constant variance, σ_v^2, independent of the u_is, which were assumed to be i.i.d. exponential or half-normal random variables.

The model, defined by equation 8.3, is called the *stochastic* frontier production function because the output values are bounded above by the stochastic (random) variable, $\exp(x_i\beta + v_i)$. The random error, v_i, can be positive or negative and so the stochastic frontier outputs vary about the deterministic part of the frontier model, $\exp(x_i\beta)$.

---

[2] The term *deterministic* is used because, in the frontier model of equation (8.1), the observed output, y_i, is bounded above by the non-stochastic (i.e., deterministic) quantity, $\exp(x_i\beta)$. The models of Aigner and Chu (1968), Afriat (1972) and Schmidt (1976) are examples of deterministic frontiers.

The basic features of the stochastic frontier model are illustrated in two dimensions in Figure 8.1. The inputs are represented on the horizontal axis and the outputs on the vertical axis. The deterministic component of the frontier model, $y = \exp(x\beta)$, is drawn assuming that diminishing returns to scale apply. The observed outputs and inputs for two firms, i and j, are presented on the graph. The i-th firm uses the level of inputs, x_i, to produce the output, y_i. The observed input-output value is indicated by the point marked with × above the value of x_i. The value of the stochastic frontier output, $y_i^* \equiv \exp(x_i\beta + v_i)$, is marked by the point ⊗ above the production function because the random error, v_i, is positive. Similarly, the j-th firm uses the level of inputs, x_j, and produces the output, y_j. However, the frontier output, $y_j^* \equiv \exp(x_j\beta + v_j)$, is below the production function because the random error, v_j, is negative. Of course, the stochastic frontier outputs, y_i^* and y_j^*, are not observed because the random errors, v_i and v_j, are not observable. However, the deterministic part of the stochastic frontier model is seen to lie between the stochastic frontier outputs. The observed outputs may be greater than the deterministic part of the frontier if the corresponding random errors are greater than the corresponding inefficiency effects (i.e., $y_i > \exp(x_i\beta)$ if $v_i > u_i$).

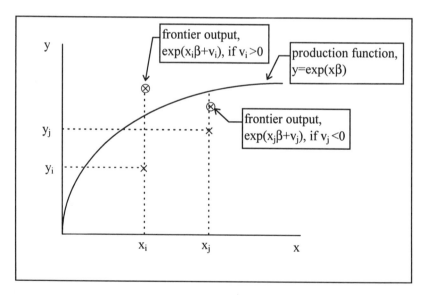

Figure 8.1: The Stochastic Frontier Production Function

This stochastic frontier model permits the estimation of standard errors and tests of hypotheses using traditional maximum-likelihood methods, which were not possible with the earlier deterministic models because of the violation of certain ML regularity conditions (refer to Schmidt 1976).[3]

The stochastic frontier model is not, however, without problems. The main criticism is that there is generally no *a priori* justification for the selection of any particular distributional form for the u_is. The specifications of more general distributional forms, such as the truncated-normal (Stevenson 1980) and the two-parameter gamma (Greene 1990), have partially alleviated this problem, but the resulting efficiency measures may still be sensitive to distributional assumptions.[4] The truncated normal distribution is discussed in Chapter 9.

8.3 Maximum-Likelihood Estimation

The parameters of the stochastic frontier production function, defined by equation 8.3, can be estimated using either the maximum-likelihood (ML) method or using a variant of the COLS method, suggested by Richmond (1974). The COLS approach is not as computationally demanding as the ML method, which requires numerical maximisation of the likelihood function. This distinction, however, has lessened in recent years with the availability of computer software, such as the LIMDEP econometrics package (Greene 1992) and the FRONTIER program (Coelli 1992, 1996a), both of which automate the ML method for estimation of the parameters of stochastic frontier models.

The ML estimator is asymptotically more efficient than the COLS estimator, but the properties of the two estimators in finite samples cannot be analytically determined. The finite-sample properties of the half-normal frontier model were investigated in a Monte Carlo experiment in Coelli (1995a), in which the ML estimator was found to be significantly better than the COLS estimator when the contribution of the technical inefficiency effects to the total variance term is large.[5] Given this result and the availability of automated ML routines, the ML estimator should be used in preference to the COLS estimator whenever possible.[6] We now discuss the basic elements of obtaining ML estimators for the parameters of the stochastic frontier model.

---

[3] Greene (1980a) observed that a particular class of distributions could be assumed for the u_i which would circumvent these regularity problems with the deterministic frontier model. However, the criticism that the model does not account for random errors would still remain.

[4] Knox Lovell suggested in a personal communication with the senior author (November 22, 1995) that he is yet to see a comparative empirical analysis in which distributional assumptions have a significant influence upon predicted technical efficiencies, discussed below.

[5] Coelli (1995a) considered 11 different values of the percentage of error due to inefficiency (γ^*), ranging from 0.0 to 1.0, in steps of 0.1, for sample sizes of N=50, 100, 400, and 800. The mean squared error of the ML estimator was significantly smaller (at the 1% level) than that for the COLS estimator for 14 of the 44 cases, while the converse occurred in only one case ($\gamma^*=0.1$, N=50).

[6] Readers interested in COLS estimation are advised to check Coelli (1995a), in which the method is discussed in more detail.

This discussion deals with the case of the half-normal distribution for the technical inefficiency effects, because it has been most frequently assumed in empirical applications. Aigner, Lovell and Schmidt (1977) derived the log-likelihood function for the model, defined by equation 8.3, in which the u_is are assumed to be i.i.d. truncations (at zero) of a $N(0,\sigma^2)$ random variable, independent of the v_is which are assumed to be i.i.d. $N(0,\sigma_V^2)$. Aigner, Lovell and Schmidt (1977) expressed the likelihood function in terms of the two variance parameters, $\sigma_S^2 \equiv \sigma^2 + \sigma_V^2$ and $\lambda \equiv \sigma/\sigma_V$. Battese and Corra (1977) suggested that the parameter, $\gamma \equiv \sigma^2/\sigma_S^2$, be used because it has a value between zero and one, whereas the λ-parameter could be any non-negative value.[7] The γ-parameterisation has advantages in seeking to obtain the ML estimates because the parameter space for γ can be searched for a suitable starting value for the iterative maximisation algorithm involved.[8] Battese and Corra (1977) showed that the log-likelihood function, in terms of this parameterisation is equal to

$$\ln(L) \;=\; -\tfrac{N}{2}\ln(\pi/2) - \tfrac{N}{2}\log(\sigma_S^2) + \sum_{i=1}^{N}\ln[1 - \Phi(z_i)] - \frac{1}{2\sigma_S^2}\sum_{i=1}^{N}(\ln y_i - x_i\beta)^2 \quad (8.4)$$

where $z_i = \dfrac{(\ln y_i - x_i\beta)}{\sigma_S}\sqrt{\dfrac{\gamma}{1-\gamma}}$; and $\Phi(.)$ is the distribution function of the standard normal random variable.

The ML estimates of β, σ_S^2 and γ are obtained by finding the maximum of the log-likelihood function, defined in equation 8.4. The ML estimators are consistent and asymptotically efficient (Aigner, Lovell and Schmidt (1977), p.28).

The computer program, FRONTIER Version 4.1, can be used to obtain the ML estimates for the parameters of this model. This program uses a three-step estimation procedure:

1. The first step involves calculation of the OLS estimators of β and σ_S^2. These are unbiased estimators of the parameters in equation 8.3, with the exception of the intercept, β_0, and σ_S^2.

2. In the second step, the likelihood function is evaluated for a number of values of γ between zero and one. In these calculations, the OLS estimates of σ_S^2 and

---

[7] A value of γ of zero indicates that the deviations from the frontier are due entirely to noise, while a value of one would indicate that all deviations are due to technical inefficiency. It should be stressed, however, that γ is not equal to the ratio of the variance of the technical inefficiency effects to the total residual variance. This is because the variance of u_i is equal to $[(\pi-2)/\pi]\sigma^2$ not σ^2. The relative contribution of the inefficiency effect to the total variance term (γ^*) is equal to $\gamma^* = \gamma/[\gamma+(1-\gamma)\pi/(\pi-2)]$. See Coelli (1995a) for more details.

[8] The γ-parameterisation also has advantages in COLS estimation, as indicated in Coelli (1995a).

β_0 are adjusted by $\sigma_S^2 = \sigma_{OLS}^2[\pi(T-K)]/[T(\pi-2\hat{\gamma})]$ and $\hat{\beta}_0 = \hat{\beta}_{0(OLS)} + \sqrt{\dfrac{2\hat{\gamma}\hat{\sigma}_S^2}{\pi}}$,

respectively. The OLS estimates are used for the remaining parameters in β.

3. The final step uses the best estimates (that is, those corresponding to the largest log-likelihood value) from the second step as starting values in a Davidon-Fletcher-Powell (DFP) iterative maximisation routine which obtains the ML estimates when the likelihood function attains its global maximum.

Approximate standard errors of the ML estimators are calculated by obtaining the square roots of the diagonal elements of the direction matrix from the final iteration of the DFP routine. The direction matrix for the final iteration is usually a good approximation for the inverse of the Hessian of the log-likelihood function, unless the DFP routine terminates after only a few iterations.

8.4 Estimation of Mean Technical Efficiency

After the stochastic frontier production function was first proposed, the parameters of the model were estimated, together with the mean technical efficiency for the firms in the industry involved, for different empirical applications involving cross-sectional data. It was initially claimed that the individual technical efficiencies of firms could not be predicted. However, this is not true. The prediction of the individual technical efficiencies is addressed in the next section.

The mathematical expectation (mean) of the technical efficiency, $TE_i = \exp(-u_i)$, can be calculated, for given distributional assumptions for the technical inefficiency effects. It can be shown that, if the u_is are i.i.d. half-normal random variables, as assumed above, then

$$E[\exp(-u_i)] = 2[1-\Phi(\sigma_S\sqrt{\gamma})]\exp(-\gamma\sigma_S^2/2). \qquad (8.5)$$

The ML estimator for the mean technical efficiency is obtained by substituting the ML estimators for the relevant parameters in equation 8.5.

Because the individual technical efficiencies of sample firms can be predicted (as shown in the next section), an alternative estimator for the mean technical efficiency is the arithmetic average of the predictors for the individual technical efficiencies of the sample firms. This is what is calculated by FRONTIER. However, the arithmetic mean may not be the best estimator when the sample firms have significantly different sizes of operations or are not obtained by a simple random sample from the population of the firms involved.

8.5 Prediction of Firm-level Technical Efficiencies

Recall that the technical efficiency of the i-th firm is defined by $TE_i = \exp(-u_i)$. This involves the technical inefficiency effect, u_i, which is unobservable. Even if the true value of the parameter vector, β, in the stochastic frontier model (8.3) was known, only the difference, $e_i \equiv v_i - u_i$, could be observed. The best predictor for u_i is the conditional expectation of u_i, given the value of v_i-u_i.[9] This result was first recognised and applied in the stochastic frontier model by Jondrow, Lovell, Materov and Schmidt (1982), who derived the result[10]

$$E[u_i|e_i] = -\gamma e_i + \sigma_A \{\frac{\phi(\gamma e_i / \sigma_A)}{1 - \Phi(\gamma e_i / \sigma_A)}\} \tag{8.6}$$

where $\sigma_A = \sqrt{\gamma(1-\gamma)\sigma_S^2}$; $e_i = \ln(y_i) -x_i\beta$; and $\phi(.)$ is the density function of a standard normal random variable.

An operational predictor of u_i involves replacing the unknown parameters in equation 8.6 with the ML (or COLS) estimators. Jondrow, et al. (1982) suggested that the technical efficiency of the i-th firm be predicted using $1-E[u_i|e_i]$.[11] Other researchers predicted the technical efficiency, $\exp(-u_i)$, by substituting u_i with the predictor associated with equation 8.6. Battese and Coelli (1988) point out that the best predictor of $\exp(-u_i)$ is obtained by using

$$E[\exp(-u_i)|e_i] = \frac{1- \Phi(\sigma_A + \gamma e_i / \sigma_A)}{1- \Phi(\gamma e_i / \sigma_A)} \exp(\gamma e_i + \sigma_A^2 / 2) . \tag{8.7}$$

This predictor gives a different value from that which uses equation 8.6 to predict u_i in $\exp(-u_i)$. This is a special case of the general result that the expectation of a non-linear function of a random variable is not equal to the function of the expectation of the random variable {i.e., $E[g(x)] \neq g(E[x])$ for a non-linear function, $g(.)$}. The technical efficiency predictor implemented in the FRONTIER computer program is obtained by replacing the unknown parameters in equation 8.7 with their ML estimates.

8.6 Tests of Hypotheses

For the frontier model, defined by equation 8.3, the null hypothesis, that there are no technical inefficiency effects in the model, can be conducted by testing the null and

---

[9] This result is related to the Rao-Blackwell theorem, see Rao (1973, p.121).

[10] The following expression is in terms of γ whereas the expression in Jondrow et al. (1982) is in terms of the parameter, λ.

[11] The rationale for this predictor is that $1-u_i$ is a first-order approximation to the infinite-series, $\exp(-u_i)$ = $1-u_i + u_i^2/2 - u_i^3/3! - ....$

alternative hypotheses, H_0: $\sigma^2=0$ versus H_1: $\sigma^2>0$.[12] This hypothesis can be tested using a number of different test statistics. The Wald statistic involves the ratio of the ML estimator for σ^2 to its estimated standard error. This statistic, or a slight variant of it, has been explicitly or implicitly conducted in almost every empirical analysis involving the stochastic frontier model since the first application by Aigner, Lovell and Schmidt (1977). In applying the model in the analysis of data from the US primary metals industry, Aigner, Lovell and Schmidt (1977) found that the Wald statistic was a small (insignificant) value. In many cases, one of the equivalent sets of hypotheses, H_0:$\lambda=0$ versus H_1:$\lambda>0$, or H_0:$\gamma=0$ versus H_1:$\gamma>0$, is considered, depending upon the parameterisation used in estimation of the stochastic frontier model. Because we have adopted the Battese and Corra (1977) parameterisation, the hypotheses involving γ are considered here.

For the Wald test, the ratio of the estimate for γ to its estimated standard error is calculated. If H_0:$\gamma=0$ is true, this statistic is asymptotically distributed as a standard normal random variable. However, the test must be performed as a one-sided test because γ cannot take negative values.

Using a Monte Carlo study, Coelli (1995a) concluded that the Wald test has very poor size (i.e., probability of a Type I error) properties. For example, for a sample of 100 observations, the Wald test of desired size, $\alpha=0.05$, was observed to reject the null hypothesis 20% of times (instead of the required 5%). Coelli (1995) suggested that the one-sided generalised likelihood-ratio test should be performed when ML estimation is involved because this test has the correct size. This test is now briefly discussed.

One-sided Generalised Likelihood-Ratio Test

The generalised likelihood-ratio test requires the estimation of the model under both the null and alternate hypotheses. Under the null hypothesis, H_0:$\gamma=0$, the model is equivalent to the traditional average response function, without the technical inefficiency effect, u_i. The test statistic is calculated as

$$LR = -2\{\ln[L(H_0)/L(H_1)]\} = -2\{\ln[L(H_0)] - \ln[L(H_1)]\} \qquad (8.8)$$

where $L(H_0)$ and $L(H_1)$ are the values of the likelihood function under the null and alternative hypotheses, H_0 and H_1, respectively.

If H_0 is true, this test statistic is usually assumed to be asymptotically distributed as a chi-square random variable with degrees of freedom equal to the number of restrictions involved (in this instance one). However, difficulties arise in testing

---

[12] Recall that σ^2 is the variance of the normal distribution which is truncated at zero to obtain the distribution of u_i. If this variance is zero, then all the u_is are zero, implying that all firms are fully efficient.

$H_0:\gamma=0$ because $\gamma=0$ lies on the boundary of the parameter space for γ. In this case, if $H_0:\gamma=0$ is true, the generalised likelihood-ratio statistic, LR, has asymptotic distribution which is a mixture of chi-square distributions, namely $\frac{1}{2}\chi_0^2 + \frac{1}{2}\chi_1^2$, (Coelli 1995a).[13]

The calculation of the critical value for this one-sided generalised likelihood-ratio test of $H_0:\gamma=0$ versus $H_1:\gamma>0$ is quite simple. The critical value for a test of size α is equal to the value, $\chi_1^2(2\alpha)$, where this is the value which is exceeded by the χ_1^2 random variable with probability equal to 2α. Thus the one-sided generalised likelihood-ratio test of size α is: "Reject $H_0:\gamma=0$ in favour of $H_1:\gamma>0$ if LR exceeds $\chi_1^2(2\alpha)$". Thus the critical value for a test of size, $\alpha=0.05$, is 2.71 rather than 3.84.[14]

8.7 A Simple Numerical Example

The purpose of this section is to illustrate the estimation of a stochastic frontier production function using a simple numerical example. Unfortunately we cannot use a simple 5 observation data set to do this (as done in the DEA chapters) because the estimation method requires a reasonable number of observations to be able to estimate the production parameters and variance parameters successfully. Thus, in our illustration we consider the data from the study by Whiteman and Pearson (1993). These data were from telecommunications providers in 21 countries in 1990. Whiteman and Pearson (1993) used DEA methods to benchmark Telecom Australia (now Telstra) against world practise. The analysis involved a single output (based on revenue) and two inputs: capital (measured by kilometres of mainlines) and labour (number of employees). These data are reproduced below in Table 8.1. For more detail on the data, see Whiteman and Pearson (1993).

A Cobb-Douglas stochastic frontier production function was estimated using these data.

Stochastic Frontier Estimation using the Computer

Stochastic frontiers can be estimated using a variety of computer programs. If you are familiar with non-linear numerical optimisation methods then all you need is access to computer software that can accommodate these optimisation methods. For example, one could use the numerical optimisation routines in statistical software such as SAS or GAUSS, or one could code the methods directly using a computing language, such as C or Fortran. Alternatively, one can use a computer program which has stochastic frontier estimation routines ready to use. The LIMDEP

---

[13] Note that χ_0^2 is the unit mass at zero.

[14] The regular (two-sided) generalised likelihood-ratio test was included in the Monte Carlo experiment in Coelli (1995) and shown to have incorrect size (too small), as expected.

econometrics software and the FRONTIER computer program are two such programs. We will use FRONTIER Version 4.1 in this book because it is the software we are familiar with. A brief description of the FRONTIER computer program is provided in the Appendix. Contact addresses for all computer software mentioned in this book are listed in the Appendix.

Table 8.1 Data on Telecommunications Providers in 21 Countries in 1990

Country	Output Index	Mainlines (M km)	Employees (10^5 persons)
Australia	0.74	0.7767	0.85
Austria	0.24	0.3223	0.18
Belgium	0.36	0.399	0.26
Canada	1.26	1.5296	1.05
Denmark	0.39	0.2911	0.18
Finland	0.29	0.267	0.2
France	2.06	2.8085	1.56
Germany	1.73	2.9981	2.12
Iceland	0.02	0.0126	0.02
Ireland	0.11	0.0983	0.13
Italy	1.48	2.235	1.18
Japan	2.73	5.3236	2.77
Netherlands	0.77	0.694	0.32
New Zealand	0.16	0.1473	0.17
Norway	0.27	0.2132	0.15
Portugal	0.19	0.2379	0.23
Spain	0.59	1.2603	0.75
Sweden	0.71	0.5849	0.42
Switzerland	0.56	0.3943	0.22
Turkey	0.15	0.6893	0.36
UK	2.53	2.5404	2.27

The FRONTIER program is used in a similar way to the TFPIP and DEAP computer program described in Chapters 4 and 6, respectively. To calculate a Cobb-Douglas stochastic production frontier applied to the above sample data using the FRONTIER program the user must construct a data file and an instruction file. The data file for this example, EXA1.DTA, (refer to Table 8.2a) contains five columns each with 21 observations. The first two columns contain an integer for firm number and year number, respectively.[15] The logs of the output quantities are then listed in the third column and the logs of the two inputs are listed in the final two columns of this data file.[16]

---

[15] Note that the year number will be everywhere equal to "1" when cross-sectional data is used.
[16] The frontier program will estimate models which are linear in parameters. Hence to estimate a Cobb-Douglas production frontier we must supply the logs of the sample data to the program. This data file

The instruction file, EXA1.INS, is listed in Table 8.2b. The purpose of the majority of entries in the file should be self explanatory, due to the comments on the right-hand side of the file.[17] On the first line of this file one selects between two types of model specifications. The model that is required in this example can be estimated using either specification. Hence we arbitrarily select model "1".[18] The next two lines of the file contain the name of the data file (EXA1.DTA) and an output file name (here we have used EXA1.OUT). On the following two lines we specify that a production function will be estimated and that it will have a logged dependent variable. Then on the next four lines we specify the number of firms (21); number of time periods (1);[19] the total number of observations (21); and number of regressor variables (2). The remaining lines of this instruction file refer to parameters of models which will be discussed in the following chapter.

Finally we execute FRONTIER and type in the name of the instruction file (EXA1.INS). The program sends the output to the file that is named (EXA1.OUT). This file is reproduced in Table 8.2c.

Table 8.2a Listing of Data File, EXA1.DTA

```
1.000000    1.000000    -.3011051    -.2527011    -.1625189
2.000000    1.000000    -1.427116    -1.132272    -1.714798
3.000000    1.000000    -1.021651    -.9187939    -1.347074
4.000000    1.000000     .2311117     .4250063     .4879016E-01
5.000000    1.000000    -.9416085    -1.234088    -1.714798
6.000000    1.000000    -1.237874    -1.320507    -1.609438
7.000000    1.000000     .7227060    1.032651      .4446858
8.000000    1.000000     .5481214    1.097979      .7514161
9.000000    1.000000    -3.912023    -4.374058    -3.912023
10.00000    1.000000    -2.207275    -2.319731    -2.040221
11.00000    1.000000     .3920421     .8042412      .1655144
12.00000    1.000000    1.004302     1.672150     1.018847
13.00000    1.000000    -.2613648    -.3652833    -1.139434
14.00000    1.000000    -1.832581    -1.915284    -1.771957
15.00000    1.000000    -1.309333    -1.545525    -1.897120
16.00000    1.000000    -1.660731    -1.435905    -1.469676
17.00000    1.000000    -.5276327     .2313498    -.2876821
18.00000    1.000000    -.3424903    -.5363144    -.8675006
19.00000    1.000000    -.5798185    -.9306432    -1.514128
20.00000    1.000000    -1.897120    -.3720787    -1.021651
21.00000    1.000000     .9282193     .9323215      .8197798
```

has been constructed from the original data listed in Table 8.1 using SHAZAM. It could alternatively be constructed using any number of spreadsheet or statistics packages.

[17] It should be mentioned that the comments in this instruction file are not read by the program.

[18] These two alternative model specifications are discussed in some detail in the following chapter.

[19] Note that the number of time periods will always be equal to 1 when using cross-sectional data.

Table 8.2b Listing of Instruction File, EXA1.INS

```
1               1=ERROR COMPONENTS MODEL, 2=TE EFFECTS MODEL
exa1.dta         DATA FILE NAME
exa1.out         OUTPUT FILE NAME
1               1=PRODUCTION FUNCTION, 2=COST FUNCTION
y               LOGGED DEPENDENT VARIABLE (Y/N)
21              NUMBER OF CROSS-SECTIONS
1               NUMBER OF TIME PERIODS
21              NUMBER OF OBSERVATIONS IN TOTAL
2               NUMBER OF REGRESSOR VARIABLES (Xs)
n               MU (Y/N) [OR DELTA0 (Y/N) IF USING TE EFFECTS MODEL]
n               ETA (Y/N) [OR NUMBER OF TE EFFECTS REGRESSORS (Zs)]
n               STARTING VALUES (Y/N)
                IF YES THEN   BETA0
                              BETA1 TO
                              BETAK
                              SIGMA SQUARED
                              GAMMA
                              MU           [OR DELTA0
                              ETA           DELTA1 TO
                                            DELTAP]

                NOTE: IF YOU ARE SUPPLYING STARTING VALUES
                AND YOU HAVE RESTRICTED MU [OR DELTA0] TO BE
                ZERO THEN YOU SHOULD NOT SUPPLY A STARTING
                VALUE FOR THIS PARAMETER.
```

Table 8.2c Listing of Output File, EXA1.OUT

```
Output from the program FRONTIER (Version 4.1)

instruction file = exa1.ins
data file =        exa1.dta

Error Components Frontier (see B&C 1992)
The model is a production function
The dependent variable is logged


the ols estimates are :

                  coefficient    standard-error    t-ratio

   beta 0     -0.16368920E+00  0.17166988E+00  -0.95351152E+00
   beta 1      0.63271608E+00  0.29752595E+00   0.21265913E+01
   beta 2      0.22442639E+00  0.34443920E+00   0.65157042E+00
   sigma-squared 0.15973407E+00

log likelihood function =   -0.89195549E+01

the estimates after the grid search were :

   beta 0          0.23812805E+00
   beta 1          0.63271608E+00
```

```
  beta 2           0.22442639E+00
  sigma-squared    0.29837202E+00
  gamma            0.85000000E+00
  mu is restricted to be zero
  eta is restricted to be zero


 iteration =        0  func evals =        19  llf = -0.68917969E+01
        0.23812805E+00 0.63271608E+00 0.22442639E+00 0.29837202E+00
 0.85000000E+00
 gradient step
 iteration =        5  func evals =        51  llf = -0.58979038E+01
        0.18163692E+00 0.74980065E+00 0.93355845E-01 0.27060056E+00
 0.98648703E+00
 iteration =        8  func evals =        95  llf = -0.39795685E+01
        0.17030195E+00 0.96842667E+00-0.10016864E+00 0.28656073E+00
 0.99999998E+00


the final mle estimates are :

                   coefficient       standard-error      t-ratio

  beta 0           0.17030195E+00  0.84007595E-01  0.20272209E+01
  beta 1           0.96842667E+00  0.21660728E+00  0.44708869E+01
  beta 2          -0.10016864E+00  0.19773237E+00 -0.50658694E+00
  sigma-squared    0.28656073E+00  0.77963209E-01  0.36755892E+01
  gamma            0.99999998E+00  0.26218111E-01  0.38141573E+02
  mu is restricted to be zero
  eta is restricted to be zero

log likelihood function =  -0.39795691E+01

LR test of the one-sided error =   0.98799718E+01
with number of restrictions = 1
[note that this statistic has a mixed chi-square distribution]

number of iterations =        8

(maximum number of iterations set at :   100)

number of cross-sections =       21

number of time periods =       1

total number of observations =       21

thus there are:      0  obsns not in the panel


covariance matrix :

  0.70572760E-02 -0.13149134E-01  0.13715549E-01  0.58248810E-03
 0.11492828E-04
 -0.13149134E-01  0.46918715E-01 -0.41490025E-01  0.10554259E-02
 0.17695505E-02
  0.13715549E-01 -0.41490025E-01  0.39098091E-01 -0.62023776E-03 -
 0.17906607E-02
  0.58248810E-03  0.10554259E-02 -0.62023776E-03  0.60782620E-02
 0.23163596E-03
  0.11492828E-04  0.17695505E-02 -0.17906607E-02  0.23163596E-03
 0.68738932E-03
```

```
technical efficiency estimates :


      firm                    eff.-est.

        1                 0.78429986E+00
        2                 0.51034694E+00
        3                 0.64590491E+00
        4                 0.70759001E+00
        5                 0.91525214E+00
        6                 0.74783198E+00
        7                 0.66824584E+00
        8                 0.54322897E+00
        9                 0.78801944E+00
       10                 0.71501360E+00
       11                 0.58243999E+00
       12                 0.50494888E+00
       13                 0.82526378E+00
       14                 0.72211899E+00
       15                 0.84118873E+00
       16                 0.55561500E+00
       17                 0.38643304E+00
       18                 0.92283260E+00
       19                 0.99947125E+00
       20                 0.16374771E+00
       21                 0.93908298E+00

mean efficiency =    0.68899413E+00
```

The first results listed in Table 8.2c are the OLS estimates for the parameters of the model. These results assume that there are no technical inefficiency effects (i.e., the term u_i is not included in equation 8.3). Note that the OLS estimators of β_1 and β_2 (the capital and labour elasticities) are unbiased but the OLS estimators of the intercept, β_0, and the variance parameter, σ_s^2, are biased. (Although FRONTIER refers to the variance parameter as 'sigma-squared', what is actually estimated is σ_s^2, which is the sum of σ_v^2 and σ^2.)

These OLS estimates are used as starting values in the iterative process to obtain the ML estimates. The program does this in two steps. It firstly conducts a grid search over values of γ between 0 and 1 and chooses that value of γ which gives the largest value of the log-likelihood function. The grid search values obtained are presented in the output.[20] The next step involves using these estimates as starting values in an iterative maximisation routine. Intermediate information is printed by the program every five iterations, and the ML estimates are listed after this.[21]

Observe that the estimate of γ is 1.000, correct to the third digit behind the decimal place, and the estimated standard error is 0.026, correct to two significant

---

[20] Note that the output file refers to mu (μ) and eta (η) being set to zero. These parameters relate to a more general model specification which is discussed in Chapter 9.

[21] Observe that the labour elasticity is negative. One would normally expect production elasticities to be between 0 and 1 in value. We note, however, that the estimate is not significantly different from zero. It is interesting to note that significance information like this is not available when DEA is used.

digits. These results indicate that the vast majority of residual variation is due to the inefficiency effect, u_i, and that the random error, v_i, is approximately zero. We also observe that the one-sided generalised likelihood-ratio test of $\gamma=0$ provides a statistic of 9.88 which exceeds the 5% critical value of 2.71 (refer to Section 8.6). Hence the traditional average response function is not an adequate representation of the data. However, it appears that the stochastic frontier model is not significantly different from the deterministic frontier model with no random error included.

The predicted technical efficiencies are listed at the bottom of Table 8.2c. We observe that Australia (Country No. 1) has a technical efficiency score of 0.784, which exceeds the industry average of 0.689, but that this is less than the scores of 0.825 for The Netherlands (No. 13), 0.841 for Norway (No. 15), 0.915 for Denmark (No. 5). 0.923 for Sweden (No. 18), 0.939 for the UK (No. 21) and 0.999 for Switzerland (No. 19). The geographical differences (in particular, in population density) between Australia and Switzerland suggest that the inclusion of some environmental variables into this study may be important.

8.8 Conclusions

In this chapter the basics of frontier production functions are outlined. The subtraction of the non-negative random variable, u_i, from the right-hand side of the deterministic production function, $\ln(y_i)=x_i\beta$, is an important feature of the modelling of observed outputs which are associated with the *technical inefficiency of production*. The addition of the random error, v_i, to the model yields the *stochastic frontier* production function model, which accounts for the presence of measurement error in the output or the combined effects of unspecified explanatory variables in the production function.

Extensions of the basic stochastic frontier model are discussed in the next chapter.

9. ADDITIONAL TOPICS ON STOCHASTIC FRONTIERS

9.1 Introduction

The discussion in Chapter 8 focused upon a stochastic frontier model with the following characteristics:

- the technical inefficiency effects, u_i, had half-normal distribution;
- it specified a Cobb-Douglas functional form;
- it was a *production* function; and
- it involved cross-sectional data.

We now consider stochastic frontier models in which one or more of these characteristics are altered.

9.2 Truncated-Normal Distribution

A common criticism of the stochastic frontier method is that there is no *a priori* justification for the selection of any particular distributional form for the technical inefficiency effects, u_i. The half-normal and the exponential distributions are arbitrary selections. Since both of these distributions have a mode at zero, it implies that there is the highest probability that the inefficiency effects are in the neighbourhood of zero. This, in turn, implies relatively high technical efficiency. In practice, it may be possible to have a few very efficient firms, but a lot of quite inefficient firms.

A few researchers attempted to address this criticism by specifying more general distributional forms, such as the truncated-normal (Stevenson, 1980) and the two-parameter gamma (Greene, 1990) distributions for the technical inefficiency effects. These two distributions allow for a wider range of distributional shapes (including ones with non-zero modes), but this comes at the cost of computational complexity. The truncated-normal model appears to suffer from fewer computational problems than the gamma distribution. The generalised truncated-normal distribution is implemented in both LIMDEP and FRONTIER. We now consider this model in more detail.

The truncated-normal distribution is a generalisation of the half-normal distribution. It is obtained by the truncation at zero of the normal distribution with mean, μ, and variance, σ^2. If μ is pre-assigned to be zero, then the distribution is the half-normal. The distribution may take a variety of shapes, depending upon the size and sign of μ. This is illustrated in Figure 9.1, where truncated-normal distributions are plotted for $\sigma^2=1$, and $\mu = -2, -1, 0, 1$ and 2.

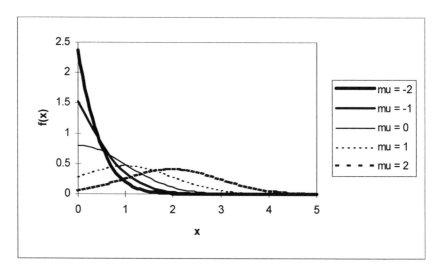

Figure 9.1 Truncated Normal Distributions

Estimation of the truncated-normal stochastic frontier involves the estimation of the parameter, μ, together with the other parameters of the model. The log-likelihood function required for the ML estimation of the parameters of the model was first given by Stevenson (1980). Expressions for appropriate predictors of the technical efficiencies of firms were given in Battese and Coelli (1988).

A number of applied studies on stochastic frontier production functions have tested the null hypothesis that the simpler half-normal model is an adequate representation of the data, given the specifications of the generalised truncated-normal model.[1] This is done by testing the null hypothesis, $H_0:\mu=0$. This can be easily conducted using either a Wald or a generalised likelihood-ratio test.

One-sided generalised likelihood-ratio test

The one-sided generalised likelihood-ratio test, recommended in Chapter 8, to test the null hypothesis that there are no technical inefficiency effects in the half-normal model, can be extended for use in the truncated-normal model. If the null hypothesis, that there are no technical inefficiency effects in the model, is true, then the generalised likelihood-ratio statistic is asymptotically distributed as a mixture of chi-square distributions. The critical value for this mixed chi-square distribution is 5.138 for a five per cent level of significance. This value is smaller than the upper five per cent point for the χ_2^2-distribution, 5.99, which has been used as the critical value in several papers, e.g., Battese and Coelli (1988). The critical value, 5.138, is taken from Table 1 in Kodde and Palm (1986). For more on the use of this test in stochastic frontier models, see Coelli and Battese (1996).

9.3 Alternative Functional Forms

The Cobb-Douglas functional form has been commonly used in the empirical estimation of frontier models. Its simplicity is a very attractive feature. A logarithmic transformation provides a model which is linear in the logarithms of the inputs and, hence, the Cobb-Douglas form is easy to estimate. This simplicity, however, is associated with a number of restrictive properties. As stated in Chapter 2, the Cobb-Douglas production function has constant input elasticities and returns to scale for all firms in the sample. Further, the elasticities of substitution for the Cobb-Douglas function are equal to one.

A number of alternative functional forms have also been used in the frontier literature. The two most popular alternative forms are the translog (e.g., Greene, 1980b) and the Zellner-Revankar generalised production function (e.g., Førsund and Hjalmarsson, 1979; and Kumbhakar, Ghosh and McGuckin, 1991). The Zellner-Revankar form removes the returns-to-scale restriction, while the translog form imposes no restrictions upon returns to scale or substitution possibilities, but has the drawback of being susceptible to multicollinearity and degrees of freedom problems. These problems can be avoided by using systems estimators, but these are more complex to compute and also have other problems which are discussed in the following section.

A number of studies have estimated both the Cobb-Douglas and the translog functional forms and then tested the null hypothesis that the Cobb-Douglas form is an adequate representation of the data, given the specifications of the translog

---

[1] Frequently, the test statistic has been significant, e.g., see Battese and Coelli (1988, 1992).

model. This can be tested by using the generalised likelihood-ratio test. For more on the generalised likelihood-ratio test, see Griffiths, Hill and Judge (1993, p.455).

9.4 Panel Data Models

The above discussion assumes that cross-sectional data on N firms are available for the estimation of the parameters of the stochastic frontier. If a number of firms are observed over a number of time periods, then the data obtained are known as *panel data*. Panel data have some advantages over cross-sectional data in the estimation of stochastic frontier models. The availability of panel data generally implies that there are a larger number of degrees of freedom for estimation of parameters. More importantly, panel data permit the simultaneous investigation of both technical change and technical efficiency change over time, given that technical change is defined by an appropriate parametric model and the technical inefficiency effects in the stochastic frontier model are stochastic and have the specified distribution.

Pitt and Lee (1981) specified a panel-data version of the Aigner, Lovell and Schmidt (1977) half-normal model:

$$\ln(y_{it}) = x_{it}\beta + v_{it} - u_{it} \qquad , i=1,2,...,N; \ t=1,2,...,T; \qquad (9.1)$$

where y_{it} denotes the output for the i-th firm at the t-th time period;

x_{it} denotes a $(1 \times K)$ vector of values of inputs and other appropriate variables associated with a suitable functional form (e.g., the Cobb-Douglas model);

β is a $(K \times 1)$ vector of unknown scalar parameters to be estimated;

the v_{it}s are random errors, assumed to be i.i.d. and have $N(0, \sigma_v^2)$-distribution, independent of the u_{it}s; and

the u_{it}s are the technical inefficiency effects in the model.

Different cases were assumed for the distribution of the u_{it}s in the panel-data model. The first basic model specified that they were i.i.d. random variables, which implies that there are no particular advantages in obtaining additional observations on a given firm versus obtaining observations on more firms at particular time periods. The second basic model assumed that the technical inefficiency effects were time-invariant,

$$u_{it} = u_i \qquad ,i=1,2,...,N; \ t=1,2,...,T. \qquad (9.2)$$

Battese and Coelli (1988) extended this model so that the u_is had the generalised truncated-normal distribution, originally proposed by Stevenson (1980). Battese, Coelli and Colby (1989) further extended the model to permit unbalanced panel data. The assumption that technical inefficiency effects are time-invariant is more difficult to justify as T becomes larger. One would expect that managers learn from their previous experience in the production process and so their technical inefficiency effects would change in some persistent pattern over time.

Kumbhakar (1990) suggested a stochastic frontier model for panel data, in which the technical inefficiency effects vary systematically with time, according to the time-varying specification,

$$u_{it} = [1 + \exp(bt + ct^2)]^{-1} u_i, \tag{9.3}$$

where the u_is were assumed to have half-normal distribution and b and c are unknown parameters to be estimated. Kumbhakar (1990) suggested that the model be estimated using ML estimation but no empirical application has yet been attempted. Battese and Coelli (1992) suggested an alternative to the Kumbhakar (1990) model, in which the u_{it}s are assumed to be an exponential function of time, involving only one unknown parameter. This model is discussed in more detail in Section 9.5 below.

Schmidt and Sickles (1984) observe that when panel data are available there is no need to specify a particular distribution for the inefficiency effects, because the parameters of the model can be estimated using the traditional panel data methods of fixed-effects estimation (dummy variables) or error-components estimation.[2] In the fixed-effects approach, the largest estimated firm intercept is used to estimate the intercept parameter so that all firm effects are estimated to be zero or negative. Measures of the technical efficiencies of the sample firms are obtained relative to the most efficient firm(s).

The use of traditional panel data methods in stochastic frontier estimation has certain advantages and disadvantages relative to the more commonly used ML methods. One criticism that can be levelled at the traditional panel data approaches (and all other COLS-type methods) is that the inefficient and efficient firms both have equivalent influence upon the shape of the estimated frontier, whereas the most efficient firms have a greater influence upon the shape of the estimated frontier when ML estimation is used. However, one advantage of the traditional panel data methods is that if one has strong reasons to believe that the inefficiency effects and the regressors are not independent then the fixed-effects panel data model can accommodate this case (while the ML methods assume that the inefficiency effects and the regressors are independent).

Cornwell, Schmidt and Sickles (1990) and Lee and Schmidt (1993) proposed generalisations of the Schmidt and Sickles (1984) model to account for time-varying inefficiency effects. Cornwell, Schmidt and Sickles (1990) specified that the intercept parameters for different firms in different time periods were a quadratic

---

[2] See Griffiths, Hill and Judge (1993) for discussion on these methods.

function of time, in which the time variables have firm-specific parameters. Lee and Schmidt (1993) specified that the technical inefficiency effects for firms in different time periods were defined by the product of individual firm and time effects. The models for temporal variation of the firm effects, proposed by Cornwell, Schmidt and Sickles (1990) and Lee and Schmidt (1993), are more flexible than the Kumbhakar (1990) and Battese and Coelli (1992) models, however, this comes with the cost of having many more parameters to estimate.

Stochastic frontier methods have been used with panel data to calculate Malmquist indices of TFP growth, along with the technical change and technical inefficiency change components. For more on this, see Grosskopf (1993, pp.186-9) and the discussion in Chapter 10.

9.5 Time-varying Inefficiency Model

Battese and Coelli (1992) proposed a time-varying model for the technical inefficiency effects in the stochastic frontier production function for panel data (equation 9.1). The technical inefficiency effects are assumed to be defined by

$$u_{it} = \{\exp[-\eta(t-T)]\}u_i \, , \, i=1, 2, \, ..., \, N; \, t=1, 2, \, ..., \, T; \tag{9.4}$$

where the u_is are assumed to be i.i.d. as the generalised truncated-normal random variable, defined in Section 9.2;[3] and η is an unknown scalar parameter to be estimated.

In the specification of equation (9.4), if the i-th firm is observed in the last period of the panel, period T, then $u_{iT} = u_i$, because the exponential function, $\exp[-\eta(t-T)]$, has value one when $t=T$. Thus the random variable, u_i, can be considered as the technical inefficiency effect for the i-th firm in the last period of the panel. For earlier periods in the panel, the technical efficiency effects are the product of the technical inefficiency effect for the i-th firm at the last period of the panel and the value of the exponential function, $\exp[-\eta(t-T)]$, whose value depends on the parameter, η, and the number of periods before the last period of the panel, $-(t-T) \equiv T-t$. If the parameter, η, is positive , then $-\eta(t-T) \equiv \eta(T-t)$ is non-negative and so $\exp[-\eta(t-T)]$ is no smaller than one, which implies that $u_{it} \geq u_i$. Conversely, if $\eta < 0$, then $-\eta(t-T) \leq 0$ and so $u_{it} \leq u_i$.

Another feature of the time-varying inefficiency model of equation (9.4) is that the technical inefficiency effects of different firms at any given time period, t, are equal to *same* exponential function, $\exp[-\eta(t-T)] \equiv \exp[\eta(T-t)]$, of the corresponding firm-specific inefficiency effects at the last period of the panel (the u_is). This implies that the ordering of the firms according to the magnitude of the technical

---

[3] The inefficiency effect, u_i, is the non-negative truncation of the $N(\mu, \sigma^2)$-distribution.

inefficiency effects is the same at all time periods. Thus the time-varying model of equation (9.4) does not account for situations in which some firms may be relatively inefficient initially but become relatively more efficient in subsequent periods.[4]

The basic features of the time-varying inefficiency model of equation (9.4) are presented in Figure 9.2, in which the two situations of decreasing and increasing technical inefficiency effects are depicted. In each case, the lines which give the values of the technical inefficiency effects at different time periods are given for two firms, whose technical inefficiency effects at the last period of the panel (period 10) are 0.4 and 0.3. In both cases, the absolute value of the η-parameter is specified to be 0.1.

In the case of the declining technical inefficiency effects, the two exponential lines decline monotonically towards their values at the last period of the panel, but the differences between the values also decrease. In the case of the increasing technical inefficiency effects, the two exponential lines increase monotonically towards their respective values at the last period of the panel, but the differences between the lines increase.

A special case of the time-varying inefficiency model of equation (9.4) is the time-invariant model, which arises when $\eta=0$. Thus it may be of interest to test the null hypothesis of no change in the technical inefficiency effects over time, H_0: $\eta=0$, given the specifications of the time-varying inefficiency model.

A composite null hypothesis which may also be of interest is H_0: $\eta=\mu=0$, which specifies that the stochastic frontier has time-invariant inefficiency effects with half-normal distribution, given the specifications of the general frontier model, defined by equations 9.1 and 9.4.

Battese and Coelli (1992) presented the logarithm of the likelihood function for the stochastic frontier model (9.1) with time-varying inefficiency effects (9.4), together with the first partial derivatives of the log-likelihood function, in the Appendix of the paper. The ML estimators of the parameters of this stochastic frontier model can be obtained by specifying in the *instruction file* for FRONTIER that "Model 1" is to be estimated.[5] FRONTIER calculates the predicted technical efficiencies for sample firms in all the time periods for which they are observed.

One of the advantages of the time-varying inefficiency model (9.4) is that the technical inefficiency changes over time can be distinguished from technical change, provided the latter is appropriately specified in the vector, x_{it}, in the frontier function (9.1). This discrimination of technical change and technical inefficiency change over

---

[4] The Cornwell, Schmidt and Sickles (1990) and the Lee and Schmidt (1993) specifications do accommodate this possibility.

[5] In FRONTIER, this model is called the "error components model", which may cause some confusion for those readers who have some knowledge of the random-effects (or error-components) models in the panel-data literature.

time is only possible given that the technical inefficiency effects are stochastic and have the specified distributions.

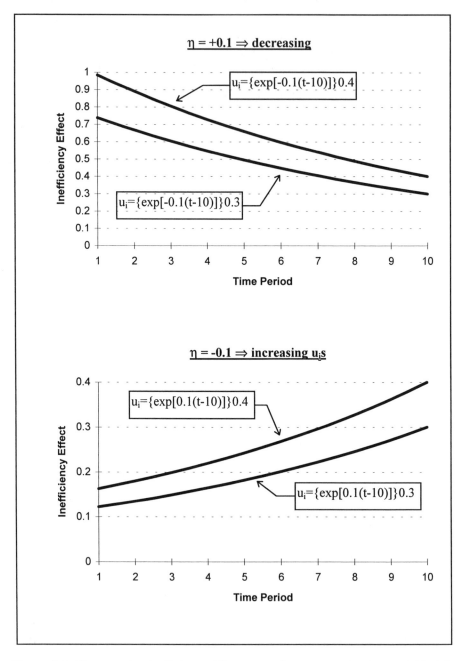

Figure 9.2: Time-varying Inefficiency Effects in the Battese and Coelli (1992) Model

9.6 Modeling Inefficiency Effects

A number of empirical studies (e.g., Pitt and Lee, 1981; and Kalirajan, 1981) have investigated the determinants of technical inefficiencies among firms in an industry by regressing the predicted inefficiency effects, obtained from an estimated stochastic frontier, upon a vector of firm-specific factors, such as firm size, age and education of the manager, etc., in a second-stage analysis. There is, however, a significant problem with this two-stage approach. In the first stage, the inefficiency effects are assumed to be independently and *identically* distributed in order to use the approach of Jondrow, et al. (1982) to predict the values of the technical inefficiency effects. However, in the second stage, the predicted inefficiency effects are assumed to be a function of a number of firm-specific factors, which implies that they are *not* identically distributed, unless all the coefficients of the factors are simultaneously equal to zero.

Kumbhakar, Ghosh and McGuckin (1991) and Reifschneider and Stevenson (1991) noted this inconsistency and specified stochastic frontier models in which the inefficiency effects were defined to be explicit functions of some firm-specific factors, and all parameters were estimated in a single-stage ML procedure. Huang and Liu (1994) also presented a model for a stochastic frontier production function, in which the technical inefficiency effects were specified to be a function of some firm-specific factors, together with their interactions with the input variables of the frontier function. Battese and Coelli (1995) extended these approaches to accommodate panel data, which permits the estimation of the parameters of the factors believed to influence the levels of the technical inefficiency effects, together with the separate components of technical inefficiency change and technical change over time. This model specification is also implemented in the FRONTIER program.

The model proposed by Battese and Coelli (1995) specifies technical inefficiency effects in the stochastic frontier model that are assumed to be independently (but not identically) distributed non-negative random variables. For the i-th firm in the t-th period, the technical inefficiency effect, u_{it}, is obtained by truncation of the N(μ_{it}, σ^2)-distribution, where

$$\mu_{it} = z_{it}\delta, \tag{9.5}$$

where z_{it} is a (1×M) vector of observable explanatory variables, whose values are fixed constants; and δ is an (M×1) vector of unknown scalar parameters to be estimated (which would generally be expected to include an intercept parameter).[6]

Equation 9.5 specifies that the means of the normal distributions, which are truncated at zero to obtain the distributions of the technical inefficiency effects, are

---

[6] It is assumed that an appropriate parametric representation of technical change, e.g., non-neutral technical change in a translog frontier, is spccified in the values of the x-vector for the frontier.

not the same, but are functions of values of observable variables and a common vector of parameters. The model is obviously a simplification, which does not account for possible correlation structures among random errors (the v_{it}s), associated with particular firms or time periods, nor heteroskedasticity in the random errors and the technical inefficiency effects.

The log-likelihood function for this stochastic frontier and inefficiency model is presented in the Appendix in Battese and Coelli (1993), together with the first partial derivatives of the log-likelihood function with respect to the different parameters of the model. These expressions are given in terms of the variance parameters,

$$\sigma_s^2 = \sigma_v^2 + \sigma^2 \text{ and } \gamma = \sigma^2 / \sigma_s^2,$$

where the γ-parameter has value between zero and one.

The ML estimation of this stochastic frontier model is programmed within FRONTIER and is called "Model 2" or the "technical efficiency (TE) effects model". The requirements of the FRONTIER program for construction of the data set and the instruction file for estimation of a particular stochastic frontier model are illustrated in the empirical example in Section 9.8.

It should be noted that, although the stochastic frontier model (9.1) with the inefficiency effects of equation 9.5, is defined in terms of panel data, it is possible to use the FRONTIER program to estimate a model in which only cross-sectional data are involved, but the technical inefficiency effects are modelled in terms of other observable explanatory variables. In fact, the application of this model, given in Section 9.8, involves cross-sectional data.

Two special cases of the frontier model, defined by equations 9.1 and 9.5, are worthy of note. First, if all the δ-parameters and the scalar parameter, γ, are equal to zero, then the model is equivalent to the average response function, which can be efficiently estimated by ordinary least-squares (OLS) regression. Second, if all the δ-parameters, except the intercept term, are zero, then the frontier model is equivalent to the panel-data version of the Aigner, Lovell and Schmidt (1977) stochastic frontier.

Tests of the above two null hypotheses, and others of interest, such as that all second-order coefficients in the translog frontier model are zero, or constant returns to scale apply in a Cobb-Douglas model, can be obtained by using the generalised likelihood-ratio test statistic, presented in Chapter 8. The generalised likelihood-ratio test for the null hypothesis, H_0: $\gamma = \delta_0 = \delta_1 = \ldots = \delta_{(M-1)} = 0$, is calculated directly by the FRONTIER program by using the values of the log-likelihood function for estimating the full frontier model and that obtained by using OLS regression to estimate the parameters of the production function only (i.e., no explanatory variables in the inefficiency model, which are not in the production function, are included).[7]

The technical efficiency for the i-th firm in the t-th time period is defined by

$$TE_{it} = \exp(-u_{it}) \qquad\qquad (9.6)$$

The prediction of these values is programmed in FRONTIER.

9.7 Duality and Modeling of Allocative Efficiencies

The discussion above concentrates upon the direct estimation of frontier production functions using single-equation methods. The three main reasons for considering the dual forms of the production technology, the cost or profit functions, are:

1. to reflect alternative behavioural objectives (such as cost minimisation);

2. to account for multiple outputs; and

3. to simultaneously predict both technical and allocative efficiency.

In the direct estimation of a production function it is assumed that either:

a) the input levels are fixed and that the managers of the firms are attempting to maximise output given these input quantities; or

b) the managers are selecting the levels of inputs and output to maximise expected (rather than actual) profit. In this instance, Zellner, Kmenta and Dreze (1966) showed that direct estimation of a production function does not suffer from simultaneous-equation bias.

If there is uncertainty regarding the output prices to be received and/or uncertainty regarding the quantity of output to be produced when a manager is making production decisions (e.g., as in agricultural industries), then the assumption of expected (rather than actual) profit maximisation may be appropriate.

However, the objective of cost minimisation may often be a more appropriate assumption. For example, if a power station is required to produce a particular level of output in a given year, it may be more appropriate to estimate a stochastic cost frontier of the form:

$$\ln c_i = C(y_i, w_i; \beta) + v_i + u_i \qquad , i=1,2,...,N, \qquad (9.7)$$

where c_i is the observed cost of production for the i-th firm;

---

[7]Note that any generalised likelihood-ratio statistic associated with a null hypothesis involving the γ-parameter will have a mixed chi-square distribution. See Coelli and Battese (1996) for an application in which composite tests involving γ are conducted.

$C(.)$ is a suitable functional form (such as the Cobb-Douglas or the translog);

y_i is the output quantity;

w_i is a $(K \times 1)$ vector of (exogenous) input prices;

β is a vector of unknown parameters to be estimated; and

u_i is a non-negative cost inefficiency effect (which is often assumed to have a half-normal or truncated-normal distribution).

Note that the inefficiency effect, u_i, is *added* in the cost frontier, instead of being *subtracted*, as in the case of the production frontier. This is because the cost function represents *minimum cost,* whereas the production function represents *maximum output.*

The u_is provide information on the level of the cost efficiency or overall economic efficiency (EE_i) of the i-th firm. This may be calculated as the ratio of frontier minimum cost (with $u_i = 0$) to observed cost, which can be shown to be equal to:[8]

$$EE_i = \exp(-u_i). \tag{9.8}$$

This measure is bounded between zero and one, and can be predicted in a similar way to that described for TE_i in the stochastic production frontier case.[9] Methods of decomposing this overall efficiency measure into its technical and allocative components (TE_i and AE_i) are discussed below.

The parameters of the cost frontier of equation (9.7) can be estimated using standard econometric methods since the y_i and w_i are assumed to be exogenously determined. Schmidt and Lovell (1979) specified a Cobb-Douglas technology for steam-powered electricity-generating plants and showed that the (half-normal) stochastic cost frontier can be estimated in a similar manner to the stochastic production frontiers using either ML or COLS estimators. (The likelihood function and COLS estimators for the cost frontier differ from those in the production frontier by only a few sign changes, see Schmidt and Lovell (1979) for further details.) Both LIMDEP and FRONTIER can be used to estimate cost frontiers.

The overall cost efficiencies (EE_i) can be decomposed into their technical and allocative components if the production function implied by the estimated cost function can be explicitly derived (which can be done when the Cobb-Douglas form is used, because it is self-dual). One then calculates the technical efficiencies

---

[8] Equation (9.8) is only appropriate for EE_i if the cost frontier is given by equation (9.7).
[9] FRONTIER calculates cost (in)efficiency predictions as the <u>inverse</u> of EE_i in equation (9.8).

relative to this derived production frontier, and the allocative efficiencies are estimated by using the expression, AE=EE/TE, which is obtained from the relationship, EE=TE×AE.

A maximum-likelihood systems estimator, involving the cost function and the factor-demand equations, provides more efficient estimators of the parameters of a cost function than the single-equation estimator. The systems approach also has the advantage of explicitly accounting for allocative inefficiency, which is reflected in the error terms on the factor demand equations, which represent violations of the first-order conditions for cost minimisation.

For a simple example of the systems approach, consider a translog cost function involving one output and two inputs:

$$\ln c_i = \beta_0 + \beta_1 \ln w_{1i} + \beta_2 \ln w_{2i} + \beta_3 \ln y_i + \beta_{12} \ln w_{1i} \ln w_{2i} + \beta_{13} \ln w_{1i} \ln y_i$$

$$+ \beta_{23} \ln w_{2i} \ln y_i + (1/2)[\beta_{11}(\ln w_{1i})^2 + \beta_{22}(\ln w_{2i})^2 + \beta_{33}(\ln y_i)^2] + v_i + u_i. \qquad (9.9)$$

The input-demand equations (derived using Shephard's Lemma) are the share equations in the case of the translog. For this two-input example, they are:

$$(w_{1i} x_{1i}/c_i) = \beta_1 + \beta_{11} \ln w_{1i} + \beta_{12} \ln w_{2i} + \beta_{13} \ln y_i + \varepsilon_{1i}, \qquad (9.10a)$$

$$(w_{2i} x_{2i}/c_i) = \beta_2 + \beta_{12} \ln w_{1i} + \beta_{22} \ln w_{2i} + \beta_{23} \ln y_i + \varepsilon_{2i}, \qquad (9.10b)$$

where the dependent variables are the shares of total cost for that input, and the ε_{ji}s are error terms which are likely to contain both allocative errors and noise.

The cost-frontier approach appears to be a significant improvement, because it accounts for the possibility of exogenous output and endogenous inputs, permits the measurement of technical and allocative inefficiency, and can be easily extended to account for multiple outputs. However, it suffers from the following problems:

- The cost-frontier approach requires input-price data to be available and to vary among firms. In many cases, firms in an industry either face the same prices, or, if they do not face the same prices, the price data are difficult to obtain.

- The frontier systems estimator is not as yet automated in any computer package. Hence one would need to write code for it in some way (using say SAS or FORTRAN).

- The above method of decomposing overall cost efficiency into technical and allocative efficiency is limited to the use of functional forms, for which the implied production function can be explicitly derived, such as the Cobb-Douglas form. Once one specifies more flexible functional forms, such as the translog form, where the implied production function cannot be derived, this method of decomposition is no longer possible. In this case, the method proposed by Kopp and Diewert (1982), and refined by Zeischang (1983), can be used to decompose the cost efficiencies into their technical and allocative components. This method is derived using duality results and involves the numerical solution of K-1 non-linear relations. These are not trivial computations, and they are not automated in LIMDEP or FRONTIER.

•   The main problem with the systems approach for estimating cost frontiers is associated with selecting an appropriate way to represent the link between the allocative inefficiency in the error terms of the input demand equations (which forms part of the ε_{ji}s in equation 9.10), and the allocative inefficiency error which appears in the cost frontier (which is part of u_i in equation 9.9). This problem has not been solved to the satisfaction of the majority of researchers, and debate continues as to how best address this issue (see Bauer (1990) and Greene (1993) for further discussion and references).[10]

Most applied economists (without higher degrees in econometrics and computer programming) are advised to avoid flexible-systems estimators. If one of the existing approaches is applied (e.g., Greene, 1980b; or Ferrier and Lovell, 1990) then criticism from some quarter is likely. Furthermore, estimation problems often arise when one tries to numerically solve the rather complicated likelihood functions that are involved. The best approach to take (given that the cost-minimising assumption is appropriate and suitable price data are available) is to estimate the cost function using the single-equation ML method, which is automated in both LIMDEP and FRONTIER. The decomposition of the cost efficiencies can be performed using one of the two methods suggested above.

This section focuses on cost functions because cost minimisation is the assumption that is most often made in the dual frontier literature. Profit maximisation has also been considered by a number of authors. Examples of frontier studies involving profit maximisation include Ali and Flinn (1989), in which a single-equation profit frontier is estimated using the same methods as for production frontiers. Kumbhakar, Ghosh and McGuckin (1991) also specified a maximum-likelihood systems estimator under the assumption of profit maximisation.

9.8 Empirical Application: Wheat Farming in South Africa

This empirical illustration of the estimation of a stochastic frontier production function, in which the technical inefficiency effects are modelled in terms of other explanatory variables, is taken from Ngwenya, Battese and Fleming (1997). This paper analyses farm-level data on the production of wheat in the Eastern Orange Free State in South Africa in the 1988/89 agricultural year. Of particular interest in South Africa is the issue of whether small farms are more technically efficient than large farms. Hence in this study, the technical efficiency effects in the stochastic

---

[10]Note that Kumbhakar (1997) has recently proposed a solution to this problem in the case of a translog cost function. However, no empirical application has yet been conducted.

frontier production function are modelled in terms of the size of the farming operation for the sample of wheat farmers involved.

A translog stochastic frontier production function is assumed to be the appropriate model for the analysis of the data available on 71 wheat farmers. The model to be estimated is defined by

$$\ln y_i = \beta_0 + \sum_{j=1}^{4} \beta_j \ln x_{ji} + \sum_{j \le}^{4} \sum_{k=1}^{4} \beta_{jk} \ln x_{ji} \ln x_{ki} + v_i - u_i,$$

(9.11)

where i indicates an observation for the i-th farmer in the survey, i=1, 2,...,71;

y represents the total value of all agricultural outputs (expressed in Rands) on the given farm;

x_1 represents the total amount of land (in hectares) operated by the wheat farmer, excluding farmyard and waste land;

x_2 is the total of machinery costs (expressed in Rands);

x_3 is the total of the remuneration for the labour of black and white workers (expressed in Rands);

x_4 is the cost of other inputs for the directly allocatable expenditures in the production of wheat (expressed in Rands);

the v_is are assumed to be independent and identically distributed as normal random variables with mean zero and variance, σ_v^2, independent of the u_is;

the u_is are non-negative technical inefficiency of production,[11] which are assumed to be independently distributed, such that u_i is obtained by truncation (at zero) of the $N(m_i, \sigma^2)$-distribution, where the mean is defined by

$$m_i = \delta_0 + \delta_1 \ell n \, (Land_i) + \delta_2 (Pasture_i/Land_i) + \delta_3 (Variable_i/Fixed \, Costs_i),$$ (9.12)

where $Pasture_i/Land_i$ is the ratio of the area of pasture land to the total area of land operated; and

---

[11] Given that the *value of output* is the dependent variable in the frontier function, rather than physical output, the inefficiency effects in the model may be influenced by allocative inefficiencies, in addition to technical inefficiencies of production.

Variable$_i$/Fixed Costs$_i$ is the ratio of the cost of other inputs to the fixed costs of the farming operation.

In order to estimate the parameters of this frontier production function, the data set for the variables involved has to be created in the form required by FRONTIER for the estimation of what it calls "Model 2". The data set involved was an text file in which observations on the variables were separated by blanks, in the following order:

1. Farm number (values from 1 to 71 are required);

2. Year of observation (This must be 1 for all observations, because only cross-sectional data are involved in this case.);

3. The logarithm of the value of agricultural output for the wheat farmers;

4. The values of all the relevant x-variables for the frontier (the values are the logs of the four input variables, followed by their squares and different cross products);[12]

5. The values of the z-variables in the inefficiency model. (These are the log of land, the ratio of pasture to total land and the ratio of variable to fixed costs.)[13]

This translog model involves a total of 14 x-variables and three z-variables. The instruction file for FRONTIER to estimate the stochastic frontier model, defined by equations 9.11 and 9.12, is listed in Table 9.1. The values in this instruction file are self-explanatory.

The output file obtained from FRONTIER is listed next in Table 9.2. Note that in the output file, the log-likelihood function for the full stochastic frontier model is calculated to be -17.999 and the value for the OLS fit of the production function is -28.889, which is less than that for the full frontier model. This implies that the generalised likelihood-ratio statistic for testing for the absence of the technical inefficiency effects from the frontier is calculated to be

$$LR = -2\{ -28.889 -(-17.999)\} = 21.78.$$

This value is calculated by FRONTIER and reported as the "LR test of the one-sided error". This value is significant, because it exceeds 10.371, which is the critical value obtained from Table 1 of Kodde and Palm (1986) for the degrees of freedom equal to 5. Hence the null hypothesis of no technical inefficiency effects in wheat production in South Africa is rejected.

---

[12] FRONTIER assumes that the production function includes an intercept parameter, so that the first x-variable is NOT specified to be 1 for all observations.

[13] Note that the variable, ln(Land$_i$), occurs in the data set as both an x-variable in the frontier function and as a z-variable in the model for the technical inefficiency effects.

Table 9.1: FRONTIER Instruction File for Estimation of the Translog Stochastic Frontier Model for Wheat Farmers in South Africa

```
2            1=ERROR COMPONENTS MODEL, 2=TE EFFECTS MODEL
logltl.dta   DATA FILE NAME
logltl.out   OUTPUT FILE NAME
1            1=PRODUCTION FUNCTION, 2=COST FUNCTION
y            LOGGED DEPENDENT VARIABLE (Y/N)
71           NUMBER OF CROSS-SECTIONS
1            NUMBER OF TIME PERIODS
71           NUMBER OF OBSERVATIONS IN TOTAL
14           NUMBER OF REGRESSOR VARIABLES (Xs)
y            MU (Y/N) [OR DELTA0 (Y/N) IF USING TE EFFECTS MODEL]
3            ETA (Y/N) [OR NUMBER OF TE EFFECTS REGRESSORS (Zs)]
n            STARTING VALUES (Y/N)
```

We note that the ML estimate for γ is 0.999999 with estimated standard error of 0.00035. These results are consistent with the conclusion that the true γ-value is concluded to be greater than zero (in the test above). However, we also see that the γ-estimate is not significantly different from one, which indicates that the stochastic frontier model may not be significantly different from the deterministic frontier, in which there are no random errors in the production function. This is a surprising result for an agricultural production function where one would normally expect data noise to play a larger role.[14]

We note that the estimate for δ_1, the coefficient of the $\ln(Land_i)$ variable in the model for the inefficiency effects, is negative, which indicates that the larger wheat farms in the sample tend to have smaller values of the inefficiency effects. However, the ML estimate is small relative to its standard error. Hence it is of interest to know if the true value is likely to be zero. By estimating the model with $\ell n\,(Land_i)$ deleted from the set of z-variables for the inefficiency effect, the log-likelihood function was found to be -23.148. This value is significantly less than the value of the log-likelihood function for the full frontier model, reported in Table 9.2.

A further hypothesis of interest is whether the Cobb-Douglas production function is an adequate representation of the data, given the specifications of the translog model. To test the null hypothesis that the second-order coefficients of the translog frontier are simultaneously zero, H_0: $\beta_{ij} = 0$, for all $i \le j = 1,2,3,4$, the data set for the Cobb-Douglas model must be created. Thus the last 10 x-variables for the data set for the translog model are deleted to obtain the required data set for the Cobb-

---

[14]Note that both of the stochastic frontier empirical examples in this book have obtained estimates of γ which are very close to one. There is no reason for one to expect this to occur regularly. The γ-parameter can take any value between zero and one, depending upon the relative contribution of noise and inefficiency.

Douglas model. The instruction file for estimating the Cobb-Douglas model with four x-variables and the three z-variables is given in Table 9.3.

Table 9.2: Output from FRONTIER for Estimation of the Translog Stochastic Frontier Production Function for Wheat Farmers in South Africa

```
instruction file = logltl.ins
data file =       logltl.dta

Tech. Eff. Effects Frontier (see B&C 1993)
The model is a production function
The dependent variable is logged

the ols estimates are :
                        coefficient          standard-error
t-ratio

    beta 0         0.16609290E+01   0.10749695E+02   0.15450941E+00
    beta 1        -0.31911130E+01   0.26267270E+01  -0.12148628E+01
    beta 2        -0.84553661E+00   0.15092290E+01  -0.56024408E+00
    beta 3         0.56238303E+00   0.78706798E+00   0.71452916E+00
    beta 4         0.35088621E+01   0.16026216E+01   0.21894514E+01
    beta 5        -0.43015875E+00   0.34101855E+00  -0.12613940E+01
    beta 6         0.51434901E-01   0.53888317E-01   0.95447220E+00
    beta 7        -0.39444165E-01   0.42037822E-01  -0.93830182E+00
    beta 8        -0.15345676E+00   0.12742122E+00  -0.12043265E+01
    beta 9         0.17743459E+00   0.22117534E+00   0.80223496E+00
    beta10         0.28223108E+00   0.18122983E+00   0.15573103E+01
    beta11         0.34197291E+00   0.27438526E+00   0.12463239E+01
    beta12        -0.40341623E-01   0.76019841E-01  -0.53067228E+00
    beta13        -0.76019284E-01   0.13979927E+00  -0.54377456E+00
    beta14        -0.96694632E-01   0.11167410E+00  -0.86586448E+00
    sigma-squared  0.16749843E+00

log likelihood function =   -0.28888747E+02

the estimates after the grid search were :
    beta 0         0.20128305E+01
    beta 1        -0.31911130E+01
    beta 2        -0.84553661E+00
    beta 3         0.56238303E+00
    beta 4         0.35088621E+01
    beta 5        -0.43015875E+00
    beta 6         0.51434901E-01
    beta 7        -0.39444165E-01
    beta 8        -0.15345676E+00
    beta 9         0.17743459E+00
    beta10         0.28223108E+00
    beta11         0.34197291E+00
    beta12        -0.40341623E-01
    beta13        -0.76019284E-01
    beta14        -0.96694632E-01
    sigma-squared  0.25594612E+00
    gamma          0.76000000E+00
    delta 0        0.00000000E+00
    delta 1        0.00000000E+00
    delta 2        0.00000000E+00
    delta 3        0.00000000E+00

(Information on Iterations is Deleted)
```

```
the final mle estimates are :
                        coefficient         standard-error
t-ratio
  beta  0        -0.11847659E+02   0.18597196E+01  -0.63706692E+01
  beta  1        -0.44985211E+01   0.33178744E+00  -0.13558443E+02
  beta  2         0.16523171E+01   0.17688942E+00   0.93409606E+01
  beta  3         0.13127570E+01   0.93103147E-01   0.14100028E+02
  beta  4         0.35910408E+01   0.20337535E+00   0.17657208E+02
  beta  5        -0.71437733E+00   0.28994883E-01  -0.24638048E+02
  beta  6         0.67525560E-03   0.27237125E-02   0.24791735E+00
  beta  7        -0.56406620E-01   0.13253170E-01  -0.42560853E+01
  beta  8        -0.95245089E-01   0.12797195E-01  -0.74426534E+01
  beta  9         0.15360601E+00   0.21061149E-01   0.72933348E+01
  beta10          0.49278322E+00   0.14300194E-01   0.34459897E+02
  beta11          0.63707530E+00   0.23318571E-01   0.27320512E+02
  beta12         -0.12430754E-01   0.13490822E-01  -0.92142307E+00
  beta13         -0.19583915E+00   0.20069212E-01  -0.97581882E+01
  beta14         -0.29865449E+00   0.22666982E-01  -0.13175845E+02
  sigma-squared   0.13514042E+01   0.30388817E+00   0.44470444E+01
  gamma           0.99999949E+00   0.35011164E-04   0.28562303E+05
  delta  0        0.74517489E+00   0.86210032E+01   0.86437143E-01
  delta  1       -0.34163568E+00   0.13954600E+01  -0.24481941E+00
  delta  2        0.30614391E+01   0.88294256E+01   0.34673140E+00
  delta  3       -0.88023162E+00   0.14168148E+01  -0.62127500E+00

log likelihood function =  -0.17998761E+02

LR test of the one-sided error =   0.21779973E+02
with number of restrictions = 5
[note that this statistic has a mixed chi-square distribution]

number of iterations =     136

(maximum number of iterations set at :   500)

number of cross-sections =     71

number of time periods =     1

total number of observations =     71

thus there are:    0  obsns not in the panel

covariance matrix :
```

(The covariance matrix for the ML estimators is deleted)

```
technical efficiency estimates:
     firm  year          eff.-est.
      1     1          0.29727157E+00
      2     1          0.80407824E+00
      3     1          0.56178490E+00
```

(The TE values for observations 4 to 69 are deleted from this output)

```
     70     1          0.44135033E+00
     71     1          0.86163487E+00

     mean efficiency =  0.67082286E+00
```

Table 9.3: FRONTIER Instruction File for Estimation of the Cobb-Douglas Frontier Model for Wheat Farmers in South Africa

```
2              1=ERROR COMPONENTS MODEL, 2=TE EFFECTS MODEL
loglcd.dta     DATA FILE NAME
loglcd.out     OUTPUT FILE NAME
1              1=PRODUCTION FUNCTION, 2=COST FUNCTION
y              LOGGED DEPENDENT VARIABLE (Y/N)
71             NUMBER OF CROSS-SECTIONS
1              NUMBER OF TIME PERIODS
71             NUMBER OF OBSERVATIONS IN TOTAL
4              NUMBER OF REGRESSOR VARIABLES (Xs)
y              MU (Y/N) [OR DELTA0 (Y/N) IF USING TE EFFECTS MODEL]
3              ETA (Y/N) [OR NUMBER OF TE EFFECTS REGRESSORS (Zs)]
n              STARTING VALUES (Y/N)
```

The output file for estimating this Cobb-Douglas model using FRONTIER gives the value of the log-likelihood function as -30.388. (The output file is not presented here to save space.) Hence the value of the generalised likelihood-ratio statistic for testing the null hypothesis, H_0: $\beta_{ij} = 0$, is calculated to be

$$LR = -2\{-30.388 - (-17.999)\} = 24.78.$$

This value is compared with the upper five per cent point for the χ_{10}^2-distribution, which is 18.31. Thus the null hypothesis that the Cobb-Douglas frontier is an adequate representation of the data is rejected, given the specifications of the translog frontier.

Ngwenya, Battese and Fleming (1997) report the technical efficiencies of the wheat farmers, together with input elasticities of production and returns to scale estimates. Interested readers are referred to that paper for these details.

9.9 Conclusions

Of the list of eleven possible pitfalls in DEA analyses presented in Chapter 7, most are applicable (in varying degrees) to stochastic frontiers. Stochastic frontiers have a few particular problems of their own, namely:

- The selection of a distributional form for the inefficiency effects may be arbitrary, but general distributions, such as the truncated-normal, are best.

- The production technology must be specified by a particular functional form, for which the flexible functional forms are recommended.

- The stochastic frontier approach is only well-developed for single-output technologies, unless one is willing to assume a cost-minimising objective.[15]

However, stochastic frontiers also have some advantages relative to DEA:

- DEA assumes all deviations from the frontier are due to inefficiency. If any noise is present (e.g., due to measurement error, weather, strikes, etc.) then this may influence the placement of the DEA frontier (and hence the measurement of efficiencies) more than would be the case with the stochastic frontier approach.

- Tests of hypotheses regarding the existence of inefficiency and also regarding the structure of the production technology can be performed in a stochastic frontier analysis.

Stochastic frontiers are likely to be more appropriate than DEA in agricultural applications, especially in developing countries, where the data are heavily influenced by measurement error and the effects of weather, disease, etc. However, in the non-profit service sector, where

- random influences are less of an issue;

- multiple-output production is important;

- prices are difficult to define; and

- behavioural assumptions, such as cost minimisation or profit maximisation, are difficult to justify,

the DEA approach may often be the optimal choice. The selection of the appropriate method should be made on a case-by-case basis.

---

[15]A multiple-output industry can be studied if one is willing to aggregate output into a single measure. This is often done using the index number methods, discussed in Chapters 4 and 5, which require knowledge of output prices (or values). Alternatively, one could consider multi-output distance function estimation. See Coelli and Perelman (1996) for an empirical example.

10. PRODUCTIVITY MEASUREMENT USING EFFICIENCY MEASUREMENT METHODS

10.1 Introduction

In this chapter we draw upon much of what has been covered in earlier chapters. We illustrate how, with access to suitable panel data, one can use the frontier estimation methods discussed in the previous four chapters to obtain estimates of TFP growth which do not require one to accept the restrictive assumptions inherent in the Tornqvist/Fisher index approach discussed in Chapter 5. That is, we do not need to assume that all firms are cost minimisers and revenue maximisers. This is of particular benefit when we are analysing public sector and not-for-profit organisations where these assumptions are unlikely to be valid.

The approaches discussed in this chapter have the additional benefits (over the Tornqvist/Fisher methods) that price data are not required, and that the TFP indices obtained may be decomposed into two components, one part due to technical efficiency change (firms getting closer to the frontier) and another part due to technical change (shifts in the frontier itself). The one principal drawback of these methods is that panel data are required, while the Tornqvist/Fisher methods may be calculated with only a single observation in each time period.

The remainder of this chapter is organised as follows. In Section 10.2 we discuss the Malmquist TFP index which was first discussed in Chapter 5. In Section 10.3 we describe how one can estimate these indices using both parametric and non-parametric frontier estimation methods. In Section 10.4 we provide a detailed application of some of these methods using panel data on Australian thermal electricity generation, and in Section 10.5 we make some brief concluding comments.

10.2 The Malmquist TFP Index

The methods discussed in this chapter are based either explicitly or implicitly upon a Malmquist TFP index. The seminal papers in this area are Nishimizu and Page (1982) and Färe, Grosskopf, Norris and Zhang (1994). The first of these papers uses the Aigner and Chu (1968) linear programming methods applied to social sector panel data of Yugoslavia to construct parametric production frontiers and subsequently measure TFP growth as the sum of an efficiency change component and a technical change component. The Färe et al (1994) paper takes the Malmquist index of TFP growth, defined in Caves, Christensen and Diewert (1982b), and illustrates how the component distance functions can be estimated using DEA-like methods. They also showed how the resulting TFP indices could be decomposed into technical efficiency change and technical change components.

The essential differences between these two papers is that Nishimizu and Page (1982) use parametric methods, calculate technical change and technical efficiency change directly and sum these to provide a TFP change measure, while Färe et al (1994) use non-parametric methods, calculate the component distance functions so that they may then calculate the Malmquist TFP change indices, and then decompose these into technical change and technical efficiency change components. With these differences aside, the two papers attempt to do essentially the same thing.

For more on these and other similar methods, see survey papers by Grosskopf (1993) and Färe, Grosskopf and Roos (1997).

Distance Functions

The Malmquist index is defined using distance functions. Hence we briefly revise our definitions of distance functions which were introduced in Chapter 3. Distance functions allow one to describe a multi-input, multi-output production technology without the need to specify a behavioural objective (such as cost minimisation or profit maximisation). One may define input distance functions and output distance functions. An input distance function characterises the production technology by looking at a minimal proportional contraction of the input vector, given an output vector. An output distance function considers a maximal proportional expansion of the output vector, given an input vector. We only consider an output distance function in detail in this chapter. However, input distance functions can be defined and used in a similar manner.

Recall from Chapter 3 that a production technology may be defined using the output set, $P(x)$, which represents the set of all output vectors, y, which can be produced using the input vector, x. That is,

$$P(x) = \{y : x \text{ can produce } y\}. \tag{10.1}$$

We assume that the technology satisfies the axioms listed in Chapter 3.

The output distance function is defined on the output set, $P(x)$, as:

$$d_o(x,y) = \min\{\delta : (y/\delta) \in P(x)\}. \tag{10.2}$$

The distance function, $d_o(x,y)$, will take a value which is less than or equal to one if the output vector, y, is an element of the feasible production set, $P(x)$. Furthermore, the distance function will take a value of unity if y is located on the outer boundary of the feasible production set, and will take a value greater than one if y is located outside the feasible production set.

Malmquist TFP Index

The Malmquist TFP index was first introduced in Chapter 5. It measures the TFP change between two data points by calculating the ratio of the distances of each data point relative to a common technology. Following Färe et al (1994), the Malmquist (output-orientated) TFP change index between period s (the base period) and period t is given by

$$m_o\left(y_s, x_s, y_t, x_t\right) = \left[\frac{d_o^s\left(y_t, x_t\right)}{d_o^s\left(y_s, x_s\right)} \times \frac{d_o^t\left(y_t, x_t\right)}{d_o^t\left(y_s, x_s\right)}\right]^{1/2}, \tag{10.3}$$

where the notation $d_o^s(x_t, y_t)$ represents the distance from the period t observation to the period s technology. A value of M_o greater than one will indicate positive TFP growth from period s to period t while a value less than one indicates a TFP decline. Note that equation 10.3 is, in fact, the geometric mean of two TFP indices. The first is evaluated with respect to period s technology and the second with respect to period t technology.

As noted in Section 5.9.2, an equivalent way of writing this productivity index is

$$m_o\left(y_s, x_s, y_t, x_t\right) = \frac{d_o^t\left(y_t, x_t\right)}{d_o^s\left(y_s, x_s\right)}\left[\frac{d_o^s\left(y_t, x_t\right)}{d_o^t\left(y_t, x_t\right)} \times \frac{d_o^s\left(y_s, x_s\right)}{d_o^t\left(y_s, x_s\right)}\right]^{1/2}, \tag{10.4}$$

where the ratio outside the square brackets measures the change in the output-oriented measure of Farrell technical efficiency between periods s and t. That is, the efficiency change is equivalent to the ratio of the Farrell technical efficiency in period t to the Farrell technical efficiency in period s. The remaining part of the index in equation 10.4 is a measure of technical change. It is the geometric mean of the shift in technology between the two periods, evaluated at x_t and also at x_s. Thus the two terms in equation 10.4 are:

$$\text{Efficiency change} = \frac{d_o^t(y_t, x_t)}{d_o^s(y_s, x_s)} \tag{10.5}$$

and

$$\text{Technical change} = \left[\frac{d_o^s(y_t, x_t)}{d_o^t(y_t, x_t)} \times \frac{d_o^s(y_s, x_s)}{d_o^t(y_s, x_s)} \right]^{1/2} \tag{10.6}$$

This decomposition is illustrated in Figure 10.1 where we have depicted a constant returns to scale technology involving a single input and a single output. The firm produces at the points D and E in periods s and t, respectively. In each period the firm is operating below the technology for that period. Hence there is technical inefficiency in both periods. Using equations 10.5 and 10.6 we obtain:

$$\text{Efficiency change} = \frac{y_t / y_c}{y_s / y_a} \tag{10.7}$$

$$\text{Technical change} = \left[\frac{y_t / y_b}{y_t / y_c} \times \frac{y_s / y_a}{y_s / y_b} \right]^{1/2} \tag{10.8}$$

In an empirical application we must calculate the four distance measures which appear in equation 10.3 for each firm in each pair of adjacent time periods. This can be done using either mathematical programming or econometric techniques. These methods are discussed in Section 10.3.

One issue that must be stressed is that the returns to scale properties of the technology is very important in TFP measurement. Grifell-Tatjé and Lovell (1995) use a simple one-input, one-output example to illustrate that a Malmquist TFP index may not correctly measure TFP changes when VRS is assumed for the technology. Hence it is important that CRS be imposed upon any technology that is used to estimate distance functions for the calculation of a Malmquist TFP index. Otherwise the resulting measures may not properly reflect the TFP gains or losses resulting from scale effects.

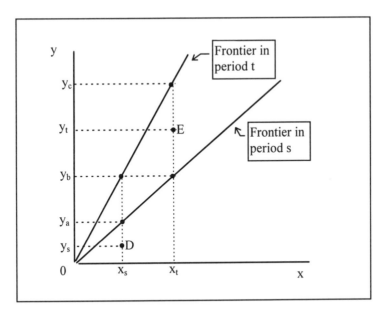

Figure 10.1 Malmquist Productivity Indices

Some Comments

Before we discuss how one may be able to obtain the distance measures, required to construct the Malmquist TFP index, we first make some brief comments regarding Malmquist TFP indices and related indices. Our discussion is based primarily upon the comprehensive survey of Malmquist TFP index methods in Färe, Grosskopf and Roos (1997).

Firstly, as noted above (and in Chapter 5), the Malmquist TFP index defined in equation 10.3 is, in fact, the geometric mean of two Malmquist TFP indices, one measured relative to the period s technology and one measured relative to period t technology. As noted by Färe, Grosskopf and Roos (1997), these two (period s and period t) indices are only equivalent if the technology is Hicks output neutral. That is, if the output distance functions may be represented as $d_o^t(x,y) = A(t)d_o(x,y)$, for all t. To avoid the necessity to either impose this restriction or to arbitrarily choose one of the two technologies, the Malmquist TFP index in equation 10.3 is defined as the geometric mean of these two indices, in the spirit of Fisher (1922) and Caves, Christensen and Diewert (1982b).

The notion of a TFP index is often motivated as the ratio of an index of outputs to an index of inputs. Diewert (1992) suggests an alternative Malmquist TFP index which is defined as the ratio of a Malmquist output index to a Malmquist input index. This index has become known as the Hicks-Moorsteen TFP index. It has been applied in a number of TFP analyses in recent years (e.g., Bjurek, 1996). Färe, Grosskopf and Roos (1997) observe that this index will equal the Malmquist TFP index defined in equation 10.3 when the technology is inverse homothetic[1] and exhibits CRS.

A variety of additional issues are raised in the Färe, Grosskopf and Roos (1997) survey paper. These include the observation that the Malmquist TFP index is not transitive (as noted by Førsund, 1990). It may be argued that transitivity is not a big issue in TFP studies because of the temporal nature of many of these studies. Färe and Grosskopf (1996) show that Hicks output neutrality is a sufficient condition to ensure transitivity of the Malmquist index. We also note that if transitivity is required, one could alternatively apply the EKS method, discussed in Chapter 4, to a non-transitive index to provide a transitive index.

Färe, Grosskopf and Roos (1997) also devote some space to a discussion of some possible further decompositions of the technical efficiency change and technical change components of the Malmquist TFP index (equations 10.5 and 10.6, respectively). Possibilities include the Färe et al (1994) suggestion that technical efficiency change be decomposed into scale efficiency and "pure" technical efficiency components, and the Färe and Grosskopf (1996) method of decomposing the technical change component into input bias, output bias and "magnitude" components. The interested reader is advised to consult Färe, Grosskopf and Roos (1997) for further details.

10.3 Two Estimation Methods

There are a number of different methods that could be used to measure the distance functions which make up the Malmquist TFP index. To date, the most popular method has been the DEA-like linear programming methods suggested by Färe et al (1994). These are discussed in Section 10.3.1. One can also use stochastic frontier methods such as those described in Section 10.3.2. We now discuss each of these in turn.

10.3.1 DEA-like Methods

Following Färe et al (1994), and given that suitable panel data are available, we can calculate the required distances using DEA-like linear programs. For the i-th firm, we must calculate four distance functions to measure the TFP change between two periods. This requires the solving of four linear programming (LP) problems. Färe et al (1994) assume a constant returns to scale (CRS) technology in their analysis. The required LPs are:[2]

---

[1] See Shephard (1970) for a definition of inverse hometheticity. Note that a single output production function of the form y=f(x) always satisfies this property.

[2] All notation follows directly from that used in Chapters 6 and 7. The only differences are that we now have time subscripts, s and t, to represent the two time periods of interest.

$$[d_o{}^t(y_t, x_t)]^{-1} = \max_{\phi,\lambda} \phi,$$
$$\text{st} \quad -\phi y_{it} + Y_t\lambda \geq 0,$$
$$X_{it} - X_t\lambda \geq 0,$$
$$\lambda \geq 0, \tag{10.9}$$

$$[d_o{}^s(y_s, x_s)]^{-1} = \max_{\phi,\lambda} \phi,$$
$$\text{st} \quad -\phi y_{is} + Y_s\lambda \geq 0,$$
$$X_{is} - X_s\lambda \geq 0,$$
$$\lambda \geq 0, \tag{10.10}$$

$$[d_o{}^t(y_s, x_s)]^{-1} = \max_{\phi,\lambda} \phi,$$
$$\text{st} \quad -\phi y_{is} + Y_t\lambda \geq 0,$$
$$X_{is} - X_t\lambda \geq 0,$$
$$\lambda \geq 0, \tag{10.11}$$

and

$$[d_o{}^s(y_t, x_t)]^{-1} = \max_{\phi,\lambda} \phi,$$
$$\text{st} \quad -\phi y_{it} + Y_s\lambda \geq 0,$$
$$X_{it} - X_s\lambda \geq 0,$$
$$\lambda \geq 0, \tag{10.12}$$

Note that in LP's 10.11 and 10.12, where production points are compared to technologies from different time periods, the ϕ parameter need not be greater than or equal to one, as it must be when calculating Farrell output-orientated technical efficiencies. The data point could lie above the feasible production set. This will most likely occur in LP 10.12 where a production point from period t is compared to technology in an earlier period, s. If technical progress has occurred, then a value of $\phi < 1$ is possible. Note that it could also possibly occur in LP 10.11 if technical regress has occurred, but this is less likely.

Some points to keep in mind are that the ϕs and λs are likely to take different values in the above four LPs. Furthermore, note that the above four LPs must be solved for each firm in the sample. Thus if there are 20 firms and 2 time periods, 80 LPs must be solved. Note also that as extra time periods are added, one must solve an extra three LP's for each firm (to construct a chained index). If there are T time periods, then (3T-2) LPs must be solved for each firm in the sample. Hence, if there are N firms, N×(3T-2) LPs need to be solved. For example, with N=20 firms and T=10 time periods, this would involve 20×(3×10-2) = 560 LPs.

Scale Efficiency

The above approach can be extended by decomposing the technical efficiency change into scale efficiency and "pure" technical efficiency components. This requires the solution of two additional LPs (when comparing two production points). These would involve repeating LPs 10.9 and 10.10 with the convexity restriction

(N1'λ=1) added to each. That is, one would calculate these two distance functions relative to a variable returns to scale (VRS), instead of a CRS, technology. One can then use the CRS and VRS values to calculate the scale efficiency measures residually, as described in Färe et al (1994, p75). For the case of N firms and T time periods, this would increase the number of LPs from Nx(3T-2) to Nx(4T-2).

Some authors suggest that all the Malmquist DEA calculations be done assuming VRS. Apart from the interpretation difficulties associated with TFP measures based upon a VRS technology (discussed in Section 10.2) this approach can also, in some cases, experience computational difficulties because the distances may not always be defined in some inter-period DEA LP's. Hence, for these two reasons, we recommend the use of the CRS methods, suggested by Färe et al (1994), to avoid these problems.

A Simple Numerical Example

Since these DEA-like methods have been used in the vast majority of studies which have used panel data to construct Malmquist TFP indices, we now work through a simple numerical example using the DEAP computer program.

In this example, we take the data from the simple one-output, one-input example introduced in Chapter 6 (see Table 6.6a) and add an extra year of data. These data are listed in Table 10.1 and are also plotted in Figure 10.2. Also plotted in Figure 10.2 are the CRS and VRS DEA frontiers for the two time periods.

The text file EG4.DTA (refer to Table 10.2a) contains observations on five firms over a three year period. These firms produce one output using one input. Data for year 1 are listed in the first five rows, year 2 data are in the second five rows and year 3 data are listed in the final five rows. Note that the year 1 and 2 data are identical to those listed in Table 10.1. Note also that the year 2 data are identical to the year 3 data. This is done to ensure that the example remains quite simple.

Table 10.1 Example Data for Malmquist DEA

firm	year	y	x
1	1	1	2
2	1	2	4
3	1	3	3
4	1	5	5
5	1	5	6
1	2	1	2
2	2	3	4
3	2	4	3
4	2	5	5
5	2	5	5

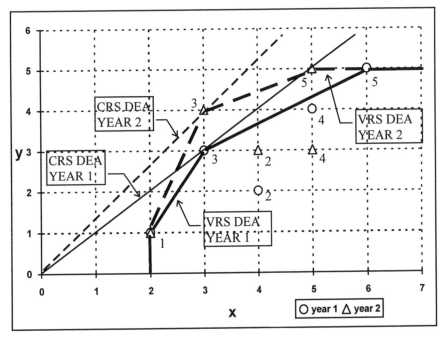

Figure 10.2 VRS Input-Orientated DEA Example

Table 10.2a Listing of Data File, EG4.DTA

```
1 2
2 4
3 3
4 5
5 6
1 2
3 4
4 3
3 5
5 5
1 2
3 4
4 3
3 5
5 5
```

The EG4.INS file is listed in Table 10.2b. The only changes relative to the EG2.INS instruction file (which was used in our VRS DEA example) listed in Table 6.6b is that:

- the input and output file names are different;

- the number of time periods is now 3;

- a "1" is entered on the third last line to indicate that an output orientation is required; and

- a "2" is entered on the last line to indicate that Malmquist DEA is required.

Note that the VRS/CRS option in the DEAP instruction file has no influence on the Malmquist DEA routine because both are used to calculate the various distances which are used to construct the Malmquist indices.

Table 10.2b Listing of Instruction File, EG4.INS

```
eg4.dta        DATA FILE NAME
eg4.out        OUTPUT FILE NAME
5              NUMBER OF FIRMS
3              NUMBER OF TIME PERIODS
1              NUMBER OF OUTPUTS
1              NUMBER OF INPUTS
1              0=INPUT AND 1=OUTPUT ORIENTATED
0              0=CRS AND 1=VRS
2              0=DEA(MULTI-STAGE), 1=COST-DEA, 2=MALMQUIST-DEA,
                  3=DEA(1-STAGE), 4=DEA(2-STAGE)
```

The output file, EG4.OUT, is reproduced in Table 10.2c. The output begins with a listing of the distances needed for the Malmquist calculations. Four distances are calculated for each firm in each year. These are relative to:

- the previous period's CRS DEA frontier;

- the current period's CRS DEA frontier;

- the next period's CRS DEA frontier; and

- the current period's VRS frontier.

Following this the Malmquist indices are presented. All indices are calculated relative to the previous year. Hence the output begins with year 2. Five indices are presented for each firm in each year. These are:

- technical efficiency change (relative to a CRS technology);

- technological change;

- pure technical efficiency change (i.e., relative to a VRS technology);

- scale efficiency change; and

- total factor productivity (TFP) change.

Following this, summary tables of these indices are presented for the different time periods (over all firms) and for the different firms (over all time periods). Note that all indices are equal to one for time period 3. This is because in the example data set used (see Table 10.2a) the data for year 3 are identical to the year 2 data.

Table 10.2c Listing of Output File, EG4.OUT

```
Results from DEAP Version 2.1

Instruction file   = eg4.ins
Data file          = eg4.dta

Output orientated Malmquist DEA


DISTANCES SUMMARY


year =      1

   firm         crs te rel to tech in yr            vrs
   no.          *************************            te
                t-1          t          t+1

    1          0.000        0.500       0.375       1.000
    2          0.000        0.500       0.375       0.545
    3          0.000        1.000       0.750       1.000
    4          0.000        0.800       0.600       0.923
    5          0.000        0.833       0.625       1.000

   mean        0.000        0.727       0.545       0.894

year =      2

   firm         crs te rel to tech in yr            vrs
   no.          *************************            te
                t-1          t          t+1

    1          0.500        0.375       0.375       1.000
    2          0.750        0.563       0.563       0.667
    3          1.333        1.000       1.000       1.000
    4          0.600        0.450       0.450       0.600
    5          1.000        0.750       0.750       1.000

   mean        0.837        0.628       0.628       0.853

year =      3

   firm         crs te rel to tech in yr            vrs
   no.          *************************            te
                t-1          t          t+1
```

```
      1        0.375          0.375          0.000       1.000
      2        0.563          0.563          0.000       0.667
      3        1.000          1.000          0.000       1.000
      4        0.450          0.450          0.000       0.600
      5        0.750          0.750          0.000       1.000

mean         0.628          0.628          0.000       0.853
```

[Note that t-1 in year 1 and t+1 in the final year are not defined]

MALMQUIST INDEX SUMMARY

year =   2

firm	effch	techch	pech	sech	tfpch
1	0.750	1.333	1.000	0.750	1.000
2	1.125	1.333	1.222	0.920	1.500
3	1.000	1.333	1.000	1.000	1.333
4	0.562	1.333	0.650	0.865	0.750
5	0.900	1.333	1.000	0.900	1.200
mean	0.844	1.333	0.955	0.883	1.125

year =   3

firm	effch	techch	pech	sech	tfpch
1	1.000	1.000	1.000	1.000	1.000
2	1.000	1.000	1.000	1.000	1.000
3	1.000	1.000	1.000	1.000	1.000
4	1.000	1.000	1.000	1.000	1.000
5	1.000	1.000	1.000	1.000	1.000
mean	1.000	1.000	1.000	1.000	1.000

MALMQUIST INDEX SUMMARY OF ANNUAL MEANS

year	effch	techch	pech	sech	tfpch
2	0.844	1.333	0.955	0.883	1.125
3	1.000	1.000	1.000	1.000	1.000
mean	0.918	1.155	0.977	0.940	1.061

MALMQUIST INDEX SUMMARY OF FIRM MEANS

firm	effch	techch	pech	sech	tfpch
1	0.866	1.155	1.000	0.866	1.000
2	1.061	1.155	1.106	0.959	1.225
3	1.000	1.155	1.000	1.000	1.155
4	0.750	1.155	0.806	0.930	0.866
5	0.949	1.155	1.000	0.949	1.095
mean	0.918	1.155	0.977	0.940	1.061

[Note that all Malmquist index averages are geometric means]

10.3.2 Stochastic Frontier Methods

The distance measures required for the Malmquist TFP index calculations can also be measured relative to a parametric technology. There are many different ways in which one could approach this. In this chapter we consider a stochastic production frontier defined as follows:

$$\ln(y_{it}) = f(x_{it}, t, \beta) + v_{it} - u_{it}, \qquad i=1,2,...,N, \quad t=1,2,...,T, \qquad (10.13)$$

where y_{it} is the output of the i-th firm in the t-th year;

$\qquad x_{it}$ denotes a $(1 \times K)$ vector of inputs;

$\qquad f(.)$ is a suitable functional form (e.g., translog);

$\qquad$ t is a time trend representing technical change;

$\qquad \beta$ is a vector of unknown parameters to be estimated;

$\qquad$ the v_{it}s are random errors, assumed to be i.i.d. and have $N(0, \sigma_v^2)$-distribution, independent of the u_{it}s; and

$\qquad$ the u_{it}s are the technical inefficiency effects.

The technical efficiencies of each firm in each year can be predicted using the approach outlined in Chapters 8 and 9. That is, we obtain the conditional expectation of $\exp(-u_{it})$, given the value of $e_{it}=v_{it}-u_{it}$. Since u_{it} is a non-negative random variable, these technical efficiency predictions are between zero and one, with a value of one indicating full technical efficiency.

In this parametric case, we can use the measures of technical efficiency and technical change to calculate the Malmquist TFP index via equations 10.4 to 10.6. The technical efficiency measures, are obtained as

$$TE_{it}=E(\exp(-u_{it})|e_{it}), \qquad (10.14)$$

where $e_{it}=v_{it} - u_{it}$, can be used to calculate the efficiency change component. That is, by observing that $d_o^t(x_{it},y_{it})=TE_{it}$ and $d_o^s(x_{is},y_{is})=TE_{is}$ we calculate efficiency change as:

$$\text{Efficiency change} = TE_{it}/TE_{is}. \qquad (10.15)$$

This measure can be compared directly to equation 10.5.

The technical change index between period s and t for the i-th firm can be calculated directly from the estimated parameters. One simply evaluates the partial derivative of the production function with respect to time (at a particular data point). If technical change is non-neutral then this technical change index may vary for different input vectors. Hence we suggest that a geometric mean be used to estimate the technical change index between adjacent periods s and t. That is,

$$
\text{Technical change} = \left\{ \left[1 + \frac{\partial f(x_{is}, s, \beta)}{\partial s} \right] \times \left[1 + \frac{\partial f(x_{it}, t, \beta)}{\partial t} \right] \right\}^{0.5}. \qquad (10.16)
$$

This measure may be compared directly with equation 10.6. The indices of technical efficiency change and technical change obtained using equations 10.15 and 10.16 may then be multiplied together to obtain a Malmquist TFP index, as defined in equation 10.4.

The above approach is similar in many ways to the Nishimizu and Page (1982) approach, but there are two small differences. First, we suggest using stochastic frontiers to estimate the technology while Nishimizu and Page (1982) use deterministic frontiers.[3] Second, Nishimizu and Page (1982) suggest estimating technical change by evaluating the two derivatives in equation 10.16 and then finding their arithmetic mean, while we have suggested that we convert these derivatives into indices and then calculate the geometric mean of these indices. These two methods of technical change calculation should provide similar measures.

Note that we could have estimated all the required distance measures directly (they would simply be ratios of observed output to predicted output for the two different input vectors for the period s and period t technologies), as is done in the DEA approach. however, we believe that the technical change measures are most easily obtained in the above manner. Note also that if sufficient observations are available, one may choose to estimate a separate stochastic frontier production function for each time period, rather than estimating a single model with technological change parameters. In this latter case, one would have no choice but to calculate the component distance values in this way.

10.4 Empirical Application: Australian Electricity Generation

This analysis utilises the data described in Coelli (1995) to construct indices of TFP growth using the two methods described in Section 10.3. The sample data comprise annual measures of output and three inputs (labour, capital and fuel) for 13 Australian coal-fired electric power generation plants from 1981/82 to 1990/91. These 13 plants are taken from three States in Australia. Four are from Victoria, six

---

[3] See Perelman (1995) for an application in which stochastic frontier methods are used in TFP calculations. That study also provides a nice comparison of the stochastic frontier results with those obtained by using the Färe et al (1994) DEA methods and Tornqvist index methods.

from New South Wales and three from Western Australia.   They represent approximately 50% of Australia's generation capacity. Some observations were not available in certain years because a few plants did not begin operating until after 1981/82, and, in some cases, because output and labour figures were missing from the data provided. Because of these omissions, the final set of data involved 114 observations (from a possible 130 observations). For further detail on data sources and variable definitions see Coelli (1995).

For the stochastic frontier approach we specify a translog stochastic frontier production function for the Australian electricity generation industry. The output of a plant is assumed to be a function of the three inputs of capital, labour and fuel; non-neutral technical change is specified; and the error term is assumed to have two components, with properties as discussed below. That is, production is assumed to be described by:

$$\ln(Q_{it}) = \beta_0 + \beta_K \ln(K_{it}) + \beta_L \ln(L_{it}) + \beta_F \ln(F_{it}) + \beta_{KK}[\ln(K_{it})]^2 + \beta_{LL}[\ln(L_{it})]^2 +$$

$$\beta_{FF}[\ln(F_{it})]^2 + 2[\beta_{KL}\ln(K_{it})\ln(L_{it}) + \beta_{KF}\ln(K_{it})\ln(F_{it}) + \beta_{LF}\ln(L_{it})\ln(F_{it})]$$

$$+ \beta_{Kt}\ln(K_{it})t + \beta_{Lt}\ln(L_{it})t + \beta_{Ft}\ln(F_{it})t + \beta_t t + \beta_{tt}t^2 + v_{it} - u_{it},$$

$$i=1,2,...,N, \quad t=1,2,...,T, \qquad (10.17a)$$

where Q_{it} = electricity generated (in kwh) by the i-th plant in the t-th year;

K_{it} = capacity (mw);

L_{it} = labour (employees);

F_{it} = fuel (terrajoules);

t = a time trend;

"ln" refers to the natural logarithm;

the β_is are unknown parameters to be estimated;

the v_{it}s are iid $N(0,\sigma_v^2)$ random errors, and are assumed to be independently distributed of the u_{it}s, which are non-negative random variables associated with technical inefficiency, which   are assumed to be independently distributed, such that the distribution of u_{it} is obtained by truncation at zero of the normal distribution with mean m_{it} and variance σ_u^2, where:

$$m_{it} = \sum_{j=1}^{3} \delta_{0j}d_j + \sum_{j=1}^{3} \delta_{tj}d_j t \qquad (10.17b)$$

where d_j is a dummy variable which takes the value 1 for the j-th State and 0 otherwise; and

the δs are unknown parameters to be estimated.

The stochastic frontier model specified above is an example of the inefficiency effects model described in Section 9.6. However, the only explanatory variables in equation 10.17b are a number of dummy intercepts and time trend variables, one for each of the three states. This model structure was inspired by the observation that the time-varying inefficiency model described in Section 9.5 is fairly restrictive in that it requires that the efficiencies of all firms follow a common trend (but allows different levels). The model, defined in equations 10.17a and 10.17b, reflects the likelihood that the different States may exhibit technical efficiencies which have different levels and follow different trends.

As noted in Section 10.2, a Malmquist TFP index is best measured relative to a CRS technology. The use of a VRS technology may result in one obtaining TFP indices which do not properly reflect the influence of scale. The restrictions required to impose CRS upon equation 10.17a are:

$$\beta_K + \beta_L + \beta_F = 1$$
$$\beta_{KK} + \beta_{KL} + \beta_{KF} = 0$$
$$\beta_{KL} + \beta_{LL} + \beta_{LF} = 0 \tag{10.18}$$
$$\beta_{KF} + \beta_{LF} + \beta_{FF} = 0$$
$$\beta_{Kt} + \beta_{Lt} + \beta_{Ft} = 0.$$

These restrictions are most easily imposed by normalising the output and the inputs by dividing them all through by one of the inputs. In our application, we have arbitrarily chosen the capital input for this purpose. Results will be invariant to the choice of this input.

The maximum-likelihood estimates of the parameters of the translog stochastic frontier model are obtained using the computer program, FRONTIER Version 4.1. These estimates are presented in Table 10.3. Asymptotic standard errors are presented beside each estimate. Note that standard errors are not reported for some estimates because these parameter estimates are calculated using the CRS restrictions in equation 10.18. Also note that the data were mean corrected prior to estimation. Hence the first order parameters may be interpreted as the elasticities at the sample means.

A number of comments can be made regarding the results in Table 10.3. Some brief observations are that the production elasticities (evaluated at the sample means) are dominated by the fuel elasticity and we also note that the labour elasticity has an unexpected negative sign. These observations conform with most past analyses of coal-fired electricity generation (see Cowing and Smith, 1980). The negative elasticity for labour suggests operation in Stage III of the production function where there is considerable congestion in the use of this input. In the case of the Australian electricity industry in the 1980s, this possibility is not unlikely. All generating plants were government owned and the labour unions were quite powerful. A lot of this surplus labour was shed in the reforms of the early 1990s (approximately 40%) without any reduction in output. If the data from the 1990s were accessible, it would be of particular interest to repeat this analysis using the 1991/92 to 1995/96 data. One would expect this labour elasticity to be much less negative, and perhaps even positive for this latter time period.

Table 10.3 Maximum-Likelihood Estimates of the Stochastic Frontier Model

Coefficient	Estimate	Standard Error	t-ratio
β_0	0.0783	0.0154	5.0883
β_F	1.0873	0.0291	37.3504
β_L	-0.1905	0.0128	-14.8588
β_K	0.1032		
β_{FF}	-0.0351	0.0297	-1.1834
β_{LL}	-0.1194	0.0155	-7.7125
β_{KK}	-0.1491		
β_{LF}	0.0027	0.0111	0.2401
β_{KF}	0.0324		
β_{KL}	0.1167		
β_{Ft}	0.0183	0.0070	2.6230
β_{Lt}	-0.0230	0.0046	-4.9973
β_{Kt}	0.0047		
β_t	0.0001	0.0034	0.0178
β_{tt}	-0.0001	0.0011	-0.0633
δ_{01}	-0.0180	0.0746	-0.2412
δ_{02}	-0.1299	0.1552	-0.8371
δ_{03}	-0.0693	0.0835	-0.8297
δ_{t1}	0.0366	0.0191	1.9180
δ_{t2}	0.0493	0.0360	1.3693
δ_{t3}	-0.0071	0.0119	-0.5968
σ^2_s	0.0049	0.0014	3.5174
γ	0.3085	0.2852	1.0819
Log-likelihood	156.70		

The estimates of the technical change parameters in Table 10.3 indicate very little technical progress during the sample period. Given the above brief discussion of the industry this observation is not surprising. The estimate of β_t suggests average annual technical progress of 0.01 percent per year. We also note that the δ_i estimates suggest that there has been a mixture of both improvements and declines in the technical efficiency of the different States.

Indices of technical change and technical efficiency change were calculated for each plant in each pair of adjacent years using the methods described in Section 10.3.2. These indices have been aggregated using geometric means and the subsequent indices were converted into cumulative (chained) indices which are reported in Table 10.4 and plotted in Figure 10.3.

Table 10.4 Cumulative Indices of Technical Efficiency Change, Technical Change and TFP Change - Stochastic Frontier Results

Year	Efficiency Change	Technical Change	TFP Change
81/82	1.000	1.000	1.000
82/83	0.999	0.992	0.991
83/84	0.999	0.990	0.989
84/85	0.998	0.988	0.986
85/86	0.996	0.985	0.980
86/87	0.992	0.984	0.975
87/88	0.985	0.983	0.968
88/89	0.978	0.985	0.964
89/90	0.970	0.989	0.959
90/91	0.938	0.993	0.931

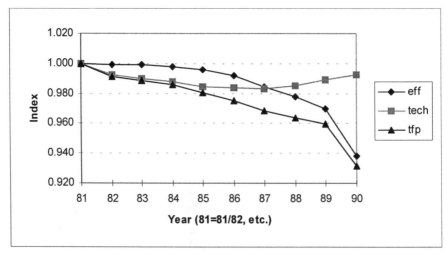

Figure 10.3 Cumulative Indices of Technical Efficiency Change, Technical Change and TFP Change - Stochastic Frontier Results

In Table 10.4 we observe a decline in technical efficiency of 6.2% during the sample period, with most of this decline occurring over the final five years of the 10 year period. This decline during the latter half of the sample period is most likely a consequence of the growth in excess capacity that was observed in the industry during this time when new plants were brought online without sufficient growth in demand.

From Table 10.4 we observe that technical change declined slightly in the first half of the sample period and then began to rise over the last half of the sample period. This small amount of technical progress in the latter half of the sample period is most likely due to the newer plants shifting the frontier because of their newer capital-embodied technologies. Overall, we observe a technical change decline of only 0.7% over the 10 year period. When this small amount of technical change is combined with the above-mentioned technical efficiency change we observe a net decline of 6.9% in TFP over the sample period.

DEA Results

The same sample data were used to calculate the same set of indices using the DEA-like methods described in Section 10.3.1. Calculations were done using a modified version of the DEAP Version 2.1 computer program (which was modified to accommodate unbalanced panel data). These results are summarised in Table 10.5 and Figure 10.4.

In Table 10.5 we observe a decline in technical efficiency of 10.3% over the 10 year period. This is larger than the 6.2% decline observed in the stochastic frontier results. However, an even greater difference is observed in the technical change index where we observe a 16.6% increase due to technical progress. This is quite different from the 0.7% *decline* observed in the stochastic frontier results. The net result of all this is an increase in TFP of 4.7% in the DEA results. This is in sharp contrast to the 6.9% decline observed in the stochastic frontier results.

Table 10.5 Cumulative Indices of Technical Efficiency Change, Technical Change and TFP Change - DEA Results

Year	Efficiency Change	Technical Change	TFP Change
81/82	1.000	1.000	1.000
82/83	0.902	1.095	0.988
83/84	0.873	1.151	1.005
84/85	0.921	1.099	1.013
85/86	0.935	1.032	0.965
86/87	0.930	1.060	0.986
87/88	0.859	1.136	0.977
88/89	0.927	1.077	0.999
89/90	0.912	1.145	1.045
90/91	0.897	1.166	1.047

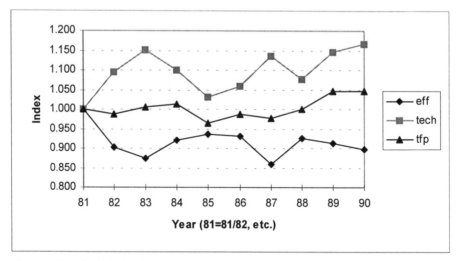

Figure 10.4 Cumulative Indices of Technical Efficiency Change, Technical Change and TFP Change - DEA Results

To obtain a better idea of how the two TFP indices compare, we have plotted them on the one graph in Figure 10.5. In this figure we observe that the two TFP indices have quite similar levels for the first eight years and then only diverge in the final two years of the sample period. We also observe that the DEA TFP series is the more volatile of the two. This suggests one possible explanation for the observed divergence in the two TFP measures in the latter part of the study period. The DEA method is much more sensitive to year-to-year changes, while the stochastic frontier method appears to smooth these effects to some degree. Hence, where the data series begins and ends can influence the measures obtained. For example, if our data series finished in 1985 we may well have observed that the DEA TFP growth was *smaller* than the stochastic frontier measure.

Alternatively, one could argue that the technical change measures obtained using the stochastic frontier model are constrained by the parameterisation and, hence, are unable to respond as quickly to a sudden shift in the technology. In general, this is a valid point. However, in the empirical application considered here, there appears to be little reason for such a large shift have been observed in the Australian electricity industry during the latter half of the 1980s.

The divergence of the results derived from the two methods is of some concern. Further research is required to attempt to ascertain the reasons for these differences. One possible avenue of future research could be to apply a window method to attempt to obtain more stable DEA frontiers by pooling the data from 2 or 3 adjacent years to construct the required frontiers.[4]

However, these issues aside, if we take the most favourable TFP measures (4.7% growth) the implied performance is still fairly poor when compared with other industries. For example, ABS (1989) estimates the rate of TFP change for the Australian market sector to be 1.5% per year over the period 1974/75 to 1987/88, while the above measures suggest, at best, a 0.47% TFP growth per year in electricity generation. This poor performance is no doubt one of the factors which provided impetus for the substantial reforms which were implemented during the early 1990s.

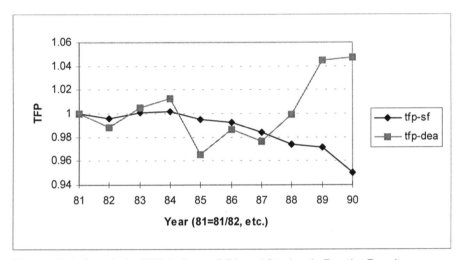

Figure 10.5 Cumulative TFP Indices - DEA and Stochastic Frontier Results

10.5 Conclusions

We conclude this chapter by summarising some of the relative merits of using frontier approaches (such as stochastic frontiers and DEA) to conduct Malmquist TFP calculations (as done in this chapter) versus using the traditional Tornqvist/ Fisher approaches. Some of the advantages of the frontier approach are:

- The frontier approach does not require price information.

- It does not assume all firms are fully efficient.

---

[4] This may prove quite useful in our example where we only have an average of 11.4 observations in each time period.

- It does not need to assume a behavioural objective such as cost minimisation or revenue maximisation.

- It permits TFP to be decomposed into technical change and technical efficiency change.

However, an important advantage of the Tornqvist approach is that it can be calculated using only two data points, while the frontier approach needs a number of firms to be observed in each time period so that the frontier technology in each year can be estimated. Thus, if one has suitable panel data, the frontier approach provides richer information and makes fewer assumptions. However, if only aggregate time-series data are available, then the Tornqvist approach allows one to obtain useful estimates of TFP change, given that the above listed assumptions are not too far from the truth.

11. CONCLUSIONS

11.1 Summary of Methods

Scattered throughout earlier chapters are a number of useful lists of points which summarise the characteristics and relative merits of the various methods that we have considered. The purpose of this final chapter is to bring together some of these lists so we can reflect upon them.

We have considered four principal methods:

1. least-squares (LS) econometric production models,
2. total factor productivity (TFP) indices (Tornqvist/Fisher),
3. data envelopment analysis (DEA), and
4. stochastic frontiers (SF).

We now summarise some key points on each of these four methods in Table 11.1 below.

Table 11.1 Summary of the Properties of the Four Principal Methods

METHOD	PROPERTY
Is the method parametric or non-parametric?	
LS	parametric
TFP	non-parametric
DEA	non-parametric

SF	parametric
Does the method account for noise?	
LS	yes
TFP	no
DEA	no
SF	yes
Does the method assume all firms are efficient?	
LS	yes
TFP	yes
DEA	no
SF	no
What behavioural assumptions are made?	

LS	it depends on the model used:
	
	    a) production or distance function - none
	
	    b) cost function - cost minimisation
	
	    c) profit function - profit maximisation

TFP	cost minimisation and revenue maximisation
DEA	none (unless allocative efficiency considered)
SF	same as for LS
What is the method used to measure?	
LS	• technical change (when time-series or panel data used) • scale economies
TFP	• TFP changes (which equals technical change when we assume CRS and no inefficiency)
DEA	• technical efficiency • scale efficiency • allocative efficiencies (if considered) • congestion efficiency (if considered) • technical change and TFP change (if panel data available and Malmquist indices calculated)
SF	• technical efficiency • scale economies • allocative efficiencies (if considered) • technical change and TFP change (if panel data available)

Data are required on what variables?	

LS	it depends on the model used:
	
	    a) production or distance function - input and output quantities
	
	    b) cost function - cost, output quantities and input prices[1,2]
	
	    c) profit function - profit and input and output prices[3,4]

TFP	input and output quantities and prices

DEA	it depends on the model used:
	
	    a) standard DEA - input and output quantities
	
	    b) cost efficiency - input and output quantities and input prices
	
	    c) revenue efficiency - input and output quantities and output prices
	
	    d) profit efficiency - input and output quantities and prices

SF	same as for LS
Time-series, cross-sectional or panel data?	
LS	can be used on all of these
TFP	can be used on all of these (but must use a transitive index when spatial comparisons are involved)
DEA	cross-sectional or panel data
SF	cross-sectional or panel data

11.2 Relative Merits of the Methods: Some Comments

Efficiency is generally measured using either DEA or stochastic frontier methods. Some of the advantages of stochastic frontiers over DEA are:

- it accounts for noise, and
- it can be used to conduct conventional tests of hypotheses.

---

[1] If some inputs are assumed fixed then quantities are required for these inputs instead of their prices.

[2] If you wish to estimate the cost function and the conditional input demand equations in a system then input quantities are also required.

[3] If some inputs and/or outputs are assumed fixed then quantities are required for these items instead of their prices.

[4] If you wish to estimate the profit function by estimating a system of input demand and output supply equations then input and output quantities are also required.

while some disadvantages are:

- the need to specify a distributional form for the inefficiency term,
- the need to specify a functional form for the production function (or cost function, etc.), and
- it is more difficult to accommodate multiple outputs (at present).

Technological change (or TFP) is usually measured using either least squares econometric methods or Tornqvist/Fisher index numbers. Some of the advantages of index numbers over least-squares econometric methods are:

- only two observations are needed,
- they are easy to calculate, and
- the method does not assume a smooth pattern of technical progress,

while the principal disadvantage is:

- it requires both price and quantity information.

Both of these approaches assume that firms are technically efficient (which is unlikely to be true). To relax this assumption one can use frontier methods (assuming panel data are available) to calculate TFP change. Some of the advantages of this frontier approach over the Tornqvist/Fisher index numbers approach are that:

- it does not require price information,
- it does not assume all firms are fully efficient,
- it does not require the assumption of cost minimisation and revenue maximisation, and
- it permits TFP to be decomposed into technical change and technical efficiency change.

However, an important advantage of the index-number approach is that it:

- only requires two data points, say observations on two firms in one time period or observations on one firm in two time periods, while the frontier approaches need a number of firms to be observed in each time period so that the frontier technology in each year can be calculated.[5]

---

[5] Note that the DEA approach can be used if only one observation in each year is available. However, in this case one must assume there is no inefficiency, or alternatively include past observations in the calculation of period-t technology. See Grosskopf (1993, p.182) for more on this.

11.3 Some Final Points

We now have a collection of very powerful and flexible tools at our disposal, to help in our analyses of efficiency and productivity. But before concluding this book we should make mention of some of the many pitfalls which a performance measurement analysis may suffer from.

- Treating inputs and/or outputs as homogenous commodities when they are heterogenous may bias results.

- There may be measurement error in the data.

- Exclusion of an important input or output may bias the results.

- Not accounting for environmental differences (both physical and regulatory) may give misleading results.

- Most methodologies do not account for multi-period optimisation or risk in management decision making.

The above points relate to all the methods considered in this book. For frontier methods, in particular, we add the points:

- The efficiency scores are only relative to the best firms in the sample. The inclusion of extra firms (say from overseas) may reduce efficiency scores.

- Be careful when comparing the mean efficiency scores from two studies. They only reflect the dispersion of efficiencies within each sample. They say nothing about the efficiency of one sample relative to the other.

- Measurement error and other noise may influence the shape and position of the frontier.

- Outliers may influence results.

To illustrate the importance of some of the above points, we pose a few questions. The following questions assume that a researcher has conducted a quick analysis of some data and is at the stage of trying to interpret the preliminary results obtained.

Q1) The researcher observes that a particular firm has lower productivity relative to other firms in an industry. Why may this be so? It could be due to one or more of:

- technical (managerial) inefficiency,

- scale inefficiency,

- omitted variables,

- quality differences in inputs and outputs,

- measurement error,

- unused capacity due to lumpy investment,

- environment:

    - physical and/or

    - regulatory.

Q2) The researcher observes that the TFP of a firm has improved from one period to the next. Why may this be so? It could be due to one or more of:

- improved technical efficiency,

- technical progress,

- scale improvements,

- changes in quality of inputs and/or outputs,

- measurement error,

- changes in environment,

- utilisation of idle capacity.

Q3) The researcher observes that the unit cost for a firm has declined from one period to the next. Why may this be so? It could be due to one or more of:[6]

- all in above list, plus:

- increased allocative efficiency (in input choices),

- favourable input price changes (need to select price indices carefully).[7]

Q4) The researcher observes that the profit for a firm has increased from one period to the next. Why may this be so? It could be due to one or more of:

- all in above list, plus:

- increased allocative efficiency (in output choices),

- favourable output price changes (need to select price indices carefully),

- the firm has simply become larger.

---

[6] Note that we are assuming no "creative" accounting methods are used.

[7] For example, if money values are not deflated or if you use an inappropriate deflator (e.g., the CPI), the cost figures may reflect more than improved performance.

Although "performance" is a somewhat slippery concept, with careful attention to the issues listed above, the performance measurement tools described in this book can provide valuable information in many situations.

APPENDIX: COMPUTER SOFTWARE

In this appendix we provide details on the computer software which is used in this book. Four computer programs are used:

1. SHAZAM - a general purpose econometrics package (White, 1993) that is used for the estimation of least-squares econometric models and the calculation of price and quantity index numbers.

2. DEAP - a data envelopment analysis (computer) program (Coelli, 1996b).

3. FRONTIER - a computer program for the estimation of stochastic frontier models (Coelli, 1996a).

4. TFPIP - a total factor productivity index (computer) program written by Tim Coelli.

The SHAZAM computer program is a widely used general econometrics software package. It can be used to estimate a large number of econometric models. For further information on this software, refer to the SHAZAM web site:

> http://shazam.econ.ubc.ca/

or to the user manual, White (1993).

The remaining three computer programs, listed above, were written by Tim Coelli, specifically for the measurement of efficiency and/or productivity. Information on these three computer programs can be obtained from the Centre for Efficiency and Productivity Analysis (CEPA) web site:

> http://www.une.edu.au/econometrics/cepa.htm

where copies of these programs (including manuals) may be downloaded.[1] We now discuss the use of these latter three computer programs.

---

[1] At the time of publishing, the TFPIP program is distributed without charge; the FRONTIER program is also distributed without charge, but a donation is suggested (i.e., shareware); and the DEAP program is sold on a commercial basis (however, a student version of the DEAP program is available free of charge). Refer to the CEPA web site for further information.

DEAP Version 2.1: A Data Envelopment Analysis (Computer) Program

This computer program has been written to conduct data envelopment analyses (DEA). The computer program can consider a variety of models. The three principal options are:

1. Standard CRS and VRS DEA models that involve the calculation of technical and scale efficiencies (where applicable). These methods are outlined in Chapter 6.

2. The extension of the above models to account for cost and allocative efficiencies. These methods are outlined in Section 7.2.

3. The application of Malmquist DEA methods to panel data to calculate indices of total factor productivity (TFP) change; technological change; technical efficiency change and scale efficiency change. These methods are discussed in Chapter 10.

All methods are available in either an input or an output orientation (with the exception of the cost efficiencies option). The output from the program includes, where applicable, technical, scale, allocative and cost efficiency estimates; slacks; peers; targets; TFP and technological change indices.

The DEAP computer program is written in Fortran (Lahey F77LEM/32) for IBM compatible PCs. It is a DOS program but can be easily run from WINDOWS using FILE MANAGER. The program involves a simple batch file system where the user creates a data file and a small file containing instructions. The user then starts the program by typing "DEAP" at the DOS prompt[2] and is then prompted for the name of the instruction file. The program then executes these instructions and produces an output file which can be read using a text editor, such as NOTEPAD or EDIT, or using a word processor, such as WORD or WORD PERFECT.

The execution of DEAP Version 2.1 on an IBM PC generally involves five files:

1. The executable file, DEAP.EXE

2. The start-up file, DEAP.000

3. A data file (for example, called TEST.DTA)

4. An instruction file (for example, called TEST.INS)

5. An output file (for example, called TEST.OUT).

The executable file and the start-up file is supplied on the disk. The start-up file, DEAP.000, is a file which stores key parameter values which the user may or may

---

[2] The program can also be run by double-clicking on the DEAP.EXE file in FILE MANAGER in WINDOWS. The use of FILE MANAGER is discussed at the end of this appendix.

not need to alter.[3] The data and instruction files must be created by the user prior to execution. The output file is created by DEAP during execution. Examples of data, instruction and output files are listed in Chapters 6 and 7.

Data file

The program requires that the data be listed in a text file[4] and expects the data to appear in a particular order. The data must be listed by observation (i.e., one row for each firm). There must be a column for each output and each input, with all outputs listed first and then all inputs listed (from left to right across the file). For example, for 40 observations on two outputs and two inputs there would be four columns of data (each of length 40) listed in the order: y1, y2, x1, x2.

The cost efficiencies option requires that price information be supplied for the inputs. These price columns must be listed to the right of the input data columns and appear in the same order. That is, for three outputs and two inputs, the order for the columns must be: y1, y2, y3, x1, x2, w1, w2, where w1 and w2 are input prices corresponding to input quantities, x1 and x2.

The Malmquist option is used with panel data. For example, for 30 firms observed in each of 4 years, all data for year 1 must be listed first, followed by the year 2 data listed underneath in the same order (of firms) and so on. Note that the panel must be "balanced", i.e., all firms must be observed in all time periods.

A data file can be produced using any number of computer packages. For example:

- using a text editor (such as DOS EDIT or NOTEPAD),

- using a word processor (such as WORD or WORD PERFECT) and saving the file in text format,

- using a spreadsheet (such as LOTUS or EXCEL) and printing to a file, or

- using a statistics package (such as SHAZAM or SAS) and writing data to a file.

Note that the data file should only contain numbers separated by spaces or tabs. It should not contain any column headings.

---

[3] At present this file only contains two parameters. One is the value of a variable (EPS) used to test inequalities with zero and the other is a flag which can suppress the printing of the firm-by-firm reports in the output file. This text file may be edited if the user wishes to alter this value.
[4] All data, instruction and output files are (ASCII) text files.

Instruction file

The instruction file is a text file which is usually constructed using a text editor or a word processor. The easiest way to create an instruction file is to make a copy of the DBLANK.INS file, which is supplied with the program (by using the FILE/COPY menus in FILE MANAGER in WINDOWS or by using the COPY command at the DOS prompt). This file is edited (using a text editor or word processor) by typing in the relevant information. The best way to describe the structure of the instruction file is via examples. Refer to the examples in Chapters 6 and 7.

Output file

As noted earlier, the output file is a text file which is produced by DEAP when an instruction file is executed. The output file can be read using a text editor, such as NOTEPAD or EDIT, or using a word processor, such as WORD or WORD PERFECT. The output may also be imported into a spreadsheet program, such as EXCEL or LOTUS, to allow further manipulation into tables and graphs for subsequent inclusion into report documents.

FRONTIER Version 4.1: A Computer Program for Stochastic Frontier Estimation

The FRONTIER computer program is very similar in construction to the DEAP computer program. It has been written to provide maximum-likelihood estimates of the parameters of a number of stochastic frontier production and cost functions. The stochastic frontier models considered can accommodate (unbalanced) panel data and assume firm effects that are distributed as truncated normal random variables. The two primary model specifications considered in the program are:

1. The Battese and Coelli (1992) time-varying inefficiencies specification, which is discussed in Section 9.5.

2. The Battese and Coelli (1995) model specification in which the inefficiency effects are directly influenced by a number of variables. This model is discussed in Section 9.6.

The computer program also permits the estimation of other models which have appeared in the literature through the imposition of simple restrictions Estimates of standard errors are calculated along with individual and mean efficiency estimates.

The program can accommodate cross-sectional and panel data; time-varying and time-invariant inefficiency effects; cost and production functions; half-normal and truncated normal distributions; and functional forms which have a dependent variable in logged or original units.

The execution of FRONTIER Version 4.1 on an IBM PC generally involves five files:

1. The executable file, FRONT41.EXE

2. The start-up file, FRONT41.000

3. A data file (for example, called TEST.DTA)

4. An instruction file (for example, called TEST.INS)

5. An output file (for example, called TEST.OUT).

The start-up file, FRONT41.000, contains values for a number of key variables, such as the convergence criterion, printing flags and so on. This text file may be edited if the user wishes to alter any values. The data and instruction files must be created by the user prior to execution.[5] The output file is created by FRONTIER during execution. Examples of data, instruction and output files are presented in Chapters 8 and 9.

The program requires that the data be stored in an text file and is quite particular about the order in which the data are listed. Each row of data should represent an observation. The columns must be presented in the following order:

1. firm number (an integer in the range 1 to N);

2. period number (an integer in the range 1 to T);

3. dependent variable;

4. regressor variables; and

5. variables influencing the inefficiency effects (if applicable).

The observations can be listed in any order but the columns must be in the stated order. There must be at least one observation on each of the N firms and there must be at least one observation in time period 1 and in time period T. If cross-sectional data are involved, then column 2 (the time-period column) must contain the value "1" throughout. Note that the data must be suitably transformed if a functional form other than a linear function is required. The Cobb-Douglas and translog functional forms are the most often used functional forms in stochastic frontier analyses. Examples involving these forms are provided in Chapters 8 and 9, respectively.

The program can receive instructions either from a file or from a terminal (keyboard). After typing "FRONT41" to begin execution, the user is asked whether instructions will come from a file or the terminal. Examples of the instruction file are listed in Chapters 8 and 9. If the interactive (terminal) option is selected, questions will be asked in the same order as they appear in the instruction file.

---

[5]Note that a model can be estimated without an instruction file if the program is used interactively.

The Three-step Estimation Method

The program follows a three-step procedure in estimating the maximum-likelihood estimates of the parameters of a stochastic frontier production function.[6] The three steps are:

1. Ordinary least-squares (OLS) estimates of the parameters of the function are obtained. All β-estimators with the exception of the intercept, β_0, will be unbiased.

2. A two-phase grid search of γ is conducted, with the β parameters (excepting β_0) set to the OLS values and the β_0 and σ^2 parameters adjusted according to the corrected ordinary least-squares formula presented in Coelli (1995c). Any other parameters (μ, η or δs) are set to zero in this grid search.

3. The values selected in the grid search are used as starting values in an iterative procedure (using the Davidon-Fletcher-Powell Quasi-Newton method) to obtain the final maximum-likelihood estimates.

Program Output

The ordinary least-squares estimates, the estimates after the grid search and the final maximum-likelihood estimates are all presented in the output file. Approximate standard errors are taken from the direction matrix used in the final iteration of the Davidon-Fletcher-Powell procedure. This estimate of the covariance matrix is also listed in the output.

Estimates of individual technical or cost efficiencies are calculated using the expressions presented in Battese and Coelli (1992, 1993). When any estimates of mean efficiencies are reported, these are simply the arithmetic averages of the individual efficiencies.

---

[6] If starting values are specified in the instruction file, the program will skip the first two steps of the procedure.

TFPIP Version 1.0: A Total Factor Productivity Index (Computer) Program

This computer program was written at the time that this book was being completed. In an earlier draft of this book, the multilateral Tornqvist and Fisher index numbers were calculated using some lengthy SHAZAM code. We decided that it would be nice to have a computer program which could be used instead of this code. TFPIP is a simple computer program which can be used to calculate Fisher and Tornqvist TFP indices (both regular and transitive). Input and output quantity indices are also reported in the output produced by the program. Refer to Chapter 4 for further details on these index numbers.

The TFPIP computer program is structured in a similar manner to the FRONTIER and DEAP computer programs. Execution generally involves four files:

1.   The executable file TFPIP.EXE

2.   A data file (for example, called TEST.DTA)

3.   An instruction file (for example, called TEST.INS)

4.   An output file (for example, called TEST.OUT).

Examples of data, instruction and output files are listed in Chapter 4.

The program requires that the data be listed in a text file and expects the data to appear in a particular order. The data must be listed by observation (i.e., one row for each firm). There must be a column for each output and input quantity and price. The data columns are listed as follows:

1.   output quantities;

2.   input quantities;

3.   output prices; and

4.   input prices.

The price columns should appear in the same order as the quantity columns. For example, for 40 observations on two outputs and three inputs, then there would be 10 columns of data (each of length 40) listed in the order: $y1$, $y2$, $x1$, $x2$, $x3$, $p1$, $p2$, $w1$, $w2$, $w3$.

Tips on using DEAP, FRONTIER or TFPIP in FILE MANAGER in WINDOWS:

The DEAP, FRONTIER and TFPIP computer programs are all DOS programs. However, they can be easily manipulated using the WINDOWS FILE MANAGER. The following steps illustrate how these programs can be used without a knowledge of DOS.

1. Use the FILE/CREATE DIRECTORY menu items to create a DEAP directory on the hard drive of the computer being used.

2. Use drag-and-drop to copy the DEAP program files (perhaps from a floppy disk) to the DEAP directory.

3. Use the FILE/ASSOCIATE menu items to associate a WINDOWS text editor (e.g., NOTEPAD) with the file extensions ".INS", ".DTA" and ".OUT". This allows these files to be edited (or viewed) by simply double-clicking on the file names. The associations need only be set once and then WINDOWS stores this association information.

4. To check that the associations have worked, double-click on EG1.INS and EG1.DTA to look at their contents (these files are supplied on the DEAP disk).

5. To practice executing DEAP, double-click on the DEAP.EXE file name. The program then asks for an instruction file name. Type in EG1.INS (and hit the RETURN key). DEAP will only take a few seconds to complete this small DEA example. To look at the output file (EG1.OUT), simply double-click on the EG1.OUT file name.

REFERENCES

ABS (1989), "Development of Multifactor Productivity Estimates for Australia 1974-75 to 1987-88", *Australian Bureau of Statistics Information Paper* No. 5229.0, Canberra.

Afriat, S.N. (1972), "Efficiency Estimation of Production Functions", *International Economic Review*, 13, 568-598.

Aigner, D.J., and S.F. Chu (1968), "On Estimating the Industry Production Function", *American Economic Review*, 58, 826-839.

Aigner, D.J., C.A.K Lovell and P. Schmidt (1977), "Formulation and Estimation of Stochastic Frontier Production Function Models", *Journal of Econometrics*, 6, 21-37.

Ali, A.I., and L.M. Seiford (1993), "The Mathematical Programming Approach to Efficiency Analysis", in Fried, H.O., C.A.K. Lovell and S.S. Schmidt (Eds.), *The Measurement of Productive Efficiency: Techniques and Applications*, Oxford University Press, New York, 120-159.

Ali, M., and J.C. Flinn (1989), "Profit Efficiency Among Basmati Rice Producers in Pakistan Punjab", *American Journal of Agricultural Economics*, 71, 303-310.

Allen, R.C., and W.E. Diewert (1981), "Direct versus Implicit Superlative Index Number Formulae", *Review of Economics and Statistics*, 63, 430-435.

Allen, R.G.D. (1975), *Index Numbers in Theory and Practice*, New York, Macmillan Press.

Althin, R. (1995), *Essays on the Measurement of Producer Performance*, Ph.D. Dissertation, Lund University, Lund.

Antle, J.M. (1984), "The Structure of U.S. Agricultural Technology, 1910-78", *American Journal of Agricultural Economics*, 66, 414-421.

Balk, B. (1995), "Axiomatic Price Index Theory: A Survey", International Statistical Review, 63, 69-93.

Balk, B. (1997), Industrial Price, Quantity, and Productivity Indices: Micro-Economic Theory", Mimeographed, Statistics Netherlands, 171.

Balk, B. and R. Althin (1996), "A New, Transitive Productivity Index", *Journal of Productivity Analysis*, 7, 19-27.

Banker, R.D. (1996), "Hypothesis Test using Data Envelopment Analysis", *Journal of Productivity Analysis*, 7, 139-160.

Banker, R.D., A. Charnes and W.W. Cooper (1984), "Some Models for Estimating Technical and Scale Inefficiencies in Data Envelopment Analysis", *Management Science*, 30, 1078-1092.

Banker, R.D., and R.C. Morey (1986a), "Efficiency Analysis for Exogenously Fixed Inputs and Outputs", *Operations Research*, 34, 513-521.

Banker, R.D., and R.C. Morey (1986b), "The Use of Categorical Variables in Data Envelopment Analysis", *Management Science*, 32, 1613-1627.

Battese, G.E. (1992), "Frontier Production Functions and Technical Efficiency: A Survey of Empirical Applications in Agricultural Economics", *Agricultural Economics*, 7, 185-208.

Battese, G.E., and G.S. Corra (1977), "Estimation of a Production Frontier Model: With Application to the Pastoral Zone of Eastern Australia", *Australian Journal of Agricultural Economics*, 21, 169-179.

Battese, G.E., and T.J. Coelli (1988), "Prediction of Firm-Level Technical Efficiencies With a Generalised Frontier Production Function and Panel Data", *Journal of Econometrics*, 38, 387-399.

Battese, G.E., and T.J. Coelli (1992), "Frontier Production Functions, Technical Efficiency and Panel Data: With Application to Paddy Farmers in India", *Journal of Productivity Analysis*, 3, 153-169.

Battese, G.E., and T.J. Coelli (1993), "A Stochastic Frontier Production Function Incorporating a Model for Technical Inefficiency Effects", *Working Papers in Econometrics and Applied Statistics*, No. 69, Department of Econometrics, University of New England, Armidale.

Battese, G.E., and T.J. Coelli (1995), "A Model for Technical Inefficiency Effects in a Stochastic Frontier Production Function for Panel Data", *Empirical Economics*, 20, 325-332.

Battese, G.E., T.J. Coelli and T.C. Colby (1989), "Estimation of Frontier Production Functions and the Efficiencies of Indian Farms Using Panel Data From ICRISAT's Village Level Studies", *Journal of Quantitative Economics*, 5, 327-348.

Bauer, P.W. (1990), "Recent Developments in the Econometric Estimation of Frontiers", *Journal of Econometrics*, 46, 39-56.

Beattie, B.R., and C.R. Taylor (1985), *The Economics of Production*, Wiley, New York.

Bessent, A.M., and E.W. Bessent (1980), "Comparing the Comparative Efficiency of Schools through Data Envelopment Analysis", *Educational Administration Quarterly*, 16, 57-75.

Bjurek, H. (1996), "The Malmquist Total Factor Productivity Index", *Scandinavian Journal of Economics*, 98, 303-313.

Blackorby, C., and R. Russell (1979), "Will the Real Elasticity of Substitution Please Stand Up?", *American Economic Review*, 79, 882-888.

Boles, J.N. (1966), "Efficiency Squared - Efficiency Computation of Efficiency Indexes", *Proceedings of the 39th Annual Meeting of the Western Farm Economics Association*, pp. 137-142.

Bortkiewicz, L. von (1923), "zweck und Struktur einer Preisindexzahl", Nordisk Statistisk Tidskrift, 369-408.

Bureau of Industry Economics (1994), *International Performance Indicators: Aviation*, Research Report No. 59, Bureau of Industry Economics, Canberra.

Call, S.T., and W.L. Holahan (1983), *Microeconomics*, 2nd Ed., Wadsworth, Belmont.

Caves, D.W., L.R. Christensen and W.E. Diewert (1982a), "Multilateral Comparisons of Output, Input and Productivity Using Superlative Index Numbers", *Economic Journal*, 92, 73-86.

Caves, D.W., L.R. Christensen and W.E. Diewert (1982b), "The Economic Theory of Index Numbers and the Measurement of Input, Output and Productivity", *Econometrica*, 50, 1393-1414.

Chambers, R.G. (1988), *Applied Production Analysis: A Dual Approach*, Cambridge University Press, New York.

Charnes, A., C.T. Clark, W.W. Cooper and B. Golany (1985), "A Developmental Study of Data Envelopment Analysis in Measuring the Efficiency of Maintenance Units in the U.S. Air Forces", In R.G. Thompson and R.M. Thrall (Eds.), *Annals of Operations Research*, 2, pp.95-112.

Charnes, A., W.W. Cooper and E. Rhodes (1978), "Measuring the Efficiency of Decision Making Units", *European Journal of Operational Research*, 2, 429-444.

Charnes, A., W.W. Cooper and E. Rhodes (1981), "Evaluating Program and Managerial Efficiency: An Application of Data Envelopment Analysis to Program Follow Through", *Management Science*, 27, 668-697.

Charnes, A., W.W. Cooper, A.Y. Lewin and L.M. Seiford (1995), *Data Envelopment Analysis: Theory, Methodology and Applications*, Kluwer Academic Publishers, Boston.

Charnes, A., W.W. Cooper, B. Golany, L. Seiford and J. Stutz (1985), "Foundations of Data Envelopment Analysis for Pareto-Koopmans Efficient Empirical Production Functions", *Journal of Econometrics*, 30, 91-107.

Charnes, A., W.W. Cooper, J. Rousseau and J. Semple (1987), "Data Envelopment Analysis and Axiomatic Notions of Efficiency and Reference Sets", *Research Report CCS 558*, Center for Cybernetic Studies, The University of Texas at Austin, Austin.

Christensen, L.R., and W.H. Greene (1976), "Economies of Scale in US Electric Power Generation", *Journal of Political Economy*, 84, 655-676.

Coelli, T.J. (1992), "A Computer Program for Frontier Production Function Estimation: FRONTIER, Version 2.0", *Economics Letters*, 39, 29-32.

Coelli, T.J. (1995a), "Estimators and Hypothesis Tests for a Stochastic Frontier Function: A Monte Carlo Analysis", *Journal of Productivity Analysis*, 6, 247-268.

Coelli, T.J. (1995b), "Measurement and Sources of Technical Inefficiency in Australian Electricity Generation", paper presented at the New England Conference on Efficiency and Productivity, University of New England, Armidale, November 23-24.

Coelli, T.J. (1996a), "A Guide to FRONTIER Version 4.1: A Computer Program for Frontier Production Function Estimation", *CEPA Working Paper 96/07*, Department of Econometrics, University of New England, Armidale.

Coelli, T.J. (1996b), "A Guide to DEAP Version 2.1: A Data Envelopment Analysis (Computer) Program", *CEPA Working Paper 96/08*, Department of Econometrics, University of New England, Armidale.

Coelli, T.J. (1996c), "Measurement of Total factor Productivity Growth and Biases in Technological Change in Western Australian Agriculture", *Journal of Applied Econometrics*, 11, 77-91.

Coelli, T.J. (1996d), "Assessing the Performance of Australian Universities using Data Envelopment Analysis", mimeo, Centre for Efficiency and Productivity Analysis, University of New England.

Coelli, T.J. (1997), "A Multi-stage Methodology for the Solution of Orientated DEA Models", Paper presented to the Taipei International Conference on Efficiency and Productivity Growth, Taipei, June 20-21.

Coelli, T.J., and Battese, G.E. (1996), "Identification of Factors which Influence the Technical Efficiency of Indian Farmers", *Australian Journal of Agricultural Economics*, 40(2), 19-44.

Coelli, T.J., and S. Perelman (1996a), "Efficiency Measurement, Multiple-output Technologies and Distance Functions: With Application to European Railways", *CREPP Discussion Paper* no. 96/05, University of Liege, Liege.

Coelli, T.J., and S. Perelman (1996b), "A Comparison of Parametric and Non-parametric Distance Functions: With Application to European Railways", *CREPP Discussion Paper* no. 96/11, University of Liege, Liege.

Cornes, R. (1992), *Duality and Modern Economics*, Cambridge University Press, Melbourne.

Cornwell, C., P. Schmidt and R.C. Sickles (1990), "Production Frontiers With Cross-sectional and Time-series Variation in Efficiency Levels", *Journal of Econometrics*, 46, 185-200.

Cowing, T.G., and V.K. Smith (1980), "The Estimation of a Production Technology: A Survey of Econometric Analyses of Steam-Electric Generation", *Land Economics*, 54, 156-186.

Debreu, G. (1951), "The Coefficient of Resource Utilisation", *Econometrica*, 19, 273-292.

Deprins, D., L. Simar and H. Tulkens (1984), "Measuring Labour-Efficiency in Post Offices" in M. Marchand, P. Pestieau and H. Tulkens (Eds.), *The Performance of Public Enterprises: Concepts and Measurements*, North-Holland, Amsterdam.

Diewert, W.E. (1976), "Exact and Superlative Index Numbers", *Journal of Econometrics,* 4, 115-45.

Diewert, W.E. (1978), "Superlative Index Numbers and Consistency in Aggregation", *Econometrica,* 46, 883-900.

Diewert, W.E. (1980) "Aggregation Problems in the Measurement of Capital", In Usher, D. (Ed.), *The Measurement of Capital,* National Bureau of Economic Research, Chicago, 433-528.

Diewert, W.E. (1981), "The Economic Theory of Index Numbers: A Survey", In Deaton, A. (Ed.), *Essays in the Theory and Measurement of Consumer Behaviour (in Honour of Richard Stone),* Cambridge University Press, New York, 163-208.

Diewert, W.E. (1983), "The Theory of the Output Price Index and the Measurement of Real Output Change", In W.E. Diewert and C. Montmarquette (Eds.), *Price Level Measurement,* Statistics Canada, 1039-1113.

Diewert, W.E. (1990), *Price Level Measurement,* North-Holland, Amsterdam.

Diewert, W.E. (1992), "Fisher Ideal Output, Input and Productivity Indexes Revisited", *Journal of Productivity Analysis,* 3, 211-248.

Diewert, W.E. and A.O. Nakamura (1993), *Essays in Index Number Theory, Volume 1,* Contributions to Economic Analysis Series, No. 217, North-Holland, Amsterdam.

Diewert, W.E., and T.J. Wales (1987), "Flexible Functional Forms and Global Curvature Conditions", *Econometrica,* 55, 43-68.

Dyson, R.G., and E. Thanassoulis (1988), "Reducing Weight Flexibility in Data Envelopment Analysis", *Journal of the Operational Research Society,* 39, 563-576.

Eichorn, W. and J. Voeller (1976), "Theory of the Price Index: Fisher's Test Approach and Generalizations", *Lecture Notes in Economics and Mathematical Systems,* Vol. 140, Springer-Verlag, Berlin.

Eichorn, W. and J. Voeller (1983) "The Axiomatic Foundations of Price Indexes and Purchasing Power Parities", in Diewert and Montamarquette (Eds.) *Price Level Measurement,* Statistics Canada, 411-450.

Elteto, O. and P. Koves (1964), "On a Problem of Index Number Computation Relating to International Comparison", *Statisztikai Szemle,* 42, 507-518.

Färe, R., and C.A.K. Lovell (1978), "Measuring the Technical Efficiency of Production", *Journal of Economic Theory,* 19, 150-162.

Färe, R., and D. Primont (1995), *Multi-Output Production and Duality: Theory and Applications,* Kluwer Academic Publishers, Boston.

Färe, R., R. Grabowski and S. Grosskopf (1985), "Technical Efficiency of Philippine Agriculture", *Applied Economics,* 17, 205-214.

Färe, R., S. Grosskopf and C.A.K. Lovell (1985), *The Measurement of Efficiency of Production,* Kluwer Academic Publishers, Boston.

Färe, R., S. Grosskopf and J. Logan (1985), "The Relative Performance of Publicly-Owned and Privately-Owned Electric Utilities", *Journal of Public Economics,* 26, 89-106.

Färe, R., S. Grosskopf and P. Roos (1997), "Malmquist Productivity Indexes: A Survey of Theory and Practice", In R. Färe, S. Grosskopf and R.R. Russell (Eds.), *Index Numbers: Essays in Honour of Sten Malmquist,* Kluwer Academic Publishers, Boston, Forthcoming.

Färe, R., S. Grosskopf and R.R. Russell (1997), *Index Numbers: Essays in Honour of Sten Malmquist,* Kluwer Academic Publishers, Boston, Forthcoming.

Färe, R., S. Grosskopf and W. Weber (1997), "The Effect of Risk-based Capital Requirements on Profit Efficiency in Banking", Discussion Paper Series No. 97-12, Department of Economics, Southern Illinios University at Carbondale.

Färe, R., S. Grosskopf, and C.A.K. Lovell (1994), *Production Frontiers,* Cambridge University Press, Cambridge.

Färe, R., S. Grosskopf, C.A.K. Lovell and C. Pasurka (1989), "Multilateral Productivity Comparisons when Some Outputs are Undesirable: A Nonparametric Approach", *Review of Economics and Statistics*, 71, 90-98.

Färe, R., S. Grosskopf, C.A.K. Lovell and S. Yaisawarng (1993), "Derivation of Shadow Prices for Undesirable Outputs: A Distance Function Approach", *Review of Economics and Statistics*, 75, 374-380.

Färe, R., S. Grosskopf, M. Norris and Z. Zhang (1994), "Productivity Growth, Technical Progress, and Efficiency Changes in Industrialised Countries", *American Economic Review*, 84, 66-83.

Farrell, M.J. (1957), "The Measurement of Productive Efficiency", *Journal of the Royal Statistical Society, Series A,* CXX, Part 3, 253-290.

Ferrier, G.D., and C.A.K. Lovell (1990), "Measuring Cost Efficiency in Banking: Econometric and Linear Programming Evidence", *Journal of Econometrics*, 46, 229-245.

Fisher, F.M., and K. Shell (1972), *The Economic Theory of Price Indexes*, Academic Press, New York

Fisher, I. (1922), *The Making of Index Numbers*, Houghton Mifflin, Boston.

Førsund, F.R. (1990), "The Malmquist Productivity Index", Memorandum No. 28, Department of Economics, University of Oslo, Oslo.

Førsund, F.R. (1997), "The Malmquist Productivity Index, TFP and Scale", Memorandum No. 233, Department of Economics, Gothenburg University, Gothenburg.

Førsund, F.R., and L. Hjalmarsson (1979), "Generalised Farrell Measures of Efficiency: An Application to Milk Processing in Swedish Dairy Plants", *Economic Journal*, 89, 294-315.

Førsund, F.R., C.A.K. Lovell and P. Schmidt (1980), "A Survey of Frontier Production Functions and of their Relationship to Efficiency Measurement", *Journal of Econometrics*, 13, 5-25.

Forsyth, F.G. (1978), "The Practical Construction of a Chain Price Index Number", *Journal of the Royal Statistical Society*, Series A, 141, 348-358.

Forsyth, F.G. and R.F. Fowler (1981), "Theory and Practice of Chain Price Index Numbers", *Journal of the Royal Statistical Society, Series A*, 144, 224-226.

Fried, H.O., C.A.K. Lovell and S.S. Schmidt (1993*), The Measurement of Productive Efficiency: Techniques and Applications*, Oxford University Press, New York.

Fried, H.O., S.S. Schmidt and S. Yaisawarng (1995), "Incorporating the Operating Environment into a Measure of Technical Efficiency", mimeo, Union College, Schenectady.

Frisch, R. (1936), "Annual Survey of General Economic Theory: The Problem of Index Numbers", *Econometrica*, 4, 1-39.

Fuss, M., and D. McFadden (1978), *Production Economics: A Dual Approach to Theory and Application*, North Holland, Amsterdam.

Ganley, J.A., and J.S. Cubbin (1992), *Public Sector Efficiency Measurement: Applications of Data Envelopment Analysis*, North-Holland, Amsterdam.

Greene, W.H. (1980a), "Maximum Likelihood Estimation of Econometric Frontier Functions", *Journal of Econometrics*, 13, 27-56.

Greene, W.H. (1980b), "On the Estimation of a Flexible Frontier Production Model", *Journal of Econometrics*, 13, 101-116.

Greene, W.H. (1990), "A Gamma-distributed Stochastic Frontier Model", *Journal of Econometrics*, 46, 141-164.

Greene, W.H. (1992), *LIMDEP Version 6.0: User's Manual and Reference Guide*, Econometric Software Inc., New York.

Greene, W.H. (1993), "The Econometric Approach to Efficiency Analysis", in Fried, H.O., C.A.K. Lovell and S.S. Schmidt (Eds.), *The Measurement of Productive Efficiency: Techniques and Applications*, Oxford University Press, New York, 68-119.

Grifell-Tatjé, E., and C.A.K. Lovell (1995), "A Note on the Malmquist Productivity Index", *Economics Letters*, 47, 169-175.

Griffiths, W.E., R.C. Hill and G.G. Judge (1993), *Learning and Practicing Econometrics*, Wiley, New York.

Grosskopf, S. (1993), "Efficiency and Productivity", in Fried, H.O., C.A.K. Lovell and S.S. Schmidt (Eds.), *The Measurement of Productive Efficiency: Techniques and Applications*, Oxford University Press, New York, 160-194.

Grosskopf, S. (1996), "Statistical Inference and Nonparametric Efficiency: A Selective Survey", *Journal of Productivity Analysis*, 7, 161-176.

Henderson, J.M., and R.E. Quandt (1980), *Microeconomic Theory: A Mathematical Approach*, 3rd Ed., McGraw Hill, Tokyo.

Hicks, J.R. (1961), "Measurement of Capital in Relation to the Measurement of Other Economic Aggregates", In F.A. Lutz and D.C. Hague (Eds.), *The Theory of Capital*, Macmillan, London.

Industry Commission (1992), *Measuring the Total Factor Productivity of Government Trading Enterprises*, Industry Commission, Canberra.

Jondrow, J., C.A.K. Lovell, I.S. Materov and P. Schmidt (1982), "On Estimation of Technical Inefficiency in the Stochastic Frontier Production Function Model", *Journal of Econometrics*, 19, 233-238.

Jorgenson, D.W., L.R. Christensen and L.J. Lau (1973), "Transcendental Logarithmic Production Frontiers", *Review of Economics and Statistics*, 55, 28-45.

Kalirajan, K.P. (1981), "An Econometric Analysis of Yield Variability in Paddy Production", *Canadian Journal of Agricultural Economics*, 29, 283-294.

Kamakura, W.A. (1988), "A Note on the Use of Categorical Variables in Data Envelopment Analysis", *Management Science*, 34, 1273-1276.

Kodde, D.A., and F.C. Palm (1986), "Wald Criteria for Jointly Testing Equality and Inequality Restrictions", *Econometrica*, 54, 1243-1248.

Konus, A.A. (1924), "The Problem of the True Index of the Cost-of-Living", (translated in 1939 in), *Econometrica*, 7, 10-29.

Koopmans, T.C. (1951), "An Analysis of Production as an Efficient Combination of Activities", in T.C. Koopmans, (Ed.) *Activity Analysis of Production and Allocation*, Cowles Commission for Research in Economics, Monograph No. 13, Wiley, New York.

Kopp, R.J. (1981), "The Measurement of Productive Efficiency: A Reconsideration", *Quarterly Journal of Economics*, 96, 477-503.

Kopp, R.J., and W.E. Diewert (1982), "The Decomposition of Frontier Cost Function Deviations into Measures of Technical and Allocative Efficiency", *Journal of Econometrics*, 19, 319-331.

Kumbhakar, S.C. (1987), "The Specification of Technical and Allocative Inefficiency of Multi-product Firms in Stochastic Production and Profit Frontiers", *Journal of Quantitative Economics*, 3, 213-223.

Kumbhakar, S.C. (1990), "Production Frontiers, Panel Data and Time-Varying Technical Inefficiency", *Journal of Econometrics*, 46, 201-211.

Kumbhakar, S.C. (1997), "Modeling Allocative Inefficiency in a Translog Cost Function and Cost Share Equations: An Exact Relationship", *Journal of Econometrics*, 76, 351-356.

Kumbhakar, S.C., S. Ghosh and J.T. McGuckin (1991), "A Generalized Production Frontier Approach for Estimating Determinants of Inefficiency in U.S. Dairy Farms", *Journal of Business and Economic Statistics*, 9, 279-286.

Land, K.C., C.A.K. Lovell and S. Thore, (1993), "Chance-constrained Data Envelopment Analysis", *Managerial and Decision Economics*, 14, 541-554.

Laspeyres, E. (1871), "Die Berechnug einer mittleren Waaren-preissteigerung", *Jahrbucher fur Nationalokonomie und Statistik*, 16, 296-314.

Lee, Y.H., and P. Schmidt (1993), "A Production Frontier Model with Flexible Temporal Variation in Technical Inefficiency", in Fried, H.O., C.A.K. Lovell and S.S. Schmidt (Eds.), *The Measurement of Productive Efficiency: Techniques and Applications*, Oxford University Press, New York, 237-255.

Lovell, C.A.K. (1993), "Production Frontiers and Productive Efficiency", in Fried, H.O., C.A.K. Lovell and S.S. Schmidt (Eds.), *The Measurement of Productive Efficiency: Techniques and Applications*, Oxford University Press, New York, 3-67.

Lovell, C.A.K. (1994), "Linear Programming Approaches to the Measurement and Analysis of Productive Efficiency", *Top*, 2, 175-248.

Lovell, C.A.K., and J.T. Pastor (1995), "Units Invariant and Translation Invariant DEA Models", *Operations Research Letters*, 18, 147-151.

Malmquist, S. (1953), "Index Numbers and Indifference Surfaces", *Trabajos de Estatistica*, 4, 209-42.

McCarty, T.A., and S. Yaisawarng (1993), "Technical Efficiency in New Jersey School Districts", in Fried, H.O., C.A.K. Lovell and S.S. Schmidt (Eds.), *The Measurement of Productive Efficiency: Techniques and Applications*, Oxford University Press, New York, 271-287.

Meeusen, W. and J. van den Broeck (1977), "Efficiency Estimation from Cobb-Douglas Production Functions With Composed Error", *International Economic Review*, 18, 435-444.

Moorsteen, R.H. (1961), "On Measuring Productive Potential and Relative Efficiency", *Quarterly Journal of Economics*, 75, 451-467.

Morrison, C.J. (1993) *A Microeconomic Approach to the Measurement of Economic Performance: Productivity Growth, Capacity Utilisation, and Related Performance Indicators*, Springer-Verlag, Berlin.

Nerlove, M. (1963), "Returns to Scale in Electricity Supply", In Christ, C.F. (Ed.), *Measurement in Economics - Studies in Mathematical Economics and Econometrics in Memory of Yehuda Grunfeld*, Stanford University Press, Stanford.

Ngwenya, S., G. E. Battese and E. M. Fleming (1997), "The Relationship Between Farm Size and the Technical Inefficiency of Production of Wheat Farmers in Eastern Orange Free State, South Africa", *Agrekon* (to appear).

Nishimizu, M., and J.M. Page (1982), "Total Factor Productivity Growth, Technical Progress and Technical Efficiency Change: Dimensions of Productivity Change in Yugoslavia, 1965-78", *Economic Journal*, 92, 920-936.

Norman, M., and B. Stoker (1991), *Data Envelopment Analysis: An Assessment of Performance*, Wiley, New York.

Olesen, O.B., and N.C. Petersen (1995), "Chance Constrained Efficiency Evaluation", *Management Science*, 41, 442-457.

Paasche, H. (1874), "Ueber die Presentwicklung der letzten Jahre nach den Hamburger Borsennotirungen", *Jahrbucher fur Nationalokonomie und Statistik*, 23, 168-78.

Perelman, S. (1995), "R&D, Technological Progress and Efficiency Change in Industrial Activities", *Review of Income and Wealth*, 41, 349-366.

Pestieau, P., and H. Tulkens (1993), "Assessing and Explaining the Performance of Public Enterprises : Some Recent Evidence From the Productive Efficiency Viewpoint", *Finanz Archiv*, 50, 293-323.

Pitt, M.M., and L-F. Lee (1981), "Measurement and Sources of Technical Inefficiency in the Indonesian Weaving Industry", *Journal of Development Economics*, 9, 43-64.

Rao, C.R. (1973), *Linear Statistical Inference and Its Applications, Second Edition*, Wiley, New York.

Rao, D.S. Prasada and K.S. Banerjee (1984), "A Multilateral System of Index Numbers Based on Factorial Approach", *Statistiche Hefte*, 27, 297-312.

Reifschneider, D., and R. Stevenson (1991), "Systematic Departures from the Frontier: A Framework for the Analysis of Firm Inefficiency", *International Economic Review*, 32, 715-723.

Richmond, J. (1974), "Estimating the Efficiency of Production", *International Economic Review*, 15, 515-521.

Rousseau, J.J., and J.H. Semple (1993), "Notes: Categorical Outputs in Data Envelopment Analysis", *Management Science*, 39, 384-386.

Russell, R.R. (1997) "Distance Functions in Consumer and Producer Theory", in Färe, R., S. Grosskopf and R.R. Russell (eds.), Index Numbers: Essays In Honor of Sten Malmquist, Kluwer Academic Publishers, Forthcoming.

Samuelson, P.A., and S. Swamy (1974), "Invariant Economic Index Numbers and Canonic Duality: Survey and Synthesis", *American Economic Review*, 64, 566-93.

Schmidt, P. (1976), "On the Statistical Estimation of Parametric Frontier Production Functions", *Review of Economics and Statistics*, 58, 238-239.

Schmidt, P. (1986), "Frontier Production Functions", *Econometric Reviews*, 4, 289-328.

Schmidt, P., and C.A.K. Lovell (1979), "Estimating Technical and Allocative Inefficiency Relative to Stochastic Production and Cost Functions", *Journal of Econometrics*, 9, 343-366.

Schmidt, P., and R.C. Sickles (1984), "Production Frontiers and Panel Data", *Journal of Business and Economic Statistics*, 2, 367-374.

Seiford, L.M. (1996), "Data Envelopment Analysis: The Evolution of the State of the Art (1978-1995)", *Journal of Productivity Analysis*, 7, 99-138.

Seiford, L.M., and R.M. Thrall (1990), "Recent Developments in DEA: The Mathematical Approach to Frontier Analysis", *Journal of Econometrics*, 46, 7-38.

Seitz, W.D. (1971), "Productive Efficiency in the Steam-Electric Generating Industry", *Journal of Political Economy*, 79, 879-886.

Selvanathan, E.A., and D.S. Prasada Rao (1994), *Index Numbers: A Stochastic Approach*, Macmillan, New York.

Shephard, R.W. (1970), *Theory of Cost and Production Functions*, Princeton University Press, Princeton.

Simar, L. (1996), "Aspects of Statistical Analysis in DEA-Type Frontier Models", *Journal of Productivity Analysis*, 7, 177-186.

Squires, D. (1994), "Firm Behaviour Under Input Rationing", *Journal of Econometrics*, 61, 235-257.

Stevenson, R.E. (1980), "Likelihood Functions for Generalised Stochastic Frontier Estimation", *Journal of Econometrics*, 13, 57-66.

Szulc, B.J. (1964), "Indices for Multiregional Comparisons", *Prezeglad Statystyczny* (Statistical Review), 3, 239-254.

Szulc, B.J. (1983), "Linking Price Index Numbers", in Diewert and Montamarquette (eds.) *Price Level Measurement*, Statistics Canada, 567-598.

Theil, H. (1973), "A New Index Number Formula", *Review of Economics and Statistics*, 53, 498-502.

Theil, H. (1974), "More on log-change Index Numbers", *Review of Economics and Statistics*, 54, 552-554.

Timmer, C.P. (1971), "Using a Probabilistic Frontier Function to Measure Technical Efficiency", *Journal of Political Economy*, 79, 776-794.

Tornqvist, L. (1936), "The Bank of Finland's Consumption Price Index", *Bank of Finland Monthly Bulletin*, 10, 1-8.

Varian, H.R. (1992), *Microeconomic Analysis*, Third Edition, Norton, New York.

Weaver, R.D. (1983), "Multiple Input, Multiple Output Production Choices and Technology in the U.S. Wheat Region", *American Journal of Agricultural Economics*, 65, 45-56.

White, K.J. (1993), *SHAZAM User's Reference Manual Version 7.0*, McGraw-Hill, New York.

Whiteman, J. and K. Pearson (1993), "Benchmarking Telecommunications using Data Envelopment Analysis", *Australian Economic Papers*, 12, 97-105.

Wong, Y-H.B., and J.E. Beasley (1990), "Restricting Weight Flexibility in Data Envelopment Analysis", *Journal of the Operational Research Society*, 4, 829-835.

Zellner, A. and N.S. Revankar (1969), "Generalised Production Functions", *Review of Economic Studies*, 36, 241-250.

Zellner, A., J. Kmenta and J. Dreze (1966), "Specification and Estimation of Cobb-Douglas Production Function Models", *Econometrica*, 34, 784-795.

Zieschang, K.D. (1983), "A Note on the Decomposition of Cost Efficiency into Technical and Allocative Components", *Journal of Econometrics*, 23, 401-405.

AUTHOR INDEX

SUBJECT INDEX

P. 58

Use graphs.